Sacred Mysteries

Sacred Mysteries

Myths About Couples in Quest

Evans Lansing Smith, Ph.D.

Blue Dolphin Publishing

Published by Blue Dolphin Publishing, Inc.
P.O. Box 8, Nevada City, CA 95959
Orders: 1-800-643-0765
Web: www.bluedolphinpublishing.com

ISBN: 1-57733-126-5

Library of Congress Cataloging-in-Publication Data

Smith, Evans Lansing, 1950–
    Sacred mysteries : myths about couples in quest / Evans Lansing
Smith.

        p. cm.
Includes biographical references and index.
    ISBN 1-57733-126-5 (pbk. : alk. paper)
    1. Marriage in literature. 2. Couples in literature. 3. Mythology in
literature. I. Title.

PN56.M28S65 2003
809'.93355—dc21

                                                2003001038

Printed in the United States of America

10   9   8   7   6   5   4   3   2   1

Dedication

For My Wife, Michelle,
"Consummation of heart's desire, its root and blossoming"

And For

Our Daughter and Son-in-Law, Anita and Bob Fitzhugh
On the Occasion of Their Marriage, Saturday, June 15th, 2002

Contents

Acknowledgments

I want to thank the Midwestern State University community, and, most especially, our President, Dr. Jesse Rogers, and First Lady, Dr. Karen Rogers, for their enthusiasm, interest, and unflagging support over the past twelve years. I want also to thank Ruth Häusler, at the Zentralbibliothek in Zürich, and Naomi Pritchard, at Thames and Hudson in London, for their assistance in obtaining permission to use the image from the *Aurora consurgens* (reproduced in *Alchemy: The Secret Art,* by Stanislas Klossowski de Rola), on the front cover of this book. Finally, my thanks to Paul Clemens, for his interest, and for his expert supervision in the production and publication of this book.

Into the Labyrinth

A year or so after traveling with Joseph Campbell, first in Northern France, to study the Arthurian Romances of the Middle Ages, and then in Egypt and Kenya to pursue the mythologies of the Ancient Near East, I had a dream about him.

I was walking down one of the avenues in New York City. When I turned off into a side street, I came to a nondescript doorway, with no address and nothing written above it. On a whim, I walked up the dark stairway to an empty room on the upper floor, inside of which I sat down with Joseph Campbell. He had a bell jar in his hand, a kind of alchemical beaker, hermetically sealed. A vaporous mist hovered over some dirt on the bottom of the jar, into which we both gazed, Campbell with that marvelous smile of delight that so often illuminated his features. As we looked into the jar, the mist slowly swirled around, and became animated with the delicate colors of the rainbow. Campbell pointed to the rainbow—the *Cauda pavonis*, or peacock's tail of the alchemical marriage—and I was led to see in it the emergence of life from the mysterious, invisible forces of the universe, into which the colorful apparition would return at the end of the cycle, evaporated into "thin air," like a dream.

As we watched the phosphorescent mist swirl above the handful of earth at the bottom of the beaker, a tiny couple slowly became visible, two faery children, with nearly transparent bodies of light. They were joined at the waist, like Siamese twins, by a tiny incision.

1

Again, I was led to understand, with no words passing between us, that this was an alchemical marriage, herald of the new life, which was just then beginning for me.

Looking back at my dream of the alchemical couple in the beaker, I have come to see it as a call to adventure, initiating my own personal version of the universal archetype of spiritual development, which Joseph Campbell called the hero journey. I've been many years now on the way, devoting much of my time to the exploration of the hero journey in the classic literary works of our tradition.

In the summer of 1988, after returning home from my first teaching job, at a small college in Switzerland, I saw segments of the PBS series, "The Power of Myth," in which Joseph Campbell told Bill Moyers about his days as a student in France during the 1920s. With characteristic zeal, Campbell recalled his daily visits to the Cathedral of Chartres, during which he identified every single figure of the Biblical pantheon, whether stained in radiant glass or carved in immemorial stone. He became such a familiar figure that one day the sexton entrusted him with an extraordinary task.

"Would you like," said the sexton, "to come up with me into the belfry to ring the noontide bells?"

Who could say no?

Campbell ascended the famous steeple into the belfry, where, with a magnificent breeze whistling through the stone windows, he climbed onto one side of a seesaw to begin rocking the enormous bells beneath him.

As I listened to Campbell share this precious memory of his youth with the TV audience, equally precious memories of my own returned. I had heard that story ten years before, when, during a tour of Northern France in the fall of 1977, Campbell told it to me as we sat together on the bus, heading into Chartres at twilight.

It was near the end of a really terrific week, which had included visits to Rouen, Amiens, Mt. St. Michel, the standing stones of Carnac, the medieval forests of Brittany, the chateaux country of the Loire river valley, and then on to Paris.

Campbell beamed with delight in his window seat beside me, looking out at a host of chateaux entirely invisible to me: he had piercing blue eyes, and knew the terrain well—where to look beneath a cluster of trees, or behind a tiny copse in the distance, for the noble relics of the Middle Ages.

We'd had lunch on the grounds of one of the chateaux earlier in the day, sitting beside the still pool that surrounded the beautiful building, which was perfectly reflected on the surface of the water: spires, towers, turrets, crenellations, copes, and barbicans—all perfectly replicated, though pointing downwards, in the serene mirror of the pool's surface. The castle shimmered, above and below the water line, a dazzling white surrounded by a bevy of immemorial oaks.

It was as if we had stepped through a hole in the hedge into another world, or as if we had passed through a door of glass into the mysterious chambers of Glastonbury Abbey, where Arthur and his court danced the Nine Men's Morris.

Our group had stopped earlier in a little pub in the woods of Brittany, to have a cup of cider, some cheese, and to enjoy the fine hospitality of our perfectly darling old French host, a diminutive white-haired dwarf with a mystical sense of humor. After several glasses of cider, we strolled down the long path outside the pub, which led into the woods where Vivian had beguiled Merlin—a picture of which he had carved into the cedar panels of his bar. Stopping beneath a tremendous flowering hawthorn, the old man said to me:

"Il y'a beaucoup de choses qui n'existent pas" ('There are many things which don't exist!').

And I could well believe him.

Deep inside the woods, where our group walked after lunch, we all sat down in a circle, sitting on logs and fallen tree trunks amidst the briars and a scattering of Amanita muscaria mushrooms.

"Don't eat those," Campbell said, "or we'll never get to Paris!"

He then told the story of Merlin's marriage.

At the end of his life, the old man fell in love with Vivian, the sorceress (also known as Morgan la Fey), who coaxed his magic spells out of him, then used them to imprison the old wizard in a tower of white thorns, in which he remains eternally invisible. Only the sound of his voice—whispering with the wind blowing gently through the trees of the vast forest—comes to those knights who wander through the forests of Broceliande, in quest of love, or the Holy Grail.

As Campbell finished his story, with hounds bellowing in the distance, the sun broke free from the mist, and its shafts penetrated the tall oak trees surrounding our silent, spellbound little group. It continued to shine on the shimmering surface of the little pond where we had lunch, Campbell leaning against a standing stone on the shore, with the Lady of the Lake retrieving Excalibur in the water behind him: I imagined I saw her hand extended from beneath the rippling surface, waving the dazzling steel three times in the air, before returning to the depths.

The next day, we drove on to visit Mt. St. Michel, staying at the little hotel down the road where Eisenhower had set up offices after the Normandy invasion. In Rouen, I'd seen where machine guns had gouged gaping holes in the Cathedral, and an old woman had taken me in to her burned out basement to thank me for liberating France!

I conveyed her gratitude to my father.

In the peaceful hotel near Mt. St. Michel, Campbell sat quietly in a corner after breakfast, before his slide-illustrated lecture, for which he said he was "composing his images." The evening before, a few of us had gone out after dinner to see the Mount at night, rising mysteriously above the dark swirl of the treacherous tides, pinnacle and archangel invisible in the darkness above. We drove together with a National Geographic photographer working on a story there, and walked up along the cobbled streets of the village to the colossal arch leading into the monastery and cathedral.

I leaned back against the stone barricades to gaze up at the huge, fluted arches which supported the massive weight of the monastery, which eerily dissolved into the intangible darkness of the endless night above.

"It's the impenetrable inner Self," Fred whispered to me, as I stood with thighs trembling in the wind.

Fred was a bandy-legged, feisty little Australian analyst, who had received his Jungian calling from a hallucinatory crow, which sat on his right thigh for years, refusing to fly away until he began his analysis!

My trembling returned later in Paris, when a small group of us walked over to Notre Dame, and then down by the river, after a lengthy dinner (with lots of wine). The sight of the powerful, vaulted nave and apse of the Cathedral, seen from the Seine below, with the flurry of flying arches supporting the weight, overwhelmed me.

The trembling didn't stop until one of our companions, an older woman who ran a philanthropic foundation in California, simply melted on the stone steps climbing up from the embankment: she'd had far too much wine!

A year or so after my trip in Northern France, I was fortunate enough to travel again with Campbell to Egypt, where I saw him blow a kiss to the gods, as we rode in horse drawn carriages by the Temples of Luxor and Karnac. On another morning, he waved to a crowd of cheering teenagers on a field trip, laughing boisterously with them as we emerged from the magnificent underground tomb of Sethos I. Later that night, in a bar on an island near Aswan, I laughed as he talked over whiskey about Freud's tendency to faint in Jung's presence.

Our visit to the Valley of the Kings the next day traced the archetypal model of the hero journey cycle: beginning and ending on our floating hotel (the SS Osiris), moored on the eastern bank beneath the Temple of Luxor, and exploring the tombs beneath the rocky mountains on the western bank in between. The descent through the maze of doorways, corridors, stairways, and chambers to the grandly painted ceilings of the tombs beneath the mountains was one of the highlights of the trip, and permanently shaped my view of the symbolism of the sacred marriage.

On the walk back to the river from the Valley of the Kings, an Egyptian guide held a mirror up to the sun for me, as I stepped gingerly down a stairway into a tiny tomb beneath the desert. Looking up, I saw the guide deflecting the brilliant rays of sunlight down into the tomb, the walls of which were colorfully painted with bright images of the sacred marriage of Isis and Osiris.

During the days following, The SS Osiris took us up the Nile for excursions to the temples of Dendera and Abydos, Karnak, Esna, Edfu, and Kom Ombo, where policemen roamed the streets in front of the glowing Temple, swatting hordes of children with long papyrus reeds. We flew from there to Abu Simbel, looking down on large conical hills of volcanic rock rising mysteriously from dried up river beds. After reading Thomas Mann's great Biblical tetralogy, some years later, I thought of Joseph transported to the prisons of the Pharaoh on a boat like the SS Osiris, and I delighted in Mann's use of the imagery of the spiral dance in his portrayal of the marriage of Joseph and Asenath.

At the Temple of Dendera, I walked way back into a small chapel to look up at the ceiling, which bore a relief sculpture of the Sky Goddess Nut: her back arched over her husband Geb, and her four limbs stretched out to demarcate the cardinal points of the compass, she swallows a solar disk at sunset which then travels its stations of the cross through her body, to be reborn at dawn from her womb. It's the most concise representation I know of the marital mysteries associated with the Great Goddess.

Campbell's model of the hero journey—an archetypal narrative structure to be found in a wide variety of world literature, myths, religious tales, and rituals—has exerted a major influence on a variety of fields of study. There have been books on the hero journey for kids, the hero journey for women, the hero journey in dreams, and numerous articles on the hero journey in myths and rituals. There have been theoretical books on the hero journey as narrative, books on the nature of the hero and heroine, hundreds of books on the general theories of mythology which have sprung up in our time, and anthologies of quest narratives in contemporary literature.

But, oddly enough, no book that focuses on the sacred mysteries of marriage, as this one does.

All the more odd, in as much as the hero journey and the descent to the underworld are myths about marriage. They have been so from the very beginning. All of our earliest myths about death and resurrection have also been myths about marriage and relationship.

These myths involve couples: the Sumerian Inanna and Dumuzi, the Egyptian Isis and Osiris, the Roman Cupid and Psyche, the Greek Hades and Persephone, or Orpheus and Eurydice. One is even tempted to include Jesus and Mary Magdalene (as did D.H. Lawrence, Nikos Kazantzakis, and Hilda Doolittle).

It took me many years to realize this fundamental fact of our mythological inheritance. One day, after finishing my fourth book on myth and literature, and celebrating my fourteenth wedding anniversary, I put the two together—myths about the hero journey are myths about marriage.

They focus on couples in relationship, and transmit a millennial wisdom about life and marriage which we should not ignore.

The revelation came as something of a surprise, and produced a wry chuckle, plus a question—do all marriages require a hero journey, a descent into the underworld?

It would seem that they do.

We should remember that for the ancients, the underworld was both infernal and Elysian; it was a dual realm, part hell, and part heaven. Like marriage. Like any relationship that lasts longer than three months.

This book explores the wonderful treasury of myths and folktales about marriage bequeathed to us by our ancestors, and which we must pass on to our descendants. What we see in the magic mirror of these myths is that deeper part of ourselves created by the marriage relationship.

My book, *Sacred Mysteries*, retells and analyzes those myths and tales of marriage and relationship which involve a hero journey to the otherworld. It focuses on the archetypal symbolism in these marvelous stories, in order to provide a magic mirror of myth in which to reflect upon the mysteries of our relationships—their sorrows and joys, their ups and downs, their losses and recoveries.

Joseph Campbell once remarked that marriage is a sacred relationship because it breaks down our egos, but thereby opens us up to a deeper dimension within ourselves. James Hillman would agree, and call marriage a "soul-making" journey, one that takes us down into the depths, where the mythic images of the soul lie buried.

Sacred Mysteries celebrates and illuminates the ups and downs of couples on the quest. It focuses exclusively on myths, ballads, poems, stories, and folktales about couples who undertake a journey to the otherworlds within the soul—worlds only marriage and relationship can open up to us.

CHAPTER ONE

Ancient Mysteries

Isis and Osiris

The ancient Egyptian myth of the marriage of Isis and her brother Osiris begins before the creation of the world, in the womb of the mother goddess of the night, with the twins twisting and twining together in the throes of first love.

When they are born, the world is born with them, and the opposites of day and night, male and female, life and death emerge from the primordial abyss of the deep. Osiris has a wicked brother, Set, and Isis a sister, Nephthys, who emerge together as a divine family from the chaos of the cosmos.

As with all marriages, family complications form the context for the relationship of Isis and Osiris.

One day, Set, the wicked brother, envious of the power of Osiris, pulls a memorable prank during a wild party. He brings a coffin cut to the precise measurements of Osiris into the room, and asks who would like to try it out. At the stroke of midnight, at the peak of the party, Osiris climbs into the coffin, much to the amusement of the guests. But at that moment, 72 cohorts of Set rush out of the dark corners of the palace and nail the coffin shut, trapping Osiris inside. Then they throw it into the river, and the bier floats up the Nile like a barge, to a place called Abydos.

A princess who has just given birth takes the sweet smelling cedar wood out of the river, and erects it in the courtyard of her

8

riverside palace, where an incense-bearing tree springs up to enclose the coffin.

Meanwhile, Isis, the bereft sister-bride, tracks her brother's coffin down, and comes to the palace of Abydos. Disguising herself as a mortal nursemaid, she gets a job watching after the child born to the princess.

Each night, Isis resumes her divinity, and, after anointing the boy with ambrosia, dips him in the fire on the hearth to purge him of his mortality. As the boy sits happily squealing in the flames, Isis turns herself into a sparrow, and flits lamenting around the erica tree in the courtyard, in which Osiris lies entombed.

One night, awakened by the song of mournful sparrow, the princess bursts into the nursery—only to find her little boy cavorting in the flames. The princess lets out a shriek which breaks the spell. Isis assumes her divine form and chastises the bewildered mother:

"If only you'd let me be, your boy would have become immortal. But now, he must die, like all men and women."

The princess is overcome with grief, and awe, in the presence of the goddess.

"By the way," Isis continues, "you've got my husband's coffin in the erica tree growing in your courtyard. Would you mind giving it me please?"

The princess complies, and Isis floats off down the Nile on a barge bearing the bier of the dead Osiris. Flapping her wings over his mummy, Isis revives the dead god, and makes love to him.

This will not be the last time in the sacred mysteries of marriage that a husband or a wife is brought back to life by the power of love.

The child born from the union of Isis and Osiris represents the perennial emergence of life from death. His name is Horus, the hawk-headed deity, and he will play a crucial role in the second death and resurrection of his father Osiris.

After giving birth to Horus, Isis sits suckling the baby in the reeds alongside the river—the first Madonna, and the first savior of our religious and mythological tradition.

While she sits happily nursing the boy, the wicked brother Set finds the mummy of Osiris, and tears it to shreds, scattering the pieces of the body all over Egypt. With the help of his son Horus—who is able to get a little distance from the situation by flying high over the land—the various pieces of the dismembered corpse of the father are put back together.

What was lost is found.

Horus gets above it all, gaining that higher perspective we need in marriage to cope with its rhythms of death and rebirth.

All of the pieces are recovered, with the exception of the phallus—which a fish has swallowed! Isis has to make the first prosthetic penis, and rouse it to life by flapping her wings over her dead husband.

An eye Horus has lost in a battle with the wicked brother Set is also needed to bring the father back to life. It represents the insight we need to penetrate the mysteries of our relationships, and bring us out of the dark moments.

The resurrected Osiris becomes the Lord of the Underworld, to whom all of the dead are brought for judgement, and for rebirth in the spiritual kingdom to come. He sits on a magnificent throne, with 24 cobras sitting in a row above him. The snakes' hoods are erect, bearing solar disks on them.

Behind the throne stand Isis and her sister Nephthys, their arms uplifted in a gesture of reverential support.

Without his wife, Osiris would be a rotting corpse on the bottom of a muddy river.

Inanna and Dumuzi

The oldest literature in our tradition about marriage and the hero journey comes to us from the Sumerians, the first civilized people of the Tigris-Euphrates river valleys. The Sumerians are responsible for the origins of language, writing, crafts, architecture, statecraft, irrigation, and agriculture (not to mention the art of brewing beer).

Nearly four thousand years ago their sacred narratives were recorded on cuneiform tablets. Here we find the earliest myths of marriage, and the earliest versions of the Flood, the Creation, death and resurrection, crucifixion, and the Garden of Eden (woman, tree, serpent, and fruit).

Among the 40,000 pieces of tablets now scattered in museums all over the world, we have the oldest versions of the hero journey of marriage in our literary tradition. In the tablets devoted to Inanna, we have three separate heroine journeys recording the trials, ordeals, and initiatory transformations of her youth, maturity and marriage, and midlife and old age.

Inanna's youth is the subject of a short myth called "The Huluppu Tree."

This tale records the primordial emergence of cosmos out of chaos, but reflects upon this process from the perspective of the feminine. The emergence of civilization itself is symbolized by the three stages in the life cycle of the tree itself: in its virgin state it is a wild tree growing by the banks of the Euphrates in the fresh, early days of the Creation; in its cultivated maturity, it is a tree tended in the garden of the goddess Inanna; and finally, in death it becomes the throne bed of the royal couple after Gilgamesh has driven the Anzu bird from its branches, the demonic goddess Lilith from its stem, and the serpent from the coils of its roots.

In its pristine virgin state (which corresponds to Inanna's girl-hood), we see the Huluppu tree "in the very first days" planted by the banks of the Euphrates, from whose primal waters it derives its sustenance. The passage to the next phase is caused by a natural crisis: a whirling South Wind tears the tree up by the roots, and the floodwaters carry it downstream. These are, metaphorically, the "rough winds that shake the darling buds of May" (as Shakespeare would say, in a famous sonnet)—i.e., those tempestuous passions which afflict adolescence and persist into adulthood.

After the floodwaters subside, the Huluppu tree is retrieved by the goddess Inanna, who plants it in her holy garden in Uruk. She then sits dreaming of the day when she will have a shining throne and marriage bed. Inanna oversees the tree's transition from a wild to a cultivated plant in the gardens of the city. She preserves a fragment of her own wild girlhood from the floodwaters of biological matura-tion. It is a piece of herself that will then, with proper care and cultivation, become the basis of her new identity.

After ten years of cultivation, new trouble begins to brew for the young goddess queen and her Huluppu tree: a serpent nests in the roots, the dark maiden Lilith inhabits the trunk, and the Anzu bird roosts in the branches, brooding upon its fledgling demons. Since these three beings will not leave, Inanna must solicit male help—for the first time in her life—to drive the demons away. Utu, the sun god, refuses, but Gilgamesh, her brother, accepts the task. These three demons represent the repressed energies of the earlier stage of the tree's life cycle, in the wilderness beside the Euphrates. But those primal, instinctual drives have taken new forms, ones associated with a wildly passionate nature, untamed by cultivation.

Lilith, particularly, is associated with an unbridled sexuality, of a kind not submissive to masculine authority.[1] Lilith was Adam's legendary first wife, who left him to breed demons of death beside the Red Sea, after Adam insisted on being on top during sexual intercourse.

She represents premarital womanhood wildly sowing her oats, in furious rebellion against all authority. She has little to do with children, preferring to murder babies in childbirth than to assist in their delivery. If impregnated, abortion, not marriage, would be her first thought.

Her separation from Adam represents the first divorce!

The serpent and the Anzu bird, in the roots and branches of the Huluppu tree, suggest other wild powers of the feminine emerging during pre-marital adolescence. The serpent in the roots has the power to shed its skin to be reborn, but it is also secretive and wily, embedded in the hidden mysteries of the earth—mysteries which only profound introversion can intuit.

The Anzu bird, on the other hand, is flighty and excitable, capable of piercing cries of spiritual ecstasy and transcendent flights of the mind. But it is also nurturing, capable of long hours of sedentary brooding over eggs that will hatch into the as yet unimaginable future. This suggests a manic-depressive dynamic in the young womanhood of Inanna, an unstable oscillation between highflying enthusiasm, and terrible fits of melancholy, brooding over the past, the present, and the future.

None of these three demons—serpent, Lilith, or bird—are negative in themselves. What is needed is not repression, but integration and transformation, a mixture of matriarchal and patriarchal approaches to the problem of marriage with the "dark aspects of the feminine."[2] Since Lilith, the Anzu bird, and the serpent would apparently be inconvenient bed partners, Inanna solicits the help of her brother Gilgamesh (not the help of a lover) to drive the creatures away.

This maneuver brings the Huluppu tree towards its third and final phase of development. This too is the first task of young manhood in relation to the feminine: to help her cope with her demons, as well as with his own—here to drive them away, *not to destroy them* (it was Nietzsche who said to be careful in the casting out of your devils lest you cast out your angels as well!). He must preserve their energies, yet make sure they do not sabotage the creation of throne and bed for the young goddess, his sister.

Gilgamesh therefore strikes the serpent, scares the Anzu bird off into the mountains (where the women both of Dionysian times and of today still go to retrieve the wild freedom of virgin womanhood). He then provokes Lilith to smash up her home in order flee to the "wild, uninhabited places" from which she came. Then Gilgamesh carves a throne and a bed out of the wood of the Huluppu tree for his sister Inanna, while she gives him a staff and ring of royal rule. In these final forms the tree reaches the last stage of its cultivation, yielding (like the giving tree) the wood that—through its death—supports both royalty and procreation.

Inanna is now ready to assert the full power of her womanhood, in the context of marriage.

Before she can do so, however, and especially before her marriage (which will come only *after* her full development), Inanna must go on her first complete heroine's journey. She must acquire wisdom and retrieve the arts of civilization from her maternal grandfather, Enki, the god of the waters. This journey will take her from her city of Uruk, to Abzu (Enki's city, in the sacred precincts of Eridu), and then back to Uruk.

During the journey, Inanna will steal the royal, divine, and human powers necessary to her maturity, and return them to her people in Uruk.

Only then will she be ready for marriage.

The journey begins when Inanna has reached physical maturity, yet is untried and unattached. As she leans against an apple tree in the sheepfold—marveling at the beauty of her sexuality—she resolves to set forth in search of Enki. He is in possession of the holy laws of heaven and earth, and he receives her so amicably that they get staggering drunk on Sumerian beer. During this marvelous binge, Enki bestows upon his favorite granddaughter the priesthood, godship, kingship, and the numerous powers and skills suggestive of her maturity.

These include all the arts, rituals, judicial skills, powers of speech, lovemaking techniques, musical talents, and crafts of civilization. There is a delightful sense of Enki's participation in his own beguiling here that reminds one of Vivian's theft of Merlin's magic at the end of the old Druid's life. Inanna gathers the arts together into the "Boat of Heaven," and wisely departs before the beer wears off!

The whole episode is a wonderful example of the role played by an older man in the heroine's journey. It shows us Inanna making full use of her education, and having a good time along the way! The task now is to retain and exploit her newly won powers for the benefit of the community to which she returns as a patron goddess.

Inanna therefore flees with the treasures and defends herself against the demons sent in pursuit by the sobered up Enki. This involves threshold battles which suggest the dark turmoil necessary to win the runes of wisdom. At this point she encounters the dark side of her male mentor—the wise old man turned dragon, unwilling to relinquish his powerful lore to a young woman.

The old man sends a sequence of six monsters after Inanna, but they are repulsed by Inanna's faithful steward Ninshubur. Each monster represents an aspect of the shadow side of the wise old man, and also the abusive potentials of Inanna's own animus (her inner masculine).

The seventh monster to attack is Enki himself; only when he catches up to her, his monstrous aspect turns beneficial, as he grants his granddaughter full rights to the powers stolen, celebrates her new role as patron goddess of Uruk, and acknowledges a newly formed alliance between the cities of Eridu and Uruk (a political treaty which, psychologically, corresponds to a reconciliation between the unconscious and the ego, and between the male and the female).

Now firmly enthroned in a position of authority and power, with her own clearly defined selfhood, Inanna is ready for courtship and marriage.

This seems the proper way of proceeding: selfhood first, then marriage. The courtship of Inanna and Dumuzi (her fiancé) is beautifully related in the Sumerian poem. Inanna must choose between the shepherd and the farmer, inclining originally to the farmer and rejecting Dumuzi. The situation suggests the conflict between Cain and Abel in the Old Testament, only here a Goddess must determine whose offering will be accepted!

Out of this quarrelsome triangle, love is born, and the conflict between shepherd and farmer dissolves into a celebration of renewed fertility symbolized by the sacred marriage of Dumuzi and Inanna. The courtship is one of the most beautiful love poems in world literature, combining a delicate but powerful eroticism with universal images of natural fertility.

The final stage of development in Inanna's journey comes after her marriage, during the mid-life passage into the underworld. This journey is recorded in the most famous of the Sumerian poems, "The Descent of Inanna to the Great Below."

Her descent is self-initiated. Inanna simply "opens her ears" to the "great below." She then abandons her seven temples in the seven cities of ancient Sumer, and adorns herself elaborately with the seven symbols of her royal power—crown, neck and breast beads, breastplate, golden bracelet, lapis measuring rod and line, and royal robe.

Her clothing represents the formidable security of the Queen's worldly position, aspects of her ego, or persona, that will need to be stripped away before she can fully open her ear to the wisdom of the great below (the Jungian unconscious, perhaps).

And what better way than marriage to divest the ego of its armor!

When Inanna arrives at the first of the seven gates of the Sumerian underworld, she tells the threshold guardian, Neti, that she has come to participate in the funeral rites of Gugalanna. Known as the "Bull of Heaven," Gugalanna is the husband of Inanna's sister, Ereshkigal, Queen of the underworld. Inanna asks for the beer of the funeral rites to be poured into the cups—can she beguile her dark sister Ereshkigal as she had Enki, by getting her drunk?

But then Inanna has each article of clothing stripped from her as she passes through each of the seven gates of the underworld, until she stands naked and bowed low before Ereshkigal, in the throne room of the Queen of the Dead. Ereshkigal fastens the "eye of death" upon her, and the words of wrath and guilt are spoken against her. Inanna is then turned into a rotting corpse, and hung up like a piece of butchered meat from a hook on the wall.

The terrifying process of divestiture—of having all that one had struggled to achieve brutally taken away, leaving one naked in the presence of death—is absolutely basic to the painful mysteries of marriage. Perhaps the imagery suggests the psychological trauma of midlife—the breakdowns and divorces, the loss of jobs, of libido, of prestige, and all those hormonal changes that feel like hell and remind us that we are only rotting corpses, all 'hung up' (as Inanna is) about one problem or another.

Any identity crisis can precipitate the heroine's journey, at any time in life, of course, and it always involves a metaphorical near-death experience—during which the old personality is stripped away, leaving a sense of nothingness.[3] But the midlife problem (in the context of marriage) is represented in "The Descent of Inanna" with a concision and intensity nearly unsurpassed in the history of world literature.

We might also see Inanna's descent as a cosmological image, representing the cyclical disappearance of Venus, the morning and evening star associated with the goddess. In the Sumerian context, the seven gates through which Inanna passes may also represent the seven spheres of the planets, spheres through which the soul ascends, shedding its material sheathes after death; and through which it descends, before birth, from the spiritual realm into incarnation.

Inanna's marital descent has also to do with the fertility mysteries of the date palm, and perhaps, with an actual ritual of suttee burial.[4] Each approach to the symbolism of the seven gates yields a comprehensive view of the mysteries of our lives and marriages: our star begins to set at mid-life, our date palms bear fewer fruit, and rituals of mourning and burial become, increasingly, a part of our yearly calendars.

The mythic journey here, however, reminds us that there is a passage through death, and a return journey to be made, perhaps as perilous as the departure from life. The sacred story of Inanna and Dumuzi reminds us that what smells like death and feels like hell may actually be the labor pains of delivery—the beginning of a new life.

At the beginning of "The Descent," Inanna instructs her faithful servant, Ninshubur, to solicit help, in the event that she should fail to return in three days time. Ninshubur goes first to Enlil and then to Nanna (Inanna's father and paternal grandfather) to petition for help in beautifully poetic prayers, thrice repeated. Both relatives on the male line refuse, self-righteously blaming the goddess for her own troubles.

Only Enki, Inanna's maternal grandfather, agrees to send help.

Enki fashions two little asexual creatures from the dirt between his fingernails, gives them the food and water of life, and instructs them to go to the underworld. There they find Ereshkigal, Queen of the Dead, with her breasts uncovered and her hair swirling around her head like leeks—she is giving birth!

The creatures then repeat the six lamentations Ereshkigal utters during her labor (everything hurts—inside, outside, belly, back, heart, and liver!), until she stops and offers them a gift as reward for moaning and groaning in cadence with her agony (excellent advice for fathers here). The fingernail-fashioned emissaries then request the corpse of Inanna, which comes back to life after they sprinkle the bread and water of life upon it.

Fascinating!

This is a eucharistic meal (bread and wine) associated with death and rebirth, along with a kind of crucifixion—Inanna is hung up on a peg for three days and three nights, before she rises again. In fact, when you consider the sacred marriage rituals in the courtship of Dumuzi, and the funeral rites in this section of "The Descent of Inanna," we have right here in Sumerian literature all the basic prototypes of the sacraments of the Church: Baptism, Confirmation, Marriage, Funeral Rites, Communion, and Crucifixion—all in place by 2000 B.C.E. at the latest!

The archetypal core of meaning shared by the sacraments of both Sumerian and Catholic theologies is death and rebirth, and the revelation of their mysterious unity. This revelation is in fact the climactic moment of the marital journey. Gugalanna's funeral, the original impetus of the descent, has become the moment of his birth, and the keening of Ereshkigal's lamentation becomes the crying of childbirth.

As the "Bull of Heaven," Gugalanna represents the moon, which dies each month to be reborn, just as Inanna, the evening star, descends daily into the dark domain of Ereshkigal, in order to be reborn. Sumerian cosmology situates the underworld right above the primal waters from which all life comes—the monster of the abyss having carried Ereshkigal down there when she was a maiden. It is appropriate then to find Ereshkigal at first mourning and then giving birth, since in her domain of the underworld, birth and death are flip sides of the same coin.

Inanna's return to the upperworld, and subsequent encounter with her husband, dramatizes a power struggle between matriarchal and patriarchal authorities. Inanna is only allowed to return to her temples if a replacement is found to take her place in the underworld. Terrifying demons of death, called the *galla*, accompany her return to choose her replacement. The *galla* neither eat, drink, make offerings or libations, accept gifts, enjoy love, or have children. They are the powerful energies of the female shadow, activated by the journey into the unconscious. The witch-like hatred of the *galla* poisons everything with implacable, jealous rage, showing us what happens when a woman who has gone down into the darkness is overwhelmed by the dark powers resident there—she becomes as fearsome as Lilith.

These demons first allow Ninshubur, Inanna's servant, and her two sons, Shara and Lulal, to go free—because they dress in sackcloth, tear out their hair, and grovel in the dust at Inanna's feet when she returns.

Only Dumuzi, Inanna's husband, makes the fatal mistake of remaining seated on his throne when his wife returns from her hellish journey. He fails to grovel and groan in acknowledgment of her suffering.

The demons therefore cut him up with axes, pour the milk out of his churns, break his reed pipe, and chase him wailing off into the wilderness. Utu the sun god changes him into a snake, and he tries to wriggle out of the crisis. The entire episode is a wonderful representation of a distraught and arrogant husband unable to deal with his wife's emotional needs, during such passages of extreme crisis as menopause—which catapults Dumuzi into his own mid-life journey.

The conflict between husband and wife, however, also has a political or cultural dimension. The fathers in Inanna's family tree (Enlil and Nanna) refuse to help retrieve her from the underworld. Only Enki, her maternal grandfather, responds to her need. This confrontation with her husband—much of whose power has been conferred upon him by marriage—relates to these earlier conflicts between Inanna and the patriarchal order.

Dumuzi would like to remain on the throne provided him by his wife, while she undergoes the terrible ordeal of the descent, but he is ultimately chastened by the dark powers of the feminine deities, Inanna and her sister Ereshkigal. If the conflict between husband and wife reflects a myth of marriage at mid-life, it may also reflect the larger problem of a culture in transition from a matriarchal to a patriarchal orientation (the poetry is a mixture of Sumerian and Semitic languages).

It is interesting then that Inanna's journey results in a renewed equilibrium between masculine and feminine potencies quite unlike the denigration of the Goddess in the Hebrew Old Testament.[5]

This equilibrium is established by forcing Dumuzi to depart on his own mid-life journey to the underworld. Unlike Inanna, he must be knocked off his throne (Inanna had gone willingly, setting her ear to the great below in sympathy with the grief of Ereshkigal). Another difference between the journeys is the intensity and violence of the threshold battle inflicted upon Dumuzi by the demons unleashed by his wife's return. Inanna had simply allowed herself to be stripped down, while Dumuzi resists the descent and flees.

After Inanna fastens "the eye of death" on Dumuzi, while he stubbornly remains seated on his throne, the demons smash him around and set off in pursuit as he flees to the steppes. Dumuzi begins his mid-life journey with a return to nature (like those middle-aged males Robert Bly, Sam Keen, and others tell us about, pounding drums in the forest and embracing trees).

He also has an archetypal dream which prefigures the basic tasks of his journey. When Dumuzi lies down among the canals beside the frogs in the rushes, he dreams of the reeds and tall trees rising terribly all around him. The single reed trembles sympathetically for him; the double reeds are taken away; and his churn, drinking cup, and shepherd's crook are shattered—powerful symbols of the devastation of midlife, divorce, and separation.

Upon waking, Dumuzi takes this dream to his sister Geshtinanna for analysis: she becomes his therapist, ready to help him handle the revelations of his vision quest into the wilderness. It is quite typical for analysis to be initiated by a powerful dream. It is also typical that this first dream (which contains both the diagnosis and prognosis) has come during a violent marital conflict and a related career crisis—Dumuzi gets knocked off his throne, and loses his job and wife at the same time.

Out of the stress of this situation, a numinous dream comes bubbling up from unsuspected depths, in compensation for the devastation of the ego. Dumuzi has instinctively retreated to the rivers of life, where the rushes and the reeds whisper to him (as they will to Psyche during her marital crisis).

His sister, Geshtinanna, goes through all the details of Dumuzi's dream, seeing them as symbols of the catastrophes to be inflicted upon him by the demons, unleashed by his arrogance and by his wife's rage. These catastrophes may also be seen as the disruptions of that stage of life which we simplistically refer to as retirement—Dumuzi's means of livelihood is destroyed, his shepherd crook broken, his lambs lost to the eagle, and his sheepfold rendered a "house of desolation given to the winds."

To make matters worse, the natural pleasures of life lose their savor: the "drinking cup falls from its peg. The churn lies silent; no milk is poured. The cup lies shattered." Such poignant images of the loss of libido and the impotence of age! Gone the butter churn and the pouring of milk, images of sexuality used earlier to consecrate the sacred marriage. Only dread and the nameless anxieties of the wind remain.

Dumuzi is then betrayed by an old friend who tells the demons where to find him, in the ditches of Arali. Dumuzi prays again to Utu, who turns Dumuzi into a gazelle. He flees first to Kubiresh, then to the refuge of the goddess marvelously called "Old Belili," and finally to his sister Geshtinanna's sheepfold, where he is captured and broken to pieces.

One might see Dumuzi's behavior as typical of the male under marital stress, taking refuge with feminine family members, first his grandmother and then his sister, or simply withdrawing into the wilderness.

Dumuzi retreats all the way back to the Great Mother herself, the source of all being, as if his marital conflict with Inanna had activated the deepest archetypal layers of a mother complex which is ultimately projected onto his sister Geshtinanna, in whose "sheepfold" he finally takes refuge—that the Sumerian sheepfold is a euphemism for the womb suggests an incestuous level of attachment.

The demons sent after Dumuzi by his wife sever these apron strings. Dumuzi is forcibly removed from the sheepfold and stripped of holy crown, royal garments, royal scepter, and holy sandals, leaving him bound and naked, like Inanna in the underworld. These images poignantly express the pain of separation from one's estranged wife.

We do not have an account of Dumuzi's descent to Ereshkigal, for which he is now prepared. Instead, our story ends with the magnificently poetic lamentations of three women: Dumuzi's mother, wife, and sister. These personify the three fates and the three aspects of Dumuzi's own inner feminine principle. Inanna arranges for Dumuzi and his sister Geshtinanna to alternate terms in the underworld—perhaps an image of the cycles of the grain (Dumuzi) and the grape (Geshtinanna).

Dumuzi thus becomes the first of a long line of dying and resurrecting gods (consorts of the Triple or Great Goddess) that ends with Jesus. His relationship with his sister Geshtinanna in particular is very beautifully wrought, and it parallels the earlier brother-sister relationship between Gilgamesh and Inanna.

Taken together with the complex sister-bride relationship between Isis and Osiris in Egypt, these ancient prototypes of the hero and heroine's journey give us precious images of sibling relationships. In the Sumerian material, the relationship is important at puberty and then again at midlife: Gilgamesh drives Inanna's demons away in the former, while Geshtinanna interprets Dumuzi's dreams and does time for him in the underworld in the latter.

Our Sumerian mysteries end with Inanna's return to the temples she had left at the beginning of the descent, bringing the marital journey full circle, and restoring the goddess to a power deepened by the wisdom of the abyss.

We are left to imagine the final joys of reconciliation between husband and wife.

Odysseus and Penelope

Homer's *Odyssey* is a priceless portrayal of the mysteries of marriage and relationship. When Odysseus leaves Troy at the end of the war to return home to his wife Penelope, he stops on several islands along the way, where he meets three marvelous women—Circe, Calypso, and Nausicaa.

This threesome helps him prepare for his ultimate reunion with his wife Penelope. Hence, all four women may seen as aspects of the same woman, during the different stages of her development, or as facets of Odysseus himself—of his inner feminine, or his anima, in its progressive stages of development or integration.

It is an experience which follows the pattern of the progressive integration of the anima—a man's inner feminine—so crucial to marriage. Jung wrote that this assimilation of a man's inner image of the feminine occurs in four stages: the instinctual (Eve), the romantic (Helen), the spiritual (Mary), and the sagacious (Athena). In the *Odyssey* the four stages of the anima are represented by Circe, Calypso, Nausicaa, and Penelope.[6] Each encounter with the archetypal feminine in the poem re-enacts the death and rebirth mysteries celebrated at Eleusis, which revolved around the marriage of Hades and Persephone.

The story traces the gradual transformation of the anima from its most primitive to its most civilized levels—from Circe, to Calypso, to Nausicaa, to Penelope. Although in an actual marriage these levels are always mixed up together, Homer's poem establishes clear differentiations between facets of the anima, and posits the final destination of a fulfilled marriage as the lodestar of psychic growth.

Circe lives in a stone hut in the center of a solitary island. Her name means circle, "a fitting name for a daughter of the Sun, since the solar movement is circling" (Kerényi 10-11). As daughter of the sun, Circe is an apt initial epiphany of the Self. Rather than approach her directly (another indication of Homer's psychological *savoir faire*), Odysseus sends a scouting party, who see her surrounded by wolves and mountain lions, tamed by the drugs she feeds them.

The scouts hear Circe singing, while weaving an ambrosial fabric on her loom, "by that craft known to the goddesses of heaven." She invites the men to a meal of cheese, barley, and dark honey mixed with wine, into which she drops a drug to make the men forget their fatherland. The drug changes them into pigs, though with human minds intact, and she pens them up in a pigsty to eat acorns, cornel berries, and pig fodder.

One might say this is first impact of the feminine upon the immature male, who becomes bestial in love. The subsequent job the woman must do is turn pigs into men—a central task of marriage! Circe, therefore, is a complicated woman. As daughter of Helios, she is associated with the light of the Self, which illuminates all psychic events, and gathers them into its magnetic circle of reference.

Yet being surrounded by wolves, lions, and pigs, and with wild bucks ranging freely on her island, she also represents the Lady of the Beasts, a kind of Artemis figure at home only in the solitary wilderness of distant islands. She mediates between the spiritual domain of the heavens and the earthy, primitive kingdom of animal life, yet she still lives far from the "fatherland" of domestic life.

In addition, she is associated with Aphrodite, and her allure reduces men to the most primitive levels of sexual need and instinctual craving. Yet the land around her is traversed by "wide watercourses," and like Athena she sits weaving at her loom, and is therefore rudimentarily connected with the basic arts and crafts of a civilized world.

I say rudimentarily, because, in spite of the complexities and contradictions in her nature, Homer appears primarily to mean to present her as a primitive goddess, one who lives alone, without social relations, surrounded by animals. He tells us that there are no farms, no cultivated land on her wild island, and the acorns she feeds her "men" is the food of the most primitive stages of a hunting and gathering civilization.

The contrast with Calypso, the next goddess on the itinerary, is therefore calculated and instructive. For although Calypso is also solitary and asocial, she is associated with vegetative life and the rudimentary arts of agriculture and viniculture, unlike Circe, who is symbolic of a more primitive stage of human development.

Odysseus stays with Circe for just one year, and with Calypso for seven, an indication of his progressive growth from promiscuous sexuality towards marital commitment with Penelope. Yet Calypso is still a dangerous nymph who lives and sings alone on a distant island, far from the normal intercourse of men and the gods—in the fairy realm, that is to say, of the nymphs of the unconscious.

Nevertheless, Calypso is a step forward in the progressive integration of the anima. Homer's imagery reflects this development. Like Circe, Calypso sits weaving at her loom with a golden shuttle, while singing in a sweet voice. But, Homer adds, she sits on a stone by a hearth with a great fire blazing; whereas, in the case of Circe, there had only been wisp of smoke from her stone cottage, with no sight of the hearth.

The detail is significant, because civilization began with the establishment and adornment of the hearth. With the transition from Circe to Calypso, Homer has begun the domestication of Odysseus in relation to the feminine, and this is a crucial development in marriage.[7]

Calypso is not surrounded by animals and bestial men as Circe was, but by trees, birds, trellised vines, and beds of flowers. The anima has progressed from the wild freedom of Aphrodite towards the cultivated earth goddess, Demeter.

At precisely this point, Zeus intervenes by sending Hermes as an emissary of Athena's will to return Odysseus to the city, Ithaca, and to his wife, Penelope. He must therefore be wrested from the arms of the reluctant nymph Calypso, who attempts to detain her mortal lover by offering him immortality.

Odysseus's reply to this temptation is the classic statement of the Western attitude towards the transcendentalism of the East: faced with all the adversities of the sea, with death, old age, and shipwreck, Odysseus simply replies, "Let the trial come." Thereby he rejects the siren call of disengagement from life, and remains committed to his marriage with Penelope.

The gradual disentanglement from the snares of the unconscious begins, in the poem as in marriage, not with the ego, but with the unconscious itself: it is Zeus and Athena, archetypal figures associated with the Self, who initiate Odysseus' escape from the allure of Calypso.

That is to say, growth in marriage is very largely an act of grace, although surely Odysseus's continual longing for home has sustained the relationship. He sits weeping for seven years on a stone by the sea, longing for home and his wife Penelope. By night, however, he submits to the snares of Calypso and her dreamlike pleasures.

This longing for home distinguishes the wanderings of Odysseus from the random peregrinations of a philanderer, and establishes the special connection to the feminine and her archetypal depths that only marriage can give us. Hence, the next woman in the story appears in the context of city life, though still at one step removed from the normal conditions of a purely human civilization.

Calypso's island had been a sort of Elysium, with four springs bubbling up near one another, streaming outwards from their maternal source like the four rivers of Eden, far from the normal vicissitudes of human life.[8] Nausicaa, the third of Odysseus's encounters with the divine feminine, shares this distance from life with Calypso, but since she exists in a social context (having as her parents a King or Queen who rule an elegant kingdom of seafarers), she stands just at the gateway or return threshold which will lead Odysseus from the dream kingdom by the sea to his home in Ithaca.

Odysseus first sees Nausicaa on the seashore, where she has been advised by Athena, who came to her in a dream, to wash her laundry in the streams that run into the sea, in preparation for her marriage. Odysseus, "far gone in weariness and oblivion" after a night recuperating from his shipwreck and three day swim, is awakened by the sound of the girls playing ball and emerges from a small grove of olive trees under which he had spent the night.[9] All the nymphs flee at the sight of this lion like man, "rain-drenched, wind-buffeted ... Streaked with brine, and swollen."

Nausicaa, however—husbands much in her mind—apparently knows a good thing when she sees it. While her nymphs cower, she gives Odysseus clothes and oil, and instructs him to bathe in the river, from which he emerges refreshed and reborn, shedding the god-like splendor Athena has endowed him with. Nausicaa then returns home to her father with her prize, and Athena wraps a cloud of invisibility around Odysseus to protect him from the curiosity of the locals, and which she removes only when he throws himself at the mercy of Alkinoos by sitting abruptly down in his hearth.

It is important to note at this point that Athena has replaced Hermes as the psychopomp or tutelary spirit of the hero journey leading to marriage. This shows that Odysseus is beginning to leave the archetypal realm of dreams, nymphs, nekyias, and wanderings associated with Hermes, and to make his way back to the polis of domestic life, of which Athena is the goddess. While in the realm of the unconscious, a male deity had served to guide him through the labyrinth of the archetypal feminine; as Odysseus makes his way back to his Kingdom on Ithaca, a feminine deity becomes his guide and protector.

Yet the world Nausicaa inhabits, as civilized and refined as it is— with its athletic contests, banquets, and courtly ceremonies—is still more divine than human, and her offer of marriage with Odysseus represents the familiar temptation of the hero to remain in the magic circle of the archetypal realm, rather than to make his way back into the normal sufferings of human life. Although the Phaiakians inhabit a civilized island, where the plow has "parceled out the black land," Skheria is still just one step removed from the Calypso's Elysium, somewhere between the archetypal and the human realms. Apollonius of Rhodes tells us that "the sickle used by Cronos to castrate his father Uranus" lies buried under its soil on Skheria; that "Demeter of the underworld ... lived there once and taught the Titans to reap corn for food;" and that Macris, who "took the infant Dionysus to her bosom and moistened his parched lips with honey .... came to the remote Phaiakian land, where she lived in the sacred cave and brought abundance to the people."

The Phaiakian palace has "high rooms ... airy and luminous / as though with lusters of the sun and moon" and "with an azure molding / of lapis lazuli." Its orchard (which Homer describes at length—again in contrast to the primitive condition of the other islands of the Odyssean itinerary (Calypso, Circe, and the Cyclops)— occupies "four spacious acres planted / with trees in bloom and weighted down for picking: / pear trees, pomegranates, brilliant apples, / luscious figs, and olives ripe and dark" that grow from trees whose fruit never fails, in winter or in summer.

In addition to all of these distinguishing features of a high civilization, Homer adds the traditions of storytelling. And the story Odysseus hears in the halls of the magical palace is a complex allegory of creativity in marriage. Homer puts it right in the middle of his tale, at the crucial moment when Odysseus names himself, and begins to tells his own story, to King Alkìnoös, Queen Arete, Nausicaa, and the rest of the Phaiákian court.

The court poet of Skhèria, Demódokos, gets up to recite the story of Ares, Aphrodite, and Hephaistos. This wonderful tale is far more than a story about adultery; it is also a complex allegory about the secrets of poetry, and the world.

Hephaistos, as the craftsman of the gods, represents the artist, and the secrets of his craft art in general. The world itself was fashioned by an artist, called the Demiurge, who shaped the cosmos following the forms given by God. Aphrodite and Ares came to represent two fundamental aspects of the process: creation and destruction, fusion and separation.

In the story Demódokos tells, Hephaistos forges a powerful, invisible net to catch his wife Aphrodite (Goddess of Love) in bed with Ares (God of War). As early as Empedocles (5th century B.C.E.), the union of Aphrodite and Ares came to represent the union of "Love and Strife, concord and discord," which themselves were conceived of as "the forces, functioning in alteration, that unite and separate the four elements in a universal process of forms coming into being and dissolving" (Campbell, *Bullfinch* 8).

We recognize the same forces, in modern physics and chemistry, as fusion and fission: fusion drives atoms together to form molecules and ignite nuclei; fission separates molecules into the elements, from which new compounds may be formed. Both forces are involved in the universal processes of creation, as Renaissance painters knew when they painted scenes of the marriage of Ares and Aphrodite.

Hephaistos, therefore, synthesizes the two powers which drive all creation generally, and marriage in particular—which is always a debate between love and war.

When Hephaistos surprises Aphrodite and Ares in his bed, he holds the whole world in his net. Aphrodite fuses all things together;

while Ares separates, distinguishes, holds apart. Both processes are basic to artistry, and to epic poetry particularly, which must simultaneously gather together and keep distinct the numerous elements of its total composition (from the line, to the oral formula, to the episode).

Love and war are also the central themes of the Homeric epics, beginning with the abduction of Helen and leading to the battle between the suitors who compete for Penelope.

Fusion and fission are also basic to the mythology of marriage in alchemy, which involves breaking matter down into its constituent elements, and recombining them to form new molecules. Hence the image of Ares and Aphrodite caught in the net of Hephaistos (who is a smith) is a metaphor for the sacred mysteries behind the marriage of Sol and Luna, the Sun and the Moon, the King and the Queen.

The knotting of the net, therefore, represents the Creation, which, like a marriage, is woven together from the opposite powers of love and war, of male and female, of union and separation. We still say that we have "Tied the knot" when we get married. We have also made possible the creation of new worlds, of new lives.

Making a net requires weaving separate strands together, like rope plaiting (see below). It is an old image of the creation of the cosmos, which Hindu mythology compared to a net of gems, in which each gem reflects all of the others.

The net also symbolized the "life giving power of the Goddess." In Minoan Crete there was a deity called "The Lady of Nets." Alternatively, the net is the world of Maya, which ensnares the soul, like a captured bird, in the warp and woof of fear and desire (Ares and Aphrodite).

The image of the net is also tied up with sewing, spinning, and weaving, as traditional metaphors of creativity, and with the imagery of the knot, or the labyrinth. In the Upanishads, Brahma creates the world like a spider spinning his web of a single thread, each knot of the net a soul.

To be free of maya's network is to be released from all those knots of the heart which relationships create—we still come to therapists to say that we feel all tied up in knots. Those who have achieved liberation from it all have had the knots undone.

Hence, the revelation of the mysteries of marriage, of the soul, and of the creation lie disguised right in the center of the hero journey of Odysseus, whose story captures the attention of the entire court, like Hephaistos catching the world in the web of his own creation.

Like Odysseus, both poet and reader journey through the labyrinth of the world and text, joyfully ensnared by the twistings of the plot, all tied up in knots, until the time for shedding the mortal coils of the maze arises at last. That time comes when Odysseus is finally escorted home to Ithaka by the Phaiakians.

Odysseus brings a rich treasure hoard back with him, gathered from his oneiric wanderings on the godly sea. The Phaiakian sailors deposit him, sleeping and laden with bronze and gold, on his native shores, beside the cave of the Naiades.

These are "immortal girls" whose mystic cave contains "winebowls hollowed in the rock / and amphorai" to which bees bring honey. There are great looms of stone where "the weaving nymphs make tissues", clear springs in the cavern that flow forever, and two entrances: "one on the north allows descent of mortals, / but beings out of light alone, the undying, / can pass by the south slit; no men come there.

In a sense, Odysseus is still dripping with the ambrosial dew of archetypal seas, still very near to the wild heart of the immortal psyche. In order to make his way back to his wife Penelope, he must again bypass the magical allure of the sea-nymphs, who signify the hypnotic pull of the anima into the depths of the unconscious, and who are most dangerous just when the hero is about to return to the domestic world of marriage.

Athena disguises Odysseus as a beggar, and takes him to a swineherd's hut, where he is reunited with his old father, Laertes, and later with his son Telemachus. The atonement spans three generations, and embracing past, present and future.

It is a reconciliation of opposites that will be repeated after the slaughter of the suitors reunites Odysseus and Penelope. The reunion of husband and wife reenacts the sacred marriage of the Sun and the Moon, and hence is the climax of the marriage mysteries.

Each woman Odysseus encounters on his journey (Circe, Calypso, and Nausicaa) is progressively more humanized, more willing to be fully assimilated, yet bearing the seeds of future trials and further growth. In a sense, they are all part of one woman—Penelope—in the different stages of her life and marriage.

In the reunion of Odysseus and Penelope, the two worlds of the unconscious and conscious minds are joined in a moment of achieved individuation—which, as subsequent legend has it, simply yields to further wanderings, and the final consummation, in a land far from the sea.

Persephone and Hades

The "Homeric Hymn to Demeter" contains one of the most beautiful of all heroine journey cycles, and one of our most profound myths of marriage. It provides an image of the female journey, in counterbalance to the male, covering all the basic stages of feminine growth and development. It particularly focuses on the problems of puberty, marriage, mid-life, and old age—all of which involve journeys of a different sort.

Persephone's journey into marriage begins with the famous abduction by Hades, Lord of the Underworld, while she is picking flowers in a field, with twenty three nymphs attending her. This yields twenty-four nymphs total, counting Persephone, which suggests the diurnal symbolism of the hours. As an image of totality, the number implies the all embracing domain of the Great Goddesses of antiquity, and also establishes a cosmic parallel for Persephone's journey: like the sun, moon, seasons, and hours, she periodically undertakes the descent into Hades.

The call to adventure takes the form of a marvelous narcissus flower; when Persephone picks this "lure," the earth opens up and her husband Hades carries her down with his chariot and "immortal horses." In some versions, a herd of pigs follows the newly wed couple down into the abyss, covering up their tracks, so that Demeter is unable to follow her daughter's tracks. These two animals—the pig and the horse—will reappear throughout the ages as symbols of the Goddess and the descent into the underworld.

A thousand and one variations will also ensue on the imagery of abduction as the first phase of the hero journey, and it seems an appropriate image for marriage—when we give our daughters to those strangers who appear on our doorstep, and they carry them off in their cars.

The abduction is not only the beginning of Persephone's journey into marriage, however; it is also her mother Demeter's call to adventure, as the two heroine journeys (of mother and daughter) are intimately intertwined. Demeter hears the eerie, profound cries of Persephone echoing from mountain peak and ocean bottom, as Hades carries her daughter off to the marriage bed below.

As with the descent of Inanna, it is the act of listening which initiates the separation phase of Demeter's journey at mid-life, the time when the mother loses the daughter within, and the daughter without. And as with Inanna, clothing symbolism immediately emerges to signal the crisis: after a sharp pain grips Demeter's heart, she tears "the headband round her divine hair," casts the "dark veil" from off her shoulders, and rushes over land and sea "like a bird," searching for Persephone.

In Sumerian, Babylonian, and Egyptian art, the soul in the underworld is commonly depicted as a bird, whether it flies up or down. In Persian myth, a legendary bird called the Simurgh is said to have left an impression of its feathers upon all of our hearts, the memory of which allows the soul to take flight. Bird flight and divestiture will remain archetypal symbols of the marriage mysteries right up to the literature of the present.

Demeter wanders for nine days with bright torches in her hands, before speaking to Hekate, and then to Helios, lord of the Sun, who tells her of Persephone's fate. That the goddess Hekate hears but does not see Persephone being dragged down into Hades suggests, among other things, the importance of poetry in the religious rituals of marriage.

When Demeter hears of her daughter's fate—abducted by her "own brother from the same seed"—for this marriage has involved a family conspiracy, the males (Zeus and Hades) having teamed up against the women to barter off Persephone—she is overcome by anger and grief, which compels her separation from the Olympian gods, and further descent into the realm of mortal mankind.

Tearing at her body, Demeter wanders to Eleusis, suddenly aging, so that she now looks like an old woman "barred from childbearing and the gifts of wreath-loving Aphrodite." She has reached a turning point in her life and marriage—that of meno-pause—and she sits manically depressed by a well with an olive tree growing above it.

Four daughters from the royal household come carrying copper vessels to fetch the water for their father, and find the old woman sitting by the well. The image of the Goddess at the Well, symbolic of her power as the source of all life, has a noble pedigree and lineage to come: one thinks of Rebecca at the well in the Old Testament; of the Samaritan woman in the New; of the mysterious maidens of the well in Celtic and Arthurian mythologies; of the nymphs of the water Goddess from Northumberland; and of the three ladies of the sacred spring at Carrowburgh on Hadrian's Wall, spilling water from urns.

The woman at the well is a marvelous icon of the creative power of the Goddess. But the well is also an entrance to the otherworld, not only in Celtic myth, but also in biblical story of Joseph, whose journey down into Egypt begins when his brothers throw him into a well.

When the four daughters of Keleos return from the well, bringing Demeter to the palace, the Goddess takes the job of nursemaid for the young prince, born late in life to Queen Metaneira. The boy is Demeter's surrogate child, to compensate for the loss of her daughter Persephone (and hence of her own maternity) during midlife.

When Demeter steps into the palace, the symbolism of torches, divestiture, and sacred springs yields to a common icon of the passage between the two worlds in the sacred rituals of marriage, the doorway. After the four daughters lead Demeter through the "portico" to where their mother sits "by a pillar," they then turn to watch the Goddess step across "the threshold," and they are awestruck when Demeter's head touches the roof, and she fills "the doorway with divine radiance."

The doorway marks the incarnation of the divine into the mortal realm, Demeter's descent from Mt. Olympus into the underworld of human experience. In addition to the emphatic use of such images as the "portico," "threshold," and "doorway," the Homeric poet places the "lady mother" of the household (Metaneira) beside a "pillar," which is another archaic symbol of the Great Goddess, appearing in association with eggs, caves and crypts, snake and phallus, as symbols of her womb and tomb.

Doorway symbols also represent a state of being betwixt and between, of transition, and hence are often found in association with rites of passage like marriage (Persephone), midlife and menopause (Demeter), and death (Hecate). These are the three phases of feminine development which lie at the heart of the Homeric Hymn.

What happens next, within the confines of the sacred space of the palace—marked off by pillar, portico, threshold, and doorway—constitutes the initiatory phase of Demeter's midlife journey (the point when mother becomes mother-in-law, and grandmother).

This transition involves the imagery of death and rebirth, for whenever an old self dies, a new one is born to take its place.

Each night Demeter nurses the little prince, Demophoön. She breathes sweetly upon him, anoints him with ambrosia, and hides him "like a firebrand in the blazing fire!" The scene recalls the wanderings of Isis, who, while searching for her murdered husband Osiris, comes to Abydos, and the courtyard with the erica tree growing up around the cedar coffin in which her husband Osiris lies entombed. Like Demeter, Isis takes on the task of nursing the young prince, whom she anoints nightly and puts in the fire, meanwhile turning herself into a swallow to flit mournfully around the erica tree

Both Goddesses—Demeter and Isis—are interrupted as they perform rituals designed to confer immortality upon their charges (a task which seems appropriate to women who have just experienced the deaths of husband and child). The Queen mother bursts upon the scene and breaks the spell in terror for their children.

Demeter admonishes the Queen and then instructs her to build the temple of Eleusis, into which she retreats for a protracted period of mourning—such as many women must do at menopause—during which she creates famine by withholding the fruits of the earth.

Denied the sacrificial offerings of the harvest, Zeus sends Iris to negotiate with the grieving Demeter, who refuses to "allow the grain in the earth to sprout forth" until she is reunited with her daughter Persephone. To this end, Zeus sends Hermes down to Hades with the mission of retrieving Persephone, whose marriage journey the poem now turns to explore.[10]

After the separation from her mother, Hades, the Lord of the Underworld, takes Persephone down below, where the initiation stage of her journey, associated with death and rebirth, proceeds. During this stage, Persephone changes from maidenly resistance to joyful acceptance of the riches offered by her husband, before the god Hermes confronts Hades with the message from Zeus, which orders the Lord of the underworld to release Persephone, and allow her to return to her mother—something all young brides certainly feel the need to do.

Before Hermes persuades Hades to release Persephone, however, Hades contrives to feed her a "honey-sweet pomegranate seed," in order to ensure that "she might not spend / all her days again with dark-robed, revered Demeter." The food of the "pomegranate seed, sweet as honey to eat"—as Persephone later confesses to her mother—recalls the forbidden fruit, from the biblical tree of knowledge, "whose mortal taste / Brought death into the world and all our woe" (*Paradise Lost* 2-3).

Like the bread and water of life, which bring Inanna back to life, the honeyed pomegranate is a sacrificial offering. In the Ancient world, the dead were embalmed in honey. Hence, "'To fall into a jar of honey' became a common metaphor" for death. The Lady of the Labyrinth on Crete also received a jar of honey as an offering.

Our "honeymoons" then are intricate passages into the maze of marriage, a journey which will require many descents.

The husband in our tale, Hades, is called "Aidoneus, Ruler of Many," an epithet which brings up important ideas relevant to the sacred mysteries of marriage. James Hillman suggests that the word "Aidoneus" is related to the word "eidos," Plato's word for the perfect Forms, the ideas that give shape and significance to life.

The heroic descent to the underworld—particularly as it develops in the context of marriage—typically involves the revelation of the form or pattern guiding one's life. The revelation of destiny is a key aspect of the sacred mysteries of marriage—for the word mystery implies a secret to be made known.

The rape and marriage of Persephone to the Lord of the Underworld may also refer to a transition from a materialistic to a psychological point of view. Marriage activates the archetypal forms of the creative imagination. The first thing Persephone does when reunited with her mother is to tell the story of her marriage, rehearsing its "every point."

Persephone, that is to say, becomes a poet, a storyteller. That is another aspect of the creativity of marriage—it makes artists out of us, by deepening and enriching our humanity, and our experience.

Persephone's ecstatic reunion with her mother Demeter is one of the most moving moments in the history of the heroine's journey. She comes up from Hades on a chariot. The powerful horses surge unchecked over sea, rivers, glens, and mountain peaks, as mother rushes to daughter, like a maenad tearing through the shady woodland of Dionysus.

The theme of the atonement (the union of father and son) often marks the climax of the initiations of the male journey: the reunion of Odysseus, Laertes, and Telemachus in the shepherd's hut on Ithaka, for example, represents the reconciliation of Eternity and Time, Death and Life. In the Bible, the reunion of the Prodigal Son and his Father symbolizes the relationship between Jesus and God. The atonement combines with the symbolism of homecoming to represent the soul's arrival at its eternal destination.

But, in the "Homeric Hymn to Demeter," the great roles of the atonement are played by mother and daughter, both of whose marital journeys come full circle with their tender reunion.[11] Mother and daughter spend several months together, before Persephone returns to her husband in the underworld, for the winter season.

Which brings us to some final questions: How much relationship is too much relationship?

Do we need quality time away from each other, in separation and solitude?

Is this quality time alone and/or away a significant part of the deal?

The myth would seem to say so: Persephone spends a part of every year in the upperworld with her mother, and the rest with her husband Hades in the lower.

Must he then carry her off once every year? Reenact the old story of the dark stranger, while she reenacts that of the resistant virgin?

Could be.

Cupid and Psyche

One of the best beloved and most enduring of heroine journey cycles about marriage comes down to us in a Roman novel by Apuleius called the *Metamorphoses*, but known to the world as *The Golden Ass*.

Like the Bible, a single large hero journey cycle frames numerous smaller cycles—the most important of which concerns the marriage of Cupid and Psyche. The great age of the story and the fact that it is told by an old woman to a young bride to be, suggests a long history of oral transmission stretching back far beyond Apuleius, so that the tale condenses a powerful tradition of matrilineal wisdom regarding marriage.[12]

Psyche's journey begins with an involuntary call to adventure, when her great beauty arouses the wrathful jealousy of Venus, and Psyche is banished from her home. She is sent to a mountain ridge (threshold border between the worlds in Sumerian, Babylonian, and Egyptian myths) where it is said she will become a serpent's bride, a widespread motif in the mythologies of the Ancient Mediterranean region. This mythic image of marriage with a monster permeated the pre-biblical cultures the Near East and the Indus river valleys, until its message of joyful participation in the rhythms of life and death was transformed by the patriarchs of the Greeks and the Hebrews.[13]

Psyche is magically wafted by the wind from the mountaintop to a magnificent palace in a paradisal valley, with a fountain spewing water in the middle of a grove. As in the Bible, the fountain is a symbol of the source and origin of all life, as is the sacred vessel of the woman of the well who attends it. Soon after her arrival, Psyche crosses the threshold—where, from time immemorial, marital rituals have been performed—into the halls of the marvelous palace, which is built of gemstones, the finest citron wood and ivory, and, most significantly, golden pillars and silver walls.

Gold and silver are associated with the marriage of the Sun and the Moon, the periodic union of which became a symbol of the reconciliation of Eternity and Time, of the King and the Queen, of Male and Female.[14] The palace Psyche walks into is a castle of marvels, a motif that will become one of the standard metaphors of the initiation phase of marriage, for it represents a recovery of the imagined paradise of our childhood homes—a place where, as Apuleius puts it, no wish but finds its fulfillment, and no treasure of the world is forbidden (an Eden of the Id!).

But, as we have seen in the story of Inanna, crossing the threshold into the otherworld of marriage will take its toll. Inside the palace, Psyche loses her virginity, as her mysterious bridegroom comes to her nightly, unseen, and the passage into womanhood initiates a second, more arduous journey.

After her jealous sisters cast aspersions upon her invisible mate, Psyche succumbs to curiosity, and during one fateful night holds an oil lamp above her husband (who turns about to be Cupid himself, son of Venus, the Goddess of love), a drop of which she spills while fiddling with the arrows in his quiver (Freudians take note)! The drop burns his wing, and he flies off: first into a tree, and then back home to his mother Venus, where he will enjoy a long, lonely sulk.

James Joyce defined myth as that which never happened continuing to happen every day, and surely this sequence repeats itself with every relationship. For every marriage is a journey. 'Seeing the light,' 'getting burned,' pricking one's finger on the forbidden arrows of love, running home to mama—all have entered our vocabulary of love, and will remain so forever.

The oil lamp Psyche uses to catch a glimpse of her invisible husband is the sacred vessel of the mystery rites (and indeed a symbol of the marriage of the soul with God in the parable of the Virgins). The quiver of arrows also has a long mythological pedigree and lineage. Many heroes shoot arrows randomly to find brides in folktales (as in the Russian tale of "The Frog Princess," or Antoine Galland's "Prince Ahmed and the Fairy Pari-Banou"). The arrow itself represents the soul's directed flight to the bull's eye, symbol of the passage through the Hindu door of the sun, into the otherworld.[15]

And indeed, Psyche's marriage will ultimately take her into the heavens, to the realm of the Gods on Mt. Olympus.

Before she gets there, however, she must undergo the trials and ordeals of marriage, after being separated from her home for the second time—this time from her husband.

Cupid abandons Psyche (at this point, an unwed mother to be), and flies home to mamma. Psyche's first impulse is to jump in the river and drown (suicide is a temptation aroused by the trials and ordeals of marriage).

The river, as always, represents another threshold crossing into the underworld, and here, as elsewhere, Psyche receives assistance and guidance, just when she needs it most. The god of nature, Pan, suddenly appears, and he instructs Psyche to go in search of Venus, her mother in law to be, and the source of all her troubles!

Along the way, Psyche must encounter three goddesses— Ceres, Juno, and Proserpine—and, at the command of Venus (her rather demanding mother-in-law), perform the various tasks, with the assistance of the various helpers, for which the tale is justly famous.

With the assistance of an army of ants, Psyche sits in a lonely corner of a granary, to sort a huge pile of the seeds (lentils, barley, wheat, and poppy).

With the help of some reeds, who whisper advice in her ear, as she sits dejected in marshes, Psyche plucks strands of Golden Fleece from a flock of wild rams by the riverside.

Then she has to climb to the mountaintop to collect a crystal jar full of the water of death, which two of Jupiter's eagles help her to do.

Psyche's final task is to go down to the underworld to get a jar of beauty cream from Persephone, Queen of the Dead.

Psyche's tasks and helpers have been beautifully, and variously, interpreted in the many fine commentaries of our times. For Erich Neumann, the four tasks are associated with the four elements of the creation—the ants earth, the reeds water, the eagles air, and Cupid fire. Both Marie-Louise von-Franz and Erich Neumann suggest that the tasks embody the feminine quest for wholeness. The quaternity of Goddesses represents aspects of the feminine, which all men and women must integrate:

The maternal Ceres, mother of the grain, whose seeds must be sorted out, and whose helpers, the ants, represent the intuitive wisdom of the psyche.

The sexual Venus, who also represents the problem of the jealous stepmother (both a person to cope with and a role to be played by many women), and whose helpers, the reeds, represent the patient voices of nature, which help us to cope with the threats of aggressive rams, symbols of domestic violence.

The dutiful wife, Juno, whose husband's eagles help Psyche to 'get above it all' and gather the bitter waters of death from between the dragons' jaws.

And the dread Goddess of Death, Proserpine, who represents the last stage of growth, for which Psyche receives guidance not from nature, but from the tower, an artifact of civilization.

All four of these tasks involve four separate heroine journey cycles, all appropriate to what Gail Sheehy referred to as the "passages" typically to be navigated during a normal woman's life and marriage.

James Hillman relates the four tasks to the initiation rites of psychotherapy, ordeals by which the structure of consciousness is transformed, in preparation for the inner marriage of Cupid and psyche.

The story is so important because it provides us with a mythic model (incorporating both sexuality and spirituality) for our relationships, all of which involve "an Odyssey of the human soul." The story represents the activation of the imagination crucial to marriage, for all relationships combine psyche and eros, and, by shattering the defenses of the ego, lead us into the realm of the soul, where we may encounter the gods.

Hence, Psyche's story typifies the tendency of relationships to collapse, constantly, and repeatedly into trouble: "So quick bright things come to confusion," as Shakespeare's Lysander wisely notes in *A Midsummer Night's Dream*. But this collapse is creative: things must fall apart before they can become whole. As Crazy Jane reminds the Bishop in Yeats' great poem, "'Nothing can be sole or whole / That has not been rent.'"

For "Eros is born of Chaos," as Hillman poignantly reminds us, "and will always hearken back to its origins in chaos and will seek it for its revivification. Eros will attempt again and again to create those dark nights and confusions which are its nest. It renews itself in affective attacks, jealousies, fulminations, and turmoils. It thrives close to the dragon."

Psyche's last task, therefore, constitutes one of the most interesting versions of the descent into Hades in the entire history of the mythic marriage. Her helper this time is a talking tower, which tells Psyche that she must seek out the hole of hell and pass through a gaping door that leads down an untrodden track into the caverns of darkness.

There follows a threshold crossing of supreme importance for the sacred mysteries of marriage.

After passing through the doorway, Psyche encounters five figures before coming into Proserpine's Palace. They are Ocnus, a lame man driving a lame ass. Charon, the ferryman to the Farther Shore. A dead man floating on the surface of the Styx, who imploringly raises his rotted hands for help. Some old women weaving. And, finally, Cerberus, a colossal dog with three heads, standing guard before the threshold of the Palace (the second doorway down).

Psyche receives further instructions from the talking tower: it tells her to ignore Ocnus, to ignore the dead man on the river, and to ignore the weavers—all of whom will ask her assistance.

Perhaps there comes a time in marriage where sympathy becomes inappropriate.

Psyche must also carry two bits of money in her mouth, and she must feed the three-headed dog, Cerberus, a piece of barley-bread soaked in honey-wine.

These are fascinating, beautiful symbols of the mysteries of life, death, and marriage. Corpses have been excavated from Roman catacombs buried with coins beneath their tongues to pay Charon for the ferryboat across the river of death. The three-headed dog guarding the doorway is familiar to us from the labors of Hercules and the descent of Aeneas. The weaving women also suggest the symbolism of the Fates, typically situated in the underworld (as in the myth of Perseus).

But the symbolism of weaving, combined with the image of Ocnus, the lame ass driver, points to something far more rich and strange: oddly enough, the descent to the underworld represents an allegory of creativity in marriage. These marital mysteries revolve around the mortuary symbolism of Ocnus, the rope plaiter, whom

Psyche encounters during a descent into hell that will lead, eventually, to a happy reunion with her estranged husband.

Ocnus, like the weaving women, symbolizes the fertility of marriage, and hence of the material world—which the enlightened soul must be liberated from by death. Ocnus himself represents the creation and preservation of the material world, which he achieves by weaving together the two strands of the rope. These two strands represent the duality of nature, the procreative marriage of man and woman.

Like Ocnus the rope plaiter, therefore, the weaving women whom Psyche encounters during her descent into hell represent an allegory of creativity in marriage. They are the great, primordial goddesses of Mother Earth. The web they weave is the world itself, all of which is contained in the body of the child spun within the womb.

Psyche has found life in the tomb, birth in the midst of the death, creative power in a place she thought to have been the lowest, most miserable phase of her marriage.

The imagery of rope plaiting and weaving in Psyche's underworld hence serves as a metaphor of the creative power of maternity that follows naturally from a fruitful marriage. As in the *Odyssey*, poets may be seen as weavers too, as rope plaiters, and song as the web woven from the various strands of the poet's materials.

In fact, all of the Goddesses Psyche encounters during the course of her wanderings represent the primordial creativity of nature, of which poetry and marriage are also expressions: Ceres generates and sustains the life giving grain; Juno maintains the creativity of marriage; Venus represents the powers of human reproduction; and Proserpine, the story tells us, creates that special kind of beauty, characteristic of all fully realized relationships, that comes with the awareness of death.

After Psyche returns from the underworld, with the box of beauty cream given her by the Queen of the Dead, she is overwhelmed by curiosity, and cannot resist opening the box. She has been told not to do so: Some mysteries are perhaps better kept secret.

Must we, in fact, know everything about each other in marriage? Psyche would seem to say yes.

But when she opens the box, she falls down as if dead, and must be brought back to life by her husband. Cupid flies down from his exalted throne on Mt. Olympus, to revive Psyche with a kiss.

How many of us have been brought back from death by a kiss?

Taken all together then, the tasks of Psyche's journey, which drive her away from home into the realm of the goddesses—both of above and below—and which ends in marriage and birth, depict the dynamics of creativity.

At the end, a story is born, alongside a child named Joy.

CHAPTER TWO

Medieval Romances

The enigmatic symbols in the Grail Castle of the Arthurian Romances (the cup, the bleeding lance, the wounded King) may originally have been metaphors of the sacred marriage—sexual symbols of regeneration—in one of the late Classical mystery cults carried into Northern Europe by Roman soldiers, and gone underground after the Theodosius outlawed paganism.

In such mysteries, the imagery of sexual and seasonal cycles had developed into highly sophisticated symbols of spiritual death and rebirth which were meant to have a redemptive impact upon the psyche of the initiate. From this perspective, the Grail—as the sacred vessel of the feminine—could find remote ancestors in Greek, Christian, Celtic, Orphic, and Norse mythologies.[16]

The import of these symbolic systems may have survived in the secret initiation rituals of the esoteric societies of the Middle Ages, and in the marvelous romances of the time. Many of the most important of these romances combine the symbolism of the sacred marriage with journeys to the otherworld, thereby producing some of our most profound meditations upon the mysteries of relationship.

Orfeo and Heurodis

The Middle English poem "Sir Orfeo" retells the Classical myth of the mortal queen, Heurodis, abducted by Pluto, the lord of the underworld, a realm of fairy enchantment. Heurodis—the abducted Eurydice of Classical myth—must be retrieved by her grief-stricken, harp-playing husband, Orfeo.[17]

The journey begins with madness and grief, in the form of a dream vision, followed by the abduction of Queen Heurodis. The dream vision occurs beneath an "ympe tree" (a grafted tree) on a fine May morning, where Heurodis has gone with her maids to enjoy the fields, which are full of flowers, with blossoms on every bough of the orchard.

While sleeping in her orchard, beneath the ympe tree, Heurodis dreams of a king, with a crown of precious stone shining as brightly as the sun, who carries her off on a white pony to his palace. He then promises to abduct her again the next day, after he returns her to the orchard beneath the "ympe" tree (a curious pun, certainly, on imp or elf, which links faeries to tree spirits).

Heurodis has this dream shortly before noon, at a time of day the poet calls "undertide," a word suggestive of an underworld of time beneath natural time, yet coextensive with it.

The dream anticipates the complete heroine's journey cycle (from orchard to underworld palace and back to orchard), like one of those premonitory dreams which drive people into analysis and predict the entire course of development that lies ahead.

Indeed, this dream precipitates neurotic symptoms, as Heurodis falls into an hysterical fit, thrashing around, rubbing her hands and feet, scratching her face until it bleeds, tearing her body with her sharp nails, and ripping her robe to pieces.

It would be difficult to find a more clinically exact portrait of those ravings of witless hysteria which occasionally bedevil marriage. Heurodis refuses to speak until her husband Orfeo manages to get her back into the palace.

There is a constant association in this poem between the fairy world, marriage, and psychological turmoil. The underworld of the fairy king, Pluto, represents the dark side of the mind, and all those tempestuous emotions which may erupt at any moment, in any marriage.

There is, after all, a psychopathology of everyday marriage, and myths like "Sir Orfeo" help us to focus on the sacred mysteries within the turmoil.[18]

A cure is possible only if Orfeo, Heurodis's husband, has the love and the courage to go through madness himself, and, like Dumuzi, descend into the underworld where his wife has already been.

This is the role Sir Orfeo must commit himself to. He must endure what Jung called the alchemical marriage, the one that begins after the honeymoon is over, during which the couple is subjected to the full range of corrosive emotions which break the relationship down to its essential elements.[19]

In his grief over the loss of his wife, Orfeo hands his kingdom over to a steward and then strips off his armor to put on a pilgrim's mantle with no belt, no hood, and no shirt. He then goes barefoot into the wilderness, his various possessions cruelly stripped: he that once wore fur and slept on purple linen now lies on the moss-covered heath; he that had castle and land now is cast out into the freezing snow; he that was once surrounded by knights and ladies must now battle "wilde wormes"; he that had plenty of dainty morsels must now dig all day for roots to eat.

These lines vividly evoke the trauma of marriage at midlife.

After ten years wandering in the woods, the grieving Orfeo stumbles upon his lost his wife, and follows her and a group of faerie dancers into a rock, beneath which he finds the hidden kingdom of Pluto.

It is a fair country, shining as bright as the sun on a summer's day. In the middle of a smooth green plain, Orfeo finds a castle with walls as clear and shiny as crystal, through which he sees spacious dwellings made of precious stone. Every pillar is burnished gold, and darkness never visits the land. When it should have been the thick of night, the radiance of jewels shines brightly as the sun at midday.

Orfeo thinks he has found the court of Paradise, and he immediately gains entrance as a wandering minstrel, after the long, grueling suffering of his ordeal in the wilderness, separated from his wife.

The faerie hunt and dance are common features of Celtic legend. There is also a porter at the gates of the underworld, a kind of doorman of the dead.

At this point, Heurodis doesn't recognize her estranged husband. He looks like hell: blackened by the sun, and lean. Heurodis is still the lovely young princess, even though she is presumably in the underworld, or land of the dead.

Oddly enough, her husband from the land of the living now looks like the dark and threatening Pluto come to carry her off. The faerie King says he is too loathly a thing to be seen in company with, but nevertheless agrees to let Heurodis go.

It is to life, then, that marriage forces Heurodis to return, leaving the paradisal conditions of the faerie court behind, where there is eternal hunting and dancing among the radiance of never fading gemstones.

In this phase of her marriage, when she must return home with her husband, Heurodis represents the human soul, *Anima Mundi*— which must be "married" to the material world, i.e., must die into life to be incarnated, and achieve rebirth through death, when the soul returns to its heavenly source.

Alone again in the wilderness, after coming back from the underworld, Orfeo takes out his harp from a hollow tree on bright clear days and plays at will, so that all the beasts and birds gather round to hear his harping.[20]

Marriage can apparently make a poet out of a politician!

The intense grief, the psychological derangement, the pathology of the dream vision, the physical symptoms, the isolation in the wasteland, and the beatific vision of his wife in the court of Paradise—all raise the power of Orfeo's verse to a supernatural level.

The word "glee" used to describe the melody of the harp is derived from an Old English word (*gleo*) meaning merriment and gladness It is also used in *Sir Gawain* to designate courtly joy, where it is alliterated with *glaum*, the root of our modern word "glamour." In the Middle Ages, and in the ballad tradition, glamour was associated with the supernatural appeal of magical beauty.

Orfeo eventually returns to his rightful kingdom, though now in beggar's rags, like Odysseus. All the townspeople remark upon his long hair, his shaggy beard hanging to his knees, and his shriveled, rough, and blackened skin, still covered with the mysterious affliction the poet calls "missais."

Orfeo's harping changes all that: after shrilly tuning up, Orfeo harps the "blissfullest" notes any man ever heard. This leads to his recognition as the lost king, after which he is bathed and freshly clothed in royal garments.

This moment of recognition reminds us that the marriage journey is a search for identity, a discovery conferred upon hero and reader by the power of poetry.

There is also a deeper level of mysticism operating in this lovely poem, having to do with the marriage of this world and the other. Whereas in Christian or Gnostic thinking there is a rigid demarcation between the spiritual and the material, such dualism is blurred in Celtic circumstances.

The two worlds of the poem are equivalent rather than antithetical. Both courts are simultaneously kingdoms of the dead, and kingdoms of the living, and the soul wanders back and forth, endlessly, between them, just as the eye alternates between castle and reflection, when pondering the facade and image of a medieval chateau reflected in the lake and moat which surrounds it: this world above the water line, and the other below merge into a single image of the same mystery, transcendent yet immanent.

As Joseph Campbell puts it, "heroes may ride back and forth over the very ground of the Castle of the Grail without seeing it: and I am told that in Ireland, one may walk around and right past a fairy hill without seeing it. One seems to be walking a straight line, but actually is curving past an invisible fairy hill of glass, which is right there, but hidden—like the Hidden Truth."

Lancelot and Guenevere

One of the greatest Arthurian romances about marriage and relationship concerns the adulterous love between Lancelot and Guenevere.

Chrétien's version of the tale, called "The Knight of the Cart," begins where it will end: in the court of King Arthur at Camelot. A fully armed knight interrupts a meal to announce that he holds in captivity many knights, ladies, and maidens from Arthur's domains. They will be released on condition that one knight be allowed to accompany Queen Guenevere into the nearby woods and defend her.

Arthur's steward, Sir Kay, obtains permission to be that knight, threatening to leave Arthur's service immediately, and refusing to relent, until the Queen falls on the floor and begs Arthur to let Kay be the one.

Kay then accompanies Guenevere and the mysterious intruder, as they ride off into the woods. This causes terrific distress, grief, and dejection among the courtiers, who comment on it as outrageous, arrogant, and absurd: Kay is a steward, not a warrior to be entrusted with the Queen's safety.

As the Queen is led away, miserable and depressed, every man and woman of the court grieves as bitterly as if Guenevere lay dead in her coffin. Gawain then complains that Arthur has done an extremely silly and astonishing thing, and gets permission to ride immediately after the Queen to see how Kay fares in her defense.

Gawain finds Kay's horse with the bridle snapped (a telling detail, suggesting that all hell has broken loose!), its saddle broken and battered, and its stirrup cups bloodstained. The riderless horse signifies the removal of reason from its rightful place—something that often happens in marriage and relationship!

The court then sees Lancelot approaching on a horse that drops dead from exhaustion. Lancelot gets a new one from Gawain, which the court soon finds dead in a field trampled down and littered by broken lances and shields.

Horseless, Lancelot agrees to get on a cart pulled by a dwarf, who promises him knowledge of Guenevere's whereabouts. Lancelot hesitates two steps before climbing on the cart, because, we are told, the cart was used in those days only for criminals guilty of treason, murder, theft, or highway robbery. Anyone put in the cart would lose all legal rights and be subject to the abuse and slander which is actually heaped on Lancelot when he and Gawain arrive a castle that same evening.

This supreme public humiliation, and the gruesome details leading up to it, suggest that a serious deflation of the ego and a complete resignation of the persona is the prerequisite for the hero journey of marriage! The wounding of chivalric pride, and the violation of courtly codes, gets the story going, and deepens the relationship.

From the psychological perspective, this is typical of an onslaught of the unconscious during marriage: the disruption of normal functioning is an archetypal situation, with which every encounter with the unconscious begins. Neurotic wounding in marriage and relationship carries us into the mythical realm of the unconscious, represented in this tale by the underworld into which Guenevere is abducted, and into which Lancelot descends in order to retrieve her.

Lancelot's first ordeal occurs at midnight in the castle where he arrives in the cart. Though warned by the Lady of the castle that no knight who has been subjected to the shame of the cart would even think to lie in the magnificent bed, Lancelot asserts his right to the privilege.

This is the "Perilous Bed," popularized by the Arthurian legends in tales usually devoted to Gawain. While sleeping in the bed, Lancelot is awakened at midnight by a lance shot down from the rafters like a thunderbolt, which pins him down and bursts into flames. The head of the lance just grazes his side, and Lancelot puts the fire out, throws the weapon away, and goes back to sleep(!).

The test here is one of courage, and the temptation is of fear; the next test, therefore, is one of duty, designed to tempt Lancelot with desire. Fear, duty, and desire are the three temptations of the Buddha beneath the Boddhi Tree.

Hence, at the next castle where Lancelot spends the night, an exceedingly beautiful and elegantly dressed damsel offers her hospitality on the condition that Lancelot sleep with her, a condition which many people would have been eager to accept.

Not Lancelot, ever faithful to his King's wife.

That night, after rescuing the naked damsel from a group of rapists, he is forced to lie with her, but he does so without removing his shirt, and his fidelity to Guenevere stifles the faintest trace of desire in his heart. These two episodes at the beginning of Lancelot's journey establish Lancelot's courage and loyalty, and prepare him for a higher love (like that of the Bodhisattva's) which transcends fear and desire.

Having passed these tests, Lancelot moves more deeply into the netherworld.

First, he comes to a church with a finely sculpted and tremendously heavy sarcophagus. An inscription on the tomb says that "whosoever raises the slab will free all the people imprisoned in that land from which no traveler has as yet returned."

This is the land of the dead, Hamlet's "undiscovered country from whose bourne no traveler returns."

Lancelot astonishes the monks by raising the slab without the slightest difficulty, hence delivering all the men and women trapped in the kingdom from which no one escapes—just as Christ delivers us from death by his sacrifice and harrowing of hell.

As both the best of knights, and the worst of knights (because of his adulterous love for Guenevere), Lancelot combines godly and human traits. Like Jesus, he sacrifices himself to save others. And like a Bodhisattva, he refuses to renounce the world until all beings have been delivered from hell.

These allusions to Christ become most pronounced during the famous sword bridge crossing, a scene often depicted in Medieval art.[21]

After many preparatory ordeals, Lancelot finally arrives at the river separating this world from the next, into which Guenevere has been abducted. Lancelot arrives at this threshold late in the afternoon. The water rushing beneath the bridge is black and turbid, as horrid and terrifying as if it were the Devil's river. Two lions are tied to a stone slab at the opposite end of the bridge, which is described as a highly polished, razor sharp, glistening sword.

The peril is so formidable that one of the knights in Lancelot's company is moved to say that crossing that bridge would be like trying to return to one's mother's womb and be born again.

If Guenevere (who awaits Lancelot across the river) is the Great Goddess—with whom Lancelot will share the sexual ritual known in mythology as the *hieros gamos*, or sacred marriage, which renews all life and releases it from bondage to death—these remarks seem very cunning, especially coming from a man whom Heinrich Zimmer accused of not understanding his material!

Having been previously wounded in the side while sleeping in the Perilous Bed, Lancelot is now grievously wounded in the hands and feet while crossing the sword bridge. Upon reaching the yonder shore, blood oozing from his wounds, he looks up and sees King Bademagu and his son Meleagant anxiously watching from the window.

The wounds now include all the ones associated with Jesus, and complete the portrait of Lancelot as the Crucified Christ (bleeding from palms, feet, and side) who redeems mankind from death (remember that Lancelot had done so earlier by lifting the stone slab of the sarcophagus).

To reinforce the analogy, King Bademagu promises to heal Lancelot by using "the three Marys' ointment," the ointment brought to the tomb on Easter Sunday by three women variously identified with Mary Magdalen, Mary Salome, and Mary mother of James.[22]

But the Triple Goddess and her dying and resurrecting consort also evoke Celtic associations. Lancelot's entrance into the under-world is an entrance into the realm of the Goddess, personified by Guenevere, but also suggested by numerous other little details, such as the lions or leopards which guard the gateway of the castle at the other end of the sword bridge.

The affiliation between the lion and the Great Goddess goes all the way back to a statuette of the Goddess giving birth on a lion throne in Turkey, of about 6500 B.C.E. In Cretan myth, Lady of the Labyrinth stands on a mountain with lions on either side. And the Anatolian Goddess, Cybele, is flanked by lions.[23]

In addition to the motifs of the wounds, the sword bridge, the ointment of the three Marys, and the lions, the passage through a sequence of doorways, leading to the union of Lancelot and Guenevere, is archetypal.

Lancelot has passed through several such thresholds during his journey to the Queen: he sat on the window ledge of one castle to watch Guenevere pass by with a coffin; he defeated two armed knights at the doorway into the room where the Lady was being raped in the next castle; he broke through a gate guarded by a knight in a Stone Passage; he passed through a bailey, chamber, barred door, and narrow gate in a daunting fortress, where he needed to look at the ring given him by the Lady of the Lake to see if he was bewitched or trapped.

Now, having at last reached the castle where the Queen lies imprisoned, Lancelot is escorted through the tower gateway, guarded by lions on the other end of the sword bridge. That night, he forces his way through the barred window into the room where Guenevere waits for him.

"Why did you hesitate two steps before climbing on the cart, back down the road a pace?" Guenevere asks him, with the apparent omniscience of a Goddess.

How did she know?

Stung by her astonishing reaction to his appearance, still bleeding from the miraculous ordeal of the sword bridge, Lancelot attempts suicide—which, in the context of the mythology of the Great Goddess and her ritually slain consort, suggests the death and rebirth of the hero who ventures into the underworld to redeem the soul of the world from death.[24]

Guenevere later forgives Lancelot his two false steps, and admits him to her room, where she is adored like the Virgin Mary. After tearing through the bars outside Guenevere's window, Lancelot comes to the Queen's bed and bows in adoration, for "no holy relic inspires him with such faith." When he leaves her chamber, after a flawless night of love, he bows again, behaving just as though he were before an altar.[25]

He has experienced a love so sweet that its wonder cannot be spoken of. This is not prudery or coyness alone, but wisdom, for the modesty and restraint of this moment reflects the mysticism of love in the poetry of the Middle Ages.

It is the ineffable joy of the "Liebestod," of love in the domain of death, with the ecstasy that transcends the categories of reason, and about which we must remain silent—for it is a genuinely sacred mystery.

This mingling of the sacred and the profane captures the mood of pagan mysticism appropriate to the sacred marriage which occurs in Guenevere's bedroom. Lancelot has, in a sense, returned to his mother's womb in order to be reborn, being both the son and lover of the Goddess.

The blood left behind on the sheets is menstrual, maternal, and mortal, coming as it does from Lancelot's wounds, yet suggesting the broken hymen of virginity (for their love is ever new, just as Guenevere is ever virgin), the blood of birth, and the blood of death.

Lancelot has endured the public humiliation of the cart, and the ordeal of the sarcophagus and the sword bridge, in order to achieve the final mystery of marriage with the Goddess.

Lancelot's return to Camelot, however, reiterates the Christian allegory, and introduces new metaphors for the marriage mysteries.

To complete his journey, Lancelot has to fight the man who stole Guenevere at the beginning of the story. His name is Meleagant, and the joust is modeled on the victory of Christ on the battlefield of Armageddon. It occurs in the presence of all the lords and ladies of Arthur's court on a heath dominated by a splendid sycamore tree, planted (we are told) in the time of Abel. Fine emerald-green grass (ever fresh) grows beneath the sycamore. Beside the tree, a spring flows above a pebbled bed bright as silver, over a channel as pure and unblemished as burnished gold.

This is a Christianity modified by the archaic Celtic and alchemical motifs of the marriage of the sun and the moon (gold and silver). The fusion of gold and silver is particularly interesting in this context, for it suggests the marriage of Eternity and Time, Sol and Luna, King and Queen.

The conjunction of the solar and the lunar symbolism, in the calculation of the date of Easter, also enters into the imagery of the Crucifixion during the Middle Ages and Renaissance. Albrecht Dürer's "Great Crucifixion" of 1498, for example, shows Jesus on the Cross with the three Marys at its base, with a sun immediately to his right hand and a moon immediately to his left.

The image is an old one, as a glorious page from The Psalter of Robert de Lindesey shows—there is a sun above the right arm of the

Crucified Jesus, and a moon above his left.[26] St. John stands beneath the sun, and Mary beneath the moon.

Apparently, the fulfillment of marriage brings the divine and the human into a relationship that redeems the sorrows of life, and promises the eternal regeneration of nature.

Yvain and the Lady of the Fountain

In Chrétien's Arthurian romance called the "Knight with the Lion," there are two complete hero journey cycles, which begin and end in Camelot, and a third journey, which begins and ends in court of Lunette, the Lady of the Fountain. The three journeys chart Yvain's gradual development from an egocentric youth to a mature adult and responsible husband, more responsive to the needs of others than to his own.

One fine Pentecost Sunday, King Arthur astonishes his courtiers by retiring to his room with Guenevere after lunch. His retirement is a lovely symbol of the psychodynamics of marriage, of the retreat of the libido from an outer to an inner room of the psyche—from the ego to the unconscious self. This is so unprecedented that some members of the court are offended and do not spare their comments.

The offense is intensified when the King is detained so long by his dalliance with the Queen that he apparently 'falls asleep' by her side.

One of the courtiers, Calogrenant, then begins to tell a story which he might very well never have started in the King's company; for just as Arthur's post-Pentecostal dalliance with his wife is offensive, so the tale Calogrenant begins is a story that was not to his honor, but to his shame.

Some seven years ago, while traveling in quest of adventure, Calogrenant had come upon a right hand path through a dense forest—a difficult track full of briars and thorns—which led to a magnificent castle in Broceliande. That night, he enjoyed the splendid hospitality of a grand old man and his gloriously refined and altogether delightful daughter.

The next morning, he came to a clearing where unruly and ferocious wild bulls were fighting in front of a churlish giant some seventeen feet tall. The giant was huge and hideous, with a head longer than a pack horse, ears like an elephant, brows and eyes like an owl, nose like a cat, mouth like a wolf, and teeth like a boar!

This Wild Man of the Woods may be the great Druid, Merlin, whose magic is ultimately derived from the mysticism of the forest, into which he retires at death, wreathed round by a tower of white thorns.

The wild man directs Calogrenant to an enormous tree, with an emerald stone and a clear fountain beneath it, where the marvels and the terrors of the sacred mysteries of marriage begin. The tree is the loveliest tree that Nature ever managed to create. It never loses its leaves the whole year round. In its shade, a spring colder than marble boils up, and there is a golden cup hanging from the tree, beside a large emerald supported by four rubies bright as the sun.

Calogrenant uses the golden cup to pour water from the spring onto the emerald. When he does so, all hell breaks loose: there is a terrific clap of thunder, followed by a hailstorm coming from more than fourteen directions. The storm shatters all the neighboring trees.

When the storm ends, the branches and leaves of the tree from which the golden ladle hangs are completely covered by birds, which sing an ecstatic pastorale in a magnificently serene and transcendently pacified atmosphere.

All of the elements of this description are archetypal—tree, spring, golden cup, gemstone, and thunderbolt—and together yield one of the great moments in the Arthurian tradition.[27]

Celtic mythology revolved around a kind of archetypal arboretum which formed the very basis of their alphabet, poetry, and religious rituals.[28] In Norse myth, the world tree is called Yggdrasil; it is rooted in the underworld and ascends through Middle Earth to branch into the heavens.

But the tree is also Biblical, the place where the opposites of good and evil are reconciled by rituals of transformation: does the spring beneath it boil or freeze? Is the basin iron or gold? Is the slab rock or emerald? All are both and the same, since the tree represents the place where heaven and hell marry on earth, where tempest yields to Paradise, and where iron is transmuted into alchemical gold.[29]

Calogrenant ends his tale after the tempest ends, when he is defeated by a Black Knight, who comes charging at him down from the castle on the hill.

Inspired by Calogrenant's story, Yvain sneaks out, unobserved by the court, to beat the other courtiers to the quest.

Yvain repeats the stages of the journey up to the arrival of the Black Knight after the tempest is unleashed, when the water in the golden ladle is poured on the emerald at the base of the tree. After a long and fierce battle beside the spring, Yvain delivers a savage blow that severs the Black Knight's helmet and splits his skull, spattering bloody bits of brain all over his armor.

Mortally wounded, Esclados (the Black Knight) races back to his castle with Yvain in fast pursuit. Yvain is much concerned, at this point, for if Esclados escapes he will lose the evidence of victory needed to secure his glory and escape Kay's taunting back at Camelot.

Driven by this desire for fame, and fear of shame, Yvain follows the Black Knight through the portcullis leading into the castle. The gate contains a hidden blade that crashes down like a Devil out of Hell, slicing Yvain's horse in half and grazing his heels. The Black Knight, however, escapes through a second gateway into the city, leaving Yvain precariously trapped in a hallway between the two gates.

Yvain is now suspended between the courtly and the supernatural realms, which are divided by doorways, such as the ones Inanna, Lancelot, Sir Orfeo, and others had to pass through during their marital journeys.

The crossing this threshold (still a phrase we use for marriage) signifies a transition from the material to the spiritual world. Lunette, a beautiful maid, emerges from a secret door in the hallway to give Yvain a ring that renders him as invisible as wood covered by bark. The simile is suggestive of the mythical properties of the great tree where Yvain's threshold battle began: like Osiris buried in the cedar of the *djed* pillar, Yvain is now an invisible captive in the realm from which only his wife to be—Laudine, the Lady of the Fountain—can deliver him.

Yvain's invisibility also signifies his new existence in the spiritual realm.

Lunette takes Yvain to a secret chamber, from which he looks out at the lords and ladies of the castle, who are crazed with grief beside the bier of the Black Knight. The wounds of the corpse suddenly open up again, and the fresh blood runs clear and crimson—positive proof that the man who had killed the Black Knight is near by.

Yvain is disturbed by the burial of the corpse and the lamentations of the courtiers because it removes positive evidence of his victory, which he will need to prove himself in the face of Kay's malicious mockery and abuse.

Yvain is now wounded himself—by the sight of Laudine grieving over the bloody, mutilated corpse of the Black Knight. "Having mortally wounded her husband," Yvain wonders in his love-stricken grief, "do I think I can be reconciled with her?"

Apparently he can be, with the extended manipulations of Laudine's maid Lunette, who urges the practical exigencies facing her Queen as reasons for reconciliation and remarriage: the arrival of King Arthur is imminent, and she will need a man to defend her fountain and kingdom.

Faced with this impending crisis, Laudine, the Lady of the Fountain, now marries Yvain, the man who had slain her husband, and who will now become the next guardian of the mystical tree and fountain.

Laudine—along with her tree, emerald stone, and fountain—symbolizes the Great Goddess, the source of life, into whose mysteries Yvain is to be initiated by the sacred marriage. Those mysteries concern a reconciliation of opposites, and a transition from the material to the spiritual world.

Just as the tree embraced the creative and destructive powers nature, so Laudine enacts within her castle walls the mysteries of life and death; the funeral and the marriage ceremonies take place in only a couple of days. These two ceremonies combine the mythical powers of the Great Goddess to take life, and to give it back, through the renewed fertility made possible by marriage.

Yvain is bathed, groomed, and dressed for the wedding in a scarlet robe lined with vair and linked at the neck by a golden clasp studded with precious stones.

During the marriage festivities, a relationship develops between Yvain's friend Gawain and the maid, Lunette. Although this relationship is primarily an example of Gawain's legendary prowess as a courtly lover, it also conceals mythological symbolism important to the marriage mysteries.

Lunette is compared to the moon. She is being courted by the sun, personified by Gawain. He is indeed like the sun, since chivalry shines from him like the morning sun.

The marriage of the sun and the moon is an old symbol reaching far back beyond the medieval romances to Homer's *Odyssey*, where, as we have seen, the reunion of Odysseus and Penelope occurs at the end of a twenty year cycle, referred to as the Great Solar Year, when the new moon and summer solstice coincide.

The solar principle represents eternity, the masculine, gold, and the King; while the moon represents time, the feminine, silver, and the Queen. As we have seen, such imagery was found frequently in alchemical illustrations, and in paintings of the Crucifixion, in which we find a sun and moon on either side of the cross.[30] The reason for this is that the date of Easter is the first Sunday after the first full moon after the spring equinox.

Such are the mysteries conveyed by the mythical marriages of medieval romance.

After the marriage, Gawain persuades Yvain to return to Camelot, and in so doing to leave the timeless realms of faerie enchantment into which he has entered by marriage. His wife grants Yvain a year's leave of absence. If he should overstep this limit, she warns, her love will change to hate.

To help him remember his obligations, she gives him a ring with the power to confer a kind of immortality upon its wearer: No true lover can be held prisoner, lose any blood, or suffer any harm, provided that he wears the ring in remembrance of his beloved wife.

Such a talisman is the special gift of the Goddess, who bestows it upon her chosen mate. Because her husband is traditionally bound to the wheel of time, however, by virtue of his humanity, he cannot simply retreat into the timeless realm of transcendent bliss offered him by marriage.

Yvain therefore forgets his promise, a year later, while performing his courtly duties in Camelot—like a workaholic husband who abandons his wife and family to make a living, only to lose both, because he is never around.

Yvain remembers his broken promise with grief and great distress. A messenger from his forgotten wife arrives at Camelot and declares him to be a disloyal traitor, a liar and a deceiver, who has abandoned and duped his wife, Laudine. Since Yvain is a false, treacherous thief, he must return the ring and forsake the pleasure of his wife's company and love.

His attachment to the worldly concerns of his temporal identity has led him to forget the radiance of his eternal life in the otherworld, to which he is now recalled.

Yvain's public humiliation is as devastating as the return of Inanna from the underworld had been for her husband Dumuzi. His first thought is to flee into the wilderness, into the pit of Hell, to a land so wild that nobody would know where to look for him.

His journey to hell is caused by the marital crisis of separation; it produces a kind of psychological derangement (all-too-familiar to marriage counselors) which leads to Yvain's departure into the forests of the unconscious, and to the total disintegration of his courtly personality.

Delirious with grief, he tears off his clothes and flees into the woods, where he lives completely naked and mad. His divestiture is self-inflicted, and dramatizes the pathology of the "forest madness" of the lover so popular during the Middle Ages.[31]

There is a very real potential for growth in this moment of marital madness: only the ego that is stripped down to the bone can be transformed for the better. Yvain's breakdown obliterates his courtly self in order to initiate change.

A year later, Yvain is discovered asleep in the forest by three women (two damsels and their Lady). These three women represent Triple Goddess of Celtic mythology, and the three fates of Classical. Yvain represents the soul, lost in the material world, with which it is 'married,' and from which it must be divorced, before its return journey to, and remarriage with, the spiritual realm.

One of the maidens recognizes the true identity of the sleeping knight, and convinces her Lady of Yvain's usefulness in the defense of her domain against Count Alier, who has plundered her lands. The Lady remembers an ointment, given her by Morgan the Wise, that has the power to clear any head of madness and frenzy (a Prozac cream!).

Morgan the Wise is Morgan le Fay, the mysterious goddess of whom these three ladies represent the courtly incarnation. She is the feminine power of transformation behind Yvain's healing.

One of the maidens rubs Yvain's temples, forehead, and body until the madness and depression leave his brain. Hence, the eternal feminine is both the cause and the cure of Yvain's breakdown: Laudine, the Lady of the Fountain, drives him mad; Lady Noroison and the two maidens, incarnations of Morgan the Wise, restore his wandering wits, and bring him back to life.

Morgan's cure would still be available today, had not the maid become so enthusiastic in her application of the ointment onto Yvain's naked body that she used up the whole jar!

Yvain's return to health initiates a sequence of adventures that develop his potential qualities as a husband, and as a Christian knight in the service of the community. During this second sequence of ordeals, Yvain defeats Count Alier and reclaims the plundered lands of Lady Noroison; kills Harpin of the Mountain, a giant who is pestering Gawain's niece; rescues Lunette from the Fountain, where Laudine has condemned her to death for conspiracy; and frees three hundred maidens from an Isle of Damsels impressed into slave labor by two sons of the Devil.

Yvain's labors refashion him into a man capable of serving others, a prerequisite for marriage in a Christian community. Yvain is aided in his execution of these tasks by a lion, which Yvain saves from a dragon. In fact, during this entire second episode, Yvain is not known by his courtly name, but simply as "The Knight with the Lion," a fact which suggests the new orientation of his identity.

The transformation of "Yvain" into the "Knight with the Lion" represents a movement from honor to loyalty in love, from personal glory to selfless service.

Yvain returns, finally, to Camelot, to complete his marital journey: he is wiser, humbled, and more mature, fighting now in the defense of Noire Espine's younger daughter against Gawain, who fights for the elder. The joust ends with a stalemate, and with the revelation of Yvain's true identity, after which he returns to Laudine, who now accepts him (perhaps out of necessity, rather than love, some would argue!).

The reunion of estranged husband and wife completes the large hero journey cycle begun by Yvain's departure from Laudine's castle. All of the hero cycles taken together give us a complete vision of male development from youth to manhood, from bachelor to husband, from the Knight in Shining Armor, to the Knight with the Lion—an archetypal symbol of the Great Goddess.

Parzival and Condwiramours

Wolfram von Eschenbach's *Parzival* is the greatest of all the Arthurian poems of the Middle Ages, and indeed of any era. It is also a profound meditation on the mysteries of love and marriage, which it explores in the stories of two couples: Parzival and Condwir-amours, and Gawain and Orgeluse. Both tales converge in a grand climax at the end of the novel, in an elaborate wedding ceremony involving multiple marriages.[32]

Parzival grows up alone, far from the court, with his mother, who wants to prevent the boy from ever becoming a knight, since his father had been killed during the Crusades. One fine spring morning, three gloriously armed knights crash through the woods where Parzival is out hunting birds with his javelin. At first, Parzival thinks the knights are devils, because of the terrific noise they make, but when he sees their glittering armor, gleaming helmets, and scarlet tunics shining in the sunlight, he thinks they are angels, or even God Himself (since his mother had told him that God is Light).

In a sense, they are both: devil to the mother who will drop dead after her son resolves to follow the knights to Arthur's court; and angels of destiny to Parzival, whose vocation in life is announced by their arrival.

The first task in the young man's journey toward marriage is to break the bond with his mother, a process in which the symbolism of clothing plays a special role. Before collapsing, his mother dresses Parzival up as a country hick and sends him riding off on an old nag, hoping such attire will deny him access to Arthur's court. She also gives him a crash course in courtly love: take a kiss and a maiden's ring if she offers them, and go to church as often as you can (as yet, he doesn't know what a church is).

On his way to Camelot, Parzival comes upon a Lady alone in a pavilion beside a stream. She is asleep in bed and wakes up to fight Parzival off, but he kisses her seven times and then steals her ring—just following mother's instructions! He then devours all the food set out for her, before leaving her alone at the mercy of her jealous husband, who returns shortly thereafter.

Her husband Orilus refuses to believe the tale his wife Jeschute tells him, and therefore subsequently subjects her to years of jealous abuse.

After leaving Jeschute in her tent, Parzival is directed to Arthur's court by a crude fisherman. When he arrives in court, a maiden bursts out laughing, and the steward, Sir Kay strikes her in the face—because a prophecy had predicted that she would not laugh for more than six years, until the man who would be supreme among the knights arrived at court.

Parzival finds King Arthur, who agrees to let the young man confront the Red Knight, who has just challenged the court by throwing wine on Queen Guenevere. Parzival rides out to kill the Red Knight with his javelin, which he tosses through the visor into the eye socket, through the brain, and out the back of the neck.

Then, with a squire's help, Parzival takes the fallen knight's armor, which he puts on over the hair shirt his mother had dressed him in. The clothing signifies the transformation of the hero as he crosses the threshold to his new life. Newly attired, Parzival now sets off on a journey that will lead him to his wife.

He rides off on the Red Knight's horse, which he cannot control. It gallops all day long until arriving at a magnificent castle by the sea which seems to emerge directly from the rock: it has four handsome turrets at each of the four walled corners (it is a mandala, a Jungian symbol of the Self).

Here lives Gurnemanz, the wise old man who will instruct Parzival in courtly ways, preparing the boy for knighthood and marriage. The completion of this rite of passage is celebrated when the worthy old man brings Parzival a shirt and breeches of fine linen, a tunic of fine indigo silk woven in India, and then persuades Parzival at last to take off his mother's hair shirt. Then Gurnemanz fits the right spur to the foot, and girds the sword about the waist—ritual gestures which signify Parzival's admission to the "highest order created and ordained by God, namely the order of chivalry, which must be free of all baseness."

At this point of the passage towards marriage, Parzival is extremely anxious to return to his mother, so he heads into the desolate forests of the waste land. In the elegant simplicity of mythological language, the search for the mother leads Parzival to his wife—the psychological wisdom of these old stories is unsurpassed.

After crossing the waste land, Parzival arrives at the well-situated fortress of his wife to be, Condwiramours. Her castle is by the sea, and it is besieged by two unwelcome suitors. Condwiramours' castle has been devastated by the siege; it is the typical situation of the waste land, translated into political terms.

The houses and streets are empty and in ruins, the monks and nuns have been terrorized, and the fortress is empty of bread, wine, and ale. All are dejected and grief-stricken. Condwiramours desperately pleads for Parzival's help that night, when she climbs into bed with him, after he promises not to wrestle with her. She tells him that of the three hundred or so knights who originally manned the castle, only fifty are left, forty-eight having been killed or imprisoned by her besieger and his seneschal.

It is a social and political waste land which Parzival is called upon to regenerate. The situation has degenerated as a result of neglected love and the abusive politics of marriage during the Middle Ages. It must therefore be redeemed by a love innocent of those politics.

Parzival agrees to fight the suitors on condition that Condwiramours accept his love. They then fall asleep and don't make love until three nights later—by which time they've figured out how things work.

Hence, in the weeks that follow, the unwanted suitors are defeated and dispatched to Arthur's court, where they are instructed by Parzival to submit themselves to the service of the maiden who laughed when Parzival first arrived.

The deeper symbolism of this episode relates to the archetypical male task—to reclaim the soul, or Anima mundi (in this case Condwiramours) from its imprisonment in the material world. A tremendous rush of renewed life is therefore released by Parzival's liberation of the castle: hall and dwellings ring with jubilation, chapels and church bells peal for joy, and all give thanks to God for delivering them from a long a terrible captivity.

Their deliverer, however, still has his mother on his mind!

Soon after his marriage with Condwiramours, Parzival says he misses Mom, and asks permission of his young wife to go get his mother from the Wild Forest of his youth. No one can detain him, since he has a greater desire to go and see his mother than for anything else.

This time Parzival's regressive longing leads him to the Grail castle itself, as if there were a spiritual mystery buried in the heart of his mother complex—a goddess behind the symbolism of the complex represented by the Grail.[33]

Parzival again rides all day long, continually praying to God that he might find his mother alive and well, until at last he comes to a rushing river.

"Ah, almighty Lord!" he exclaims, "If I could cross this water, I fancy, I'd find my mother on the other side, if she's still alive."

She isn't.

But, in psychological terms, his mother still lives in his unconscious, weaving the web of his fate; she is the buried source of those complexes which compel his destiny, but cloud his marriage.

The river, however, seems impassable. A man fishing in a boat tells Parzival that no boat, ferry, bridge, or ford leads across the water, but that Parzival can take shelter that night in the house where the fisherman lives, close by the river and the surrounding woods. After climbing through a fissure in the rock, Parzival looks for, but at first does not see, the tower rising splendidly from a distant castle.

The fisherman who appears to guide Parzival is called the Angler, and we see him on a large lake beautifully dressed, wearing a hat of peacock feathers which suggests the alchemical symbolism of death and rebirth, and the Christian symbolism of the Resurrection.

He is the wounded Fisher King, who can only be healed when a certain question is asked by a wandering knight, like Parzival.

Inside the Grail Castle, he is greeted by several pages who disarm him on the green lawn within the walls, and then invests him with a cloth-of-gold cloak from Araby given him by Repanse de Schoye (the maiden whom we will later see carrying the Grail).

He is then led by a rude jester into a hall where a hundred chandeliers hang, with as many candles on each, above a hundred couches with quilts, four knights seated on each. All surround the fireplace in the middle, against which we see the old ailing lord of the castle seated in a sling bed.

A page then runs wailing out of the kitchen to carry a bleeding lance around the four walls of the great hall, accompanied by much weeping. Through another steel door at the end of the Hall comes a pair of noble maidens, with garlands of flowers in their hair, wearing brown dresses, and carrying golden candelabra. A duchess and her companion, similarly dressed, come next, carrying two ivory trestles. Together with the flower maidens, they form a group of four, and bow to the lord of castle lying in his sling by the fireplace.

Four more pairs of ladies then enter, all wearing robes of green samite, four of them carrying large candles, and four carrying a table top cut from a radiant garnet-hyacinth, which they set on the ivory trestles. This group of eight, green-clad maidens then bows to the lord.

Two princely ladies, each carrying ingeniously fashioned silver knives, then enter, preceded by four faultless virgins, each bearing a light. This makes a group of six, who bow before the lord seated in the sling in front of the fire, before joining the other twelve maidens.

Six more maidens now advance, dressed in brocade of Nineveh, cut parti-wise, like the previous group of six, and carrying vials of pure glass with burning balsam.

Then, Princess Repanse de Schoye, wearing a brocade of Araby and carrying the Grail on green achmardi, follows these six. She and her vessel are said to be the consummation of heart's desire, its root and blossoming, paradisal, transcending all earthly perfection.

The Grail is then placed before the Maimed Fisher King (while Parzival stares intently at Repanse de Schoye, whose robe he is wearing), and the seven maidens join the other eighteen to form a group of twenty-five, twelve on either side of the crowned Repanse de Schoye.

This image of Repanse de Schoye standing in the center of the Grail Castle with twelve maidens gorgeously dressed on either side of her is one of the grandest epiphanies of the Great Goddess in all of literature. She is mother universe, from whose womb are born the twelve hours of the night on her left, and the twelve hours of the day on her right. She bears the sacred vessel of the Grail as a symbol of her own power, and she balances the male Trinity of the Grail Castle.

These three men are the incarnations of her consort, in the three stages of life which she bestows upon them. Parzival is the King to be, and represents the folly of youth; the crippled Angler is the present and ailing King representing midlife; while Titurel (an extremely old man just visible in an interior room) is the King of the past, representing the inaccessible wisdom of old age.

After this grand procession, an elaborate banquet begins. Chamberlains with bowls of gold are assigned at the rate of one to every four knights, accompanied by one handsome page carrying a white towel (that's two hundred servants total!). One hundred tables are then set up before each of the one hundred couches on which the groups of four knights sit (totaling four hundred knights). Parzival and the Maimed King wash and a count's son dries their hands with a fine silk towel.

Four pages then assist the previously assigned chamberlains and towel bearers at each of the hundred tables of knights (two carve, two serve). Four trolleys bearing cups attended by one clerk enter to serve wine to the hundred tables, one at a time.

One hundred pages are then bidden to receive the loaves and abundant delicacies magically dispensed by the Grail, which is again eulogized as the very fruit of bliss, a cornucopia of the sweets of the world.

The sacred feast is one of the world's great mythic images, and hence a frequent occurrence as a symbol of the consummation of the marriage mysteries.

But Parzival observes the magnificent feast in silence, without asking the Question necessary to heal the wounded King. While he sits musing on this divine spectacle, a page appears carrying a sword with a priceless sheath and ruby hilt, which the crippled lord bestows upon him. This is a cue for him to ask the Question which could rid his host of his misfortune, but Parzival remains dumb, and the dinner ends.

As the Princess and her maidens carry the Grail back through the steel door through which they entered, Parzival glimpses the most handsome old man he had ever seen or heard of. He is Titurel, the fourth of the major attendants of the Grail. The entire castle is a magnificent mandala radiating around the Grail by the fire in the center, the still point of the turning world, surrounded by groups of four, which reiterate the mystical quaternity.

There are four knights per hundred tables, which we can imagine symmetrically arranged in groups of twenty five in each of the quadrants of the Hall; there are four knights per trolley bearing golden cups, each of which establishes a new center at each of the tables. The maidens themselves form two groups of twelve on either side of the central Repanse de Schoye.

It is a grandly elaborated symbol of that universal wholeness at the center of the sacred mysteries of marriage.

But Parzival is ignominiously expelled the morning after the Grail procession for not having asked the question that would heal the Grail King. Riding away from the castle, Parzival chances upon a maiden weeping beneath an oak tree, holding the decapitated body of a knight in her lap.

She tells Parzival that his host of the previous night was the rich Fisher King, wounded in the thigh by a javelin, and she reprimands him for not asking the healing question. She is Parzival's cousin, and she explains that he had probably been tainted by responsibility for his mother's death, and hence as yet ineligible to heal Anfortas.

No longer nameless, Parzival continues on his way, not now in search of the mother he now knows to be dead, but in pursuit of the knight who decapitated his cousin's beloved. This man turns out to be Orilus, the jealous husband of Jeschute, whose ring Parzival had stolen a while back after first leaving home.

Jeschute is now in terrible shape after long abuse from her maniacally suspicious husband: her lacerated flesh shows through a hundred holes in her garment, and her face (pale, wrinkled, and haggard) is stained by the numerous tracks of her tears.

All of this is Parzival's fault, the consequence of his youthful indiscretion. After confessing his folly to the lady's husband, known also as the Haughty Knight of the Heath, Parzival knocks him off his horse in a joust, commands him to take better care of his long-suffering wife, and then to proceed to Arthur's court.

Meanwhile, having received a steady stream of knights defeated by Parzival and sent to his court, Arthur has packed up his tents and gone in search of him (Parzival is still known to Arthur as the Red Knight). When Gawain and Kay find Parzival lost in a trance at the sight of three drops of blood in the snow (which remind him of his wife, Condwiramours), Parzival breaks Kay's arm in a joust (thus avenging Kay's humiliation of the maiden who laughed when Parzival arrived in court) and is then gently enticed into Arthur's tent by Gawain—who can tell by his trance that Parzival is in love.

This completes the first cycle of the hero journey, during the course of which Parzival has literally made a name for himself. But he is still haunted by the depressing awareness of his failings and spiritual blindness. Like many men at midlife, he has all the power and glory of worldly success, but is still poisoned by a spiritual malaise about the unanswered questions in life, and this malaise will lead to his second departure from court.

Parzival's second departure from Arthur's court is precipitated by the Loathly Damsel, Cundrie the Sorceress, who speaks all languages, knows geometry and dialectic, and has mastered astronomy! Ornately attired—a hat of peacock feathers significantly links her to the Fisher King—she rides into court on a mule harnessed by the most costly of bridles. Her appearance is conventionally loathsome. She has boar bristle hair and tusks, a dog's nose, bear's ears, lion claw hands, and so forth.

Her news is devastating: the honor of the Round Table has been tarnished by the presence of Parzival, whose perfidy is responsible for the continued sufferings of the Sorrowful Angler, since he failed to ask the fateful question. Cundrie lays it on thick, thoroughly humiliating Parzival. He is derided as a "heartless guest," a "ban on salvation, curse on felicity, disdainer of flawless fame," "sport of

Hell's guardians," a "man devoid of honor," than whom none other "was ever more perfidious."

Parzival leaves the court in a stage of deep grief and shame, the climax of which is a dark night of the soul. Parzival renounces God, after five years of wandering, as he makes his way back towards the Grail Castle in order to redeem his former failure.

But his spiritual depression leads to the complete divulgence of the mysteries of the Grail, as if the ego needed to be completely annihilated before the radiant wisdom of the soul can be released.

At this low point of his journey, Parzival comes upon the hermit Trevirizent, on Good Friday. Trevirizent is the spiritual counterpart of Gurnemanz, substituting Christian doctrine for the latter's worldly advice about chivalry. This doctrine, however, is not strictly dogmatic, since a great deal of pagan lore about the Grail and its King slips in, which opens up the symbols to a flood of universal wisdom.

Trevirizent tells Parzival about Master Kyot, who first read, in Toledo, of the thing called the Grail, in an astrological treatise by the heathen Flegetans. In this text, Master Kyot read that Flegetans deciphered the hidden secrets of the constellations, and discovered the existence of the Grail, which was left on earth by a troop of heavenly beings—the angels who remained neutral during the war in heaven when Lucifer was cast out by the Archangel Michael.

Master Kyot, Trevirizent continues, pursued the mystery in many obscure Latin texts, discovering in Anjou the text which tells the story of the Grail and delineates the pedigree of the Grail Kings (Titurel, Trimurtel, and Anfortas) and of Parzival himself.

Trevirizent then tells Parzival about the Grail. It is a stone called "Lapsit exillis" defended by the Templars of Munsalvaesche. By virtue of the stone, the Phoenix (an alchemical symbol of rebirth) molts its feathers, and the flesh and bones of mortal men are made young again. The chivalric brotherhood appointed to attend the Grail is determined by inscriptions that periodically appear under the top edge of the stone: such children who are so bidden to the Company are immune from sin and go directly to Paradise at death.

Of Anfortas, the current Maimed King, we soon learn much. During his youth he rode forth in pursuit of Love, violating the restraints of holy matrimony. Such ways being unsuitable for those in the service of the Grail, whose loves are also determined for them by magical inscriptions which appear on the stone, Anfortas is wounded in the thighs and scrotum by a poisoned lance, wielded by a heathen knight from the precincts of Paradise, where the Tigris flows.

All attempts to heal the wound have failed: herbs, Pelican blood, the heart and carbuncle stone of the unicorn, and the golden bough, which Aeneas used to ward off the hazards of Hell. In spite of all these ministrations, the Fisher King cannot die, living as he does in the continuous presence of the Grail.

As a result, the most bizarre remedies from the remote pharmacopoeia of the Middle Ages are resorted too, most significantly a bloody lance, which, when inserted into the wound when the planet Saturn or the change of the moon mark a particularly severe phase of the King's suffering, draws frost from his body around its tip.

The frost can only be removed by the silver knives which Parzival had silently observed on the occasion of his first visit to the Castle. Only by asking the Fisher King the question, Trevirizent dramatically concludes, "Uncle, what ails you?" can the wound be healed.

These revelations revolve around the mysteries of death and rebirth in marriage, and the power of love and compassion. This love involves a death of the ego, so that the higher faculties of the Self can be activated. Only when we forget about ourselves, and open our hearts to the sorrows of others, will the waste land be regenerated.

After returning to the Castle, and healing the Fisher King, Parzival is reunited with his wife, Condwiramours. He then awaits the arrival of King Arthur and Sir Gawain—whose tempestuous marital journey the tale now turns to.

Gawain and Orgeluse

Gawain's initiation into the sacred mysteries of marriage begins when a knight arrives at court and accuses him of having murdered his master. The knight challenges Gawain to combat, and he sets off on his journey.

Gawain's first trial is to defend a young girl during a tournament, after which he is unwittingly lodged in the castle of the knight who challenged him to combat. While in this knight's castle, Gawain is seduced by the young girl's sister, and attacked by her courtiers—a mess not untypical of pre-marital madness. As a result, when the lord of the castle finds out that his offer of hospitality has been abused by his people, and that the man they have attacked is none other than Gawain, he makes a special deal: Gawain can go free to find the bleeding lance of the Grail King and return in one year for the joust to avenge the death of his master.

Gawain departs and endures a series of adventures that focus on his odd relationship with an abusive woman whom Wolfram calls Orgeluse.

Their relationship begins ominously.

Gawain rides into a green meadow, where he sees a pony tethered to a battered shield hanging from a tree, and a disconsolate lady sitting nearby with a severely wounded knight lying in her lap. Gawain heals the knight, and then sets off after the man who had wounded him; the bloody tracks lead him to a splendid castle, which looks like it is spinning round, since it sits at the top of spiral pathway, lined with fruit trees.

From the top of the castle hill, Gawain gets his first sight of Orgeluse de Logroys, his wife to be, "the fairest flower of all feminine beauty," charming, shapely, and refined. She is sitting beside a spring that leaps directly out of the rock upon which the castle is built.

This is a marvelous epiphany of the divine feminine—sitting at the source of the water of life, at the end of the tortuous, spiraling ascent that leads into the labyrinthine difficulties of her domain. The terrain evokes a long association between the Great Goddess and mountains that goes back to the Minoan ladies of the maze, standing on peaks with lions on either side.

The difficulty of her situation prefigures the problems ahead, which must be resolved before their marriage. Orgeluse is haughty, rude, and arrogant. She promises Gawain "disgrace," "dishonor," and "great trouble."

But fools rush in where angels fear to tread!

Gawain accepts her first command, leaving his horse with Orgeluse, to cross a little bridge into an orchard, where her pony is tethered to an olive tree. An old knight with an ample, braided, grey beard leans on his staff beside the palfrey, lamenting Gawain's fate, and cursing Orgeluse for causing so many fine men to lose their lives! No one will stop Gawain from taking the pony, he says, but it will bring him much suffering if he does.

Leaving his fate in the hands of God, and ignoring the ominous portents, Gawain returns to Orgeluse, who calls him a goose for undertaking her service. When they ride off together, a proud squire rides up called Malcreatiure, a gift to Orgeluse from the Grail King.

Malcreatiure is Cundrie's brother, and he is just as monstrous in appearance, sporting fangs like a wild boar, and hair sharp and short as a hedgehog's—deformities produced by an herb eaten by one of the intemperate daughters of Adam when she was pregnant!

Queen Secundille of Tribalot—beside the River Ganges—sent Cundrie and Malcreatiure as gifts to the Grail King, who in turn has given the latter to Orgeluse. He rides up on a wretched nag, and immediately taunts Gawain, calling him a fool for taking Orgeluse away in this fashion, and threatening to tan his hide. Gawain grabs Malcreatiure by the hair and throws him off his nag, but cuts his hand deeply in the process—much to the delight of Orgeluse, who loves a good quarrel!

Gawain's humiliations continue, as Orgeluse heaps abuse on her would-be lover, putting him to the test. But we are warned not to condemn her appalling abusiveness, until we have learned the true state of her feelings.

Does Gawain have some intimation of the trauma at the heart of her neurotic complex? Does he intuit his role in redeeming the feminine from her demons? For this is the task of his courtship—to endure the trials and ordeals Orgeluse inflicts upon him, without excessive commotion, and without the kind of bellicose indignation her squire provokes in him.

He must endure her fury and rudeness, and accept her unrelenting mockery and scorn, if he is to heal her and win her love. Marriage, it seems, is indeed a sacred relationship—as Joseph Campbell once remarked—for it breaks down the ego so a new self may be born.

To this end, Orgeluse remains a source of much pain for Gawain, laughing at his cruel ordeal, when a knight steals his horse, forcing Gawain to ride a broken down nag with stirrups and saddle harness too flimsy to hold him up when another knight attacks him by the riverside. This knight is Lischois Gwelljus, also in the service of Orgeluse, who continues to torment and harass Gawain, even though Gawain defeats Lischois on foot, after being knocked off his nag.

Orgeluse then rudely leaves Gawain behind by crossing the river on a ferryboat.

The Castle of Marvels sits on the other side of river. Nearly four hundred ladies look down from the windows at Gawain as he approaches the quay. He strikes a deal with the ferryman to accept the defeated knight, Lischois Gwelljus, as a toll for the passage.

On the other side of the river, Gawain enjoys the meager but sincere hospitality of the ferryman, Plippalinot. The ferryman conducts souls to the yonder shore, where they will be judged and tested on the Perilous Bed. Plippalinot and his daughter live off the toll exacted for the crossing, and eat larks captured by their grey merlin.

The larks symbolize the souls of the dead, represented as birds as far back as the Egyptian Books of the Dead. Bird souls also abound in Celtic legends of the Isle of Maidens, where the dead are transformed into beautiful swans.[34]

Plippalinot, therefore, is a guide of souls to the otherworld. He tells Gawain about the Castle and its Perilous Bed, and about the mighty sorcery of Clinschor, who is responsible for the afflictions of the men and women enchanted there. He then gives Gawain a shield undented by combat and instructs him to leave his horse with a huckster selling priceless merchandise in a booth outside the Castle.

From there, Gawain goes to the room where the Perilous Bed awaits him. It sits on four ruby wheels on a slick floor made of shining jasper, chrysolite, and sardonyx, brought by Clinschor from many lands by wizardry. The floor is so glassy that Gawain can hardly stand upright, and the bed seems continually to thwart his efforts to mount it, until with one great leap he lands squarely upon it.

The bed immediately starts crashing around the room (like a reluctant bride, Heinrich Zimmer said!), and after Gawain crawls under his shield, he is attacked first by a barrage of pebbles and arrows and then by a magnificent lion, as tall as a horse. All the while, the enchanted maidens of the Castle look on. After the battle on the bed, one of the maidens determines that Gawain is still alive. Arnive, the Queen of the Castle, then treats his wounds with ointments given her by Cundrie the Sorceress.

Gawain has endured a kind of death and rebirth ritual during his night on the Perilous Bed, a ritual appropriate to a mate of the Great Goddess. The lions who attack Gawain are guardians of the passage into the realm of the mothers, like the two lions at the end of the sword bridge which leads to Guenevere in "The Knight of the Cart."

The lion is a traditional symbol of the Goddess, and is associated with the sun as a feminine power: the sun pounces on the moon, as the lion does the bull, and both the moon and the bull are then reborn from the solar fire of her womb. Hence the lion pounces on Gawain, in the Castle of the Medieval Goddess, leaving him nearly dead, but reborn and healed the next morning, when the sun rises from the darkness of the night.

He emerges from his ordeal transformed, with a new identity as the King of the Castle of Marvels, husband to be of Orgeluse. He is healed by Cundrie's magic ointment, another powerful symbol of feminine power.

The next morning Gawain awakes and explores the Castle, finding a staircase spiraling around a pillar forged by the subtle arts of Clinschor. As Gawain sits down to observe the mysterious images of the surrounding countryside (which are reflected in the polished surface of the pillar), he is greeted by four queens of the Castle: old Arnive, her daughter Sangive, and two of Sangive's daughters.

These four queens are Gawain's Grandmother, Mother, and his two sisters. His Grandmother and Mother have long been dead—his journey has taken him into the underworld.

These women are manifestations of the one Goddess who rules the underworld. They form a quaternity which parallels the male dominated quaternity in the Grail Castle. Their domain is the Realm of the Mothers, and the spell which afflicts them is the same waste land of life in death which surrounded Anfortas and the Grail Castle.

The magic pillar is another mythic image with a long lineage in the Arthurian tales. It is a still point of the turning world which Gawain reaches via an ordeal death and rebirth on the Perilous Bed. Having passed beyond the earthly domain of fear, desire, and duty,

Gawain now sits meditating upon the rapidly evolving and dissolving images of the material world, which he sees reflected in this mirror of Maya.

Unlike the Buddha, however, Gawain is forced back into the realm of action by his love for Orgeluse, whose image he now sees in the mirror, in the company of another man. More Bodhisattva than Buddha, this love for another being compels Gawain's return to the world, where he will confront a King called Gramoflanz at a mystical tree.

Gawain sees Orgeluse riding to the meadow across the river with Turkoyt, another champion who will soon be unhorsed by Gawain, after he quickly arms himself and crosses the river to confront him.

After the defeat of Turkoyt, Orgeluse leads Gawain to a rushing river, on the other side of which is a garland, hanging from the twig of a tree guarded by King Gramoflanz, which Orgeluse imperiously challenges Gawain to get for her. Gawain leaps the rushing river, but only the forelegs of his horse make it, so the two nearly drown before crawling out onto the yonder shore.

After Gawain rides up to the tree, breaks off a twig, and sets the garland on his helmet, King Gramoflanz comes riding out unarmed, wearing a peacock feather in his hat (like the Fisherman who had directed Parzival to the Grail Castle) and carrying a moulted sparrow hawk, which he says is a love token sent him by Gawain's sister from the Castle.

Gramoflanz explains that he has killed the noble husband of Orgeluse, abducted her, unsuccessfully sued for her favor, and abandoned her. For he now loves Itanje, Gawain's sister, to whom he asks Gawain to take a ring. He then goes on to say that he has taken a vow to fight only two knights at once, and to engage in single combat only with a knight named Gawain, whose father, King Lot, he accuses of having murdered his own father in the very act of greeting. Gawain identifies himself and they agree to joust on the field at Joflanze in sixteen days time in the presence of Arthur's entire court.

The ritual imagery of the sacred marriage saturates this episode. Gramoflanz approaches wearing the peacock feather, a symbol of resurrection in Christian and alchemical traditions. These symbols converge with the Celtic and Classical symbols of death and rebirth associated with the river crossing. And all occur in the context of the symbolic tree which Gramoflanz guards.

The tree with its guardian suggests the King of the Wood, husband of the Goddess Diana. Diana's man guards a golden bough hanging from a sacred oak, until he is slain by his successor. Gramoflanz, our King of the Wood, is merely defeated in a joust, and then appeased by marriage to Gawain's sister, while Gawain becomes his successor.

A complex political dimension complements these symbols, so that the death and rebirth mysteries associated with the sacred marriage are given a realistic twist. For all marriages generate changes in the social, as well as the domestic order.

When Gawain leaps back across the river, he is greeted by a newly penitent Orgeluse, who explains that her animosity stemmed from grief over her slain husband, and that she has been testing Gawain to prove his worthiness. Having found him purged and as purified as gold in the fire—an alchemical metaphor for the sacred mysteries of marriage—she now accepts his request for her favor.

The reconciled lovers then return to the Castle of Marvels. Orgeluse explains along the way that the merchandise of Thabrant which stands at the gate was a love gift from Anfortas, the Grail King, who we learn was wounded in the service of Orgeluse (hence the two marital journeys of Parzival and Gawain come together).

Orgeluse has since given the precious merchandise to Clinschor, to avoid his necromantic spells, until such time as a man achieves the adventure of the Perilous Bed and confers his favor on Orgeluse. Having done so, Gawain redeems the Castle of Maidens from its curse, just as Parzival must still redeem the Grail Castle by healing Anfortas.

The immediate sign of this redemption is an elaborately contrived sequence of multiple marriages. Back in the Castle, Gawain secretly sends a message to request Arthur's presence at the fields of Joflanze, where he will joust with Gramoflanz to assert his right to the garland from the tree. At the bidding of Orgeluse, he frees the two knights whom he has defeated in the meadow beside the ferry (they had been compelled into the service of Orgeluse to defeat

Gramoflanz). He then tactfully informs Itanje of Gramoflanz's love for her, before giving her the ring he had asked Gawain to deliver.

A wonderful feast then follows (parallel to the Grail feast), during which the captive lords and ladies of the Castle mingle in love for the first time since Clinschor had cast his evil spell upon them, which had made them invisible to each other. Gawain too is healed that night by the love of Orgeluse!

The next morning, Gawain sits with the old Queen, Arnive, who now reveals the strange mysteries of the Castle.

The Castle is the work of Clinschor, who took up magic after being castrated by the King of Sicily for sleeping with his wife. As a result of being leveled off between his legs by royal hands, Clinschor went to Persida to study the necromantic arts, with which he casts spells on anybody whose happiness provokes his wrath.

The Castle contains all precious things in such abundance that thirty years of siege could not deplete its stores. Whoever endures a night on the Perilous Bed becomes the Lord of the Castle, free from the molestation of Clinschor.

As such, Arnive now requests that Gawain allow the many subjects forced to live in the Castle by Clinschor's arts to return to their homelands (like Lancelot in "The Knight of the Cart," Gawain frees the courtiers from imprisonment in the otherworld).

Gawain's journey then comes full circle when Arthur's court arrives. Parzival appears simultaneously, and, since he has also challenged Gramoflanz, Gawain fights Parzival first until they recognize each other. Parzival then defeats Gramoflanz, and an elaborately wrought vision of medieval politics ensues, with the result that the quarrels all around come to an end, and the hero journey is completed for Gawain by an elaborate marriage ceremony.

Hence, it is with a sense of political importance as well as psychological healing and mystical revelation that Gawain's triumph allows life to begin anew, freed from the spells of Persian magic, and from the Byzantine complexities of domestic diplomacy on the home front.

These marriages are a personal triumph for Gawain, but also effect a delicate political solution to the debilitating social conflicts of Medieval Germany. The marriages reconcile oppositions between

Gawain and Gramoflanz's family, and in so doing overcome the long-standing conflict between Gramoflanz and Arthur. The reconciliations require a delicate diplomacy, which the poet develops thoroughly, creating labyrinthine social complexities, only to resolve them by political alliances and marriages.

When we add to this the fact that Parzival pulls off a similar political treaty by uniting Christian and Muslim worlds, through the baptism of his half-brother Feirefiz, who then marries Repanse de Schoye, the Grail maiden, we have a profound meditation upon the social and political importance of the sacred mysteries of marriage.

Jesus and Mary

During the Middle Ages, the chivalric portrayals of courtly lovers was often enriched by sacred themes from Christian iconography, which was itself sometimes influenced by the secular poetry of the period. In the lovely ballad, "I Sing of a Maiden," Jesus is presented as lover coming to visit his Lady, lying in her secluded bower in the woods. Here is the poem, in my slightly modernized version:

> I sing of a maiden
> Who is matchless:
> King of all kings
> To her son she chose.
>
> He came so still
> Where his mother was
> As dew in April
> That falleth on the grass.
>
> He came so still
> To his mother's bower
> As dew in April
> That falleth on the flower.
>
> He came so still
> Where his mother lay

As dew in Aprille
That falleth on the spray.

Mother and maiden
Was never none but she—
Well may such a lady
God's mother be.

"I Sing of a Maiden" is a perfectly crafted song in celebration of the Immaculate Conception of Jesus. The poem is famous for its delicate sexual imagery, and its portrayal of Jesus as a courtly lover, which it achieves through the paradox of divine genealogy.

According to the doctrine of the Trinity, the Father, Son, and Holy Spirit are one. Jesus is simultaneously the Father, husband, and Son of Mary. It is a paradox at the core of Medieval Mariolatry, well expressed by Dante in the famous address to the Virgin Mary as "figlia di tuo figlio" ("daughter of your own son").

Our poet uses the device known as incremental repetition, frequently found in ballads and folktales, to embody this paradox. The technique involves the repetition of a phrase with some slight change at the same crucial spot. With each repetition, suspense mounts powerfully until we come at last to the climax.

The sexual nature of this device is used with extreme grace and discretion in "I Sing of a Maiden," in which the first and third lines of stanzas two through four are repeated verbatim, but with a progression of the words "grass," "flower," and "spray" as suspenseful substitutions in the last line of each stanza, which indicate where the dew of April falls (dew frequently found in biblical typology as a metaphor for conceptual power of the Holy Spirit).

The progression is a natural, indeed erotic one, which follows the cycle of conception in the plant world at springtime: from the grass to the flower, which when pollinated produces the first sprigs of "spray" (fresh buds and leaves on the end of the twigs). The gentle erotic mood matches this movement to climax, as does the progression in the setting: "He" (Jesus, the Holy Ghost—Son, Lover, and Father) 'comes' in the first line in each stanza, and the pun is no doubt respectfully intended.

The setting advances accordingly: from the unspecified place where the mother "was," to her "bower," in the next stanza, and finally to the place where she "lay" in the fourth: i.e., in her bed.

It's a lovely progression, using repetition to combine the rhythms of conception and the metaphors of gestation associated with courtship and marriage. The poem explores the Medieval doctrine of the Trinity in ways which force us to notice the Oedipal complications of divine genealogy, which involves incest: that between Father and Daughter (God the Father couples with Mary, his daughter, to conceive Jesus); and that between Mother and Son (Jesus the Son mates with Mary His Mother to produce Himself!).

Indeed, the Freudian aspects of the story of Jesus have not gone unnoticed. It may be that the hypnotic appeal of the poem, and of the imagery of Mary during the Middle Ages, derives some of its power from the unconscious dynamics of the Oedipal and Electra complexes, which it combines into a single image (in a most dazzling, daring, and yet completely innocent manner).

I prefer, however, to approach the problem from the perspective of comparative mythology: one finds numerous parallels in the archetypal imagery of the Great Goddess, whose iconography Mary assumed custody of during the 12th and 13th centuries.

To give just one example, we may think of the marvelous wood sculpture from the 15th century, known as the "Vierge Ouvrante," which, when closed, shows Mary as the Madonna, with the Christ Child seated in her lap, but, when opened, shows Jesus on the Cross with God the Father contained in her womb—she is "Theotokos," "Mother of God," as the Council of Ephesus proclaimed her to be in 431 A.D.

Her father must therefore be her own Son, both having emerged from that womb to which they must return at the end of the cycle. With respect to the marital mysteries, the image suggests the complicated way in which our childish images of our parents persist in adulthood, coloring all our relationships with the forgotten fantasies, needs, and problems of our earlier lives.

Another beautiful medieval poem about marriage, in which Mary is associated with a miraculous tree, is the ballad known as "The Cherry Tree Carol":

Joseph was an old man, and an old man was he,
When he wedded Mary, in the land of Galilee.

Joseph and Mary walked through an orchard good,
Where were cherries and berries, so red as any blood.

Joseph and Mary walked, through an orchard green,
Where were berries and cherries, as thick as might be seen.

O then bespoke Mary, so meek and so mild:
"Pluck me one cherry, Joseph, for I am with child."

O then bespoke Joseph, with words most unkind:
Let him pluck thee a cherry that brought thee with child."

O then bespoke the babe, within his mother's womb:
"Bow down then the tallest tree, for my mother to have some."

Then bowed down the highest tree unto his mother's hand;
Then she cried, "See Joseph, I have cherries at command."

O then bespoke Joseph: "I have done Mary wrong;
But cheer up, my dearest, and be not cast down."

Then Mary plucked a cherry, as red as the blood,
Then Mary went home with her heavy load.

Then Mary took her babe, and sat him on her knee,
Saying, "My dear son, tell what this world will be."

"O I shall be as dead, mother, as the stones in the wall;
O the stones in the streets, mother, shall mourn for me all.

"Upon Easter-day, mother, my uprising shall be;
O the sun and the moon, mother, shall both rise with me."

The song is about the Flight into Egypt, and plays upon Medieval suspicions that Joseph misunderstood his wife Mary's pregnancy. But, as is the case with so many of the marvelous legends of the Middle Ages, the imagery draws from a reservoir of mythological wisdom.

Mary's special relationship to the cherry tree, and her child's evocation of the sun and the moon (in the prophecy of his resurrection) are both images of archetypal import—universal symbols whose presence in world myth takes us from Greek and Buddhist analogies, to the imagery of the Maya in Mesoamerica.

The Greek God Apollo is related to trees at the moment of his birth. While on her wanderings to escape the wrathful jealousy of Hera, Apollo's mother Leto comes to the island of Delos. After nine days and nine nights of labor, Leto gives birth, while throwing her arms around a palm tree. During her labor, a flock of swans circles seven times around the fragrant island, stopping their song on the eighth circle, when the god Apollo is born.

In Buddhist myth, we find the themes of the Virgin Birth and the miraculous tree combined. The soul of the Buddha is conceived after his mother Maya dreams of a white elephant; and he is born from her side in a scene clearly reminiscent of the legend of "The Cherry Tree Carol"—on the way home to see her parents, Queen Maya passes through a pleasure grove of trees in full flower, and, as she reaches up to grasp the branches of a sal tree, the great limb bends down of its own accord, as she gives birth to the Buddha from her right side.

In both legends, inanimate nature recognizes and responds to the heroic children (both world saviors) while still in the womb of the mother.

We also find the mysteries connecting Mary's conception and the nurturing of Jesus to the symbolism of miraculously flowering trees in a variety of medieval images. One of the most spectacular is "The Dream of the Virgin," a painting on a wooden panel by Christoforo dei Crocefissi. It shows the Virgin Mary dreaming on a bed, with the trunk of the tree of the Cross (bearing the Crucified Jesus) emerging from her womb. The tree is in full leaf, attended by angels gathering the blood of Jesus, and it has a Pelican feeding its young sitting in the top branches.

The similarity between this painting and the Mayan picture of the "Tree of the Middle Place," rising from two rivers of blood, which flow out from the womb of the earth goddess, with Quetzalcoatl (the feathered serpent, Mesoamerican lord of death and rebirth) sitting in the top branches, is indeed uncanny, as Joseph Campbell has shown.

The connection between the infant Jesus and food provided by trees persists throughout Christian art, as for example in Gerard David's perfectly lovely painting, "The Rest of the Flight into Egypt," of the late 15th century. Unlike "The Cherry Tree Carol," Joseph has to work for food in this painting: we see him laboriously flailing the branches of a fruit tree in the background, while the baby Jesus sits on his mother's lap in the foreground, picking from a bunch of grapes.

The flowering cross is often depicted with a sun and moon above, and a male and female couple below. An extremely beautiful page from the illuminated Psalter of Robert de Lindesey, of about 1220, shows Christ crucified upon a cross from which sprigs of foliage sprout. The wood of the Cross is a symbolic Tree of Life, promising redemption and resurrection by the sacrifice of Christ.

The image of the flowering cross goes back to the fourth century A.D., to the Holy Sepulcher at Jerusalem, where the emperor Theodosius I erected a large golden cross, encrusted with gems, and in the form of a flowering tree. Shortly thereafter, in Palestine, small ampoules appeared (containing holy oil from the Cross), inscribed with a cross in the shape of a palm tree, possibly because the Mesopotamians saw the palm as a symbol of renewal and immortality.

From then on, the flowering cross was rapidly translated into Christian symbolism, appearing in illuminated manuscripts, in Breviaries, in frescoes, and in woodcuts. Albrecht Dürer left us a particularly splendid example in his Crucifixion of 1500, which shows Joseph spading, and Mary watering the twin stems of a tree rooted at the foot of the Cross, with the branches exfoliating and bearing fruit as they coil up around the figure of Jesus.

During the Middle Ages, an anonymous Cistercian monk in France added a long chapter on the "Legend of the Tree of Life" to his magnificent *Quest of the Holy Grail*. The bed on board the Miraculous Ship in the chapter was built by King Solomon under the direction of his wife. The bed has three posts that sustain a canopy: a white and a red post inserted perpendicularly into the frame, and a green cross-post, all of naturally hued, unpainted wood.

This wood comes from the Tree of Knowledge in the Garden of Eden, a sprig of the fruit tree which Eve had taken with her after the Expulsion and planted while she was still a virgin. The sprig grew into a magnificent white tree, from which other white trees were grafted. When Adam and Eve were instructed to make love beneath the original white tree in order to conceive Abel, the white tree turned green, to betoken Eve's loss of virginity, and other grafts were subsequently planted from this green tree. When Cain killed Abel beneath this very same tree (originally white and now green), it turned blood red, and no further sprigs could be grafted, even though it continues to flourish itself.

The Tree survived until Solomon's time. One day, in consolation for the many sorrows caused Solomon by his unfaithful wife, Solomon was given foreknowledge of the coming of Mary and of the birth of Christ. Racking his wits to find some way of letting future generations know of his prescience, he consults his wife, who advises him to build the Miraculous Ship. She herself then oversees the construction of the bed, using white and green wood for the two posts from grafts, and a slice of bleeding red wood from the original tree.

This tradition linking trees to the Great Goddesses of antiquity (whose imagery passed on into the iconography of the Virgin Mary during the Middle Ages) is extremely ancient.

It is not only Biblical (as in the image of Eve tending the Tree of Knowledge in the Garden of Eden). Analogous images are to be found among the Hindus, who worshipped a Goddess of the Tree as early as 2000 B.C.; the Greeks, whose tree of golden apples was tended by Goddesses on the islands of the Hesperides; and the Babylonians, who personified Ishtar, the primeval mother Goddess, as a fig tree. The Sumerians called it the Huluppu Tree, which was sacred to the Goddess Inanna, who was imagined leaning up against an apple tree, while rejoicing in her sexuality.

These sacred trees are all connected to the same mysteries of conception celebrated in "I Sing of a Maiden," "The Cherry Tree Carol," and in the poetry and paintings celebrating the marriage and maternity of the Virgin Mary—who, according to Catholic dogma, has both human and divine consorts, a situation that generates considerable confusion on the part of the former.

CHAPTER THREE

Renaissance Relationships

The hero journey of marriage, during the Renaissance, became a philosophical allegory of the soul's departure from, and return to, a spiritual realm of Platonic ideas. Its descent is into the material world, which it animates with its radiance, but in which it feels imprisoned.

A similar allegory later became the basis of the alchemical mysteries of the late 16th and early 17th centuries, elaborately illustrated in the Rosicrucian manifestos printed in England and Germany.[35] The alchemical imagery there involves the marriage of the King and Queen (Sol and Luna).

The alchemical mysteries of marriage involve the metaphorical transformation of molecular compounds, which are reduced to base elements, and then reunited to produce the philosopher's stone. The opus, or Royal Art, as it was called, is often symbolized by the marriage of the King and Queen, Sol and Luna, whose relations follow the rhythms of the hero journey: an initial union (boy meets girl) is broken down in the alchemical bath, in which various alchemical operations reduce the couple to base elements, from which the couple emerges renewed in the form of the royal hermaphrodite.

Much of this symbolism occurs in comic drama, which involves a plot that begins the normal world of daily life, moves into the forest, and returns to the normal world. This is the basic form of the marriage mysteries in Shakespeare, and Milton.

Four Couples in the Forest

Shakespeare's *A Midsummer Night's Dream* involves no less than four couples: Theseus and Hippolyta (the King and Queen of Athens); Titania and Oberon (the King and Queen of Fairyland); and Demetrius and Helena, and Lysander and Hermia (two young courtly couples). For the lovers, the journey is a metaphor for the mysteries of marriage and of the human heart.

The forest represents more than the Freudian id—a realm of repressed sexuality and aggression where human beings become bestial. It is also a place of transformation, in which the powers of the imagination replace the dominion of reason. If the city is ruled by the patriarchy of father and King, the woods are permeated by the authority of the matriarchal Queen of the Faeries, Titania. In Shakespeare's hands, the great themes of transformation and revelation are related to the role played by the imagination in marriage and relationship.

The journey into the forest begins when an old father and a rigid society blocks the marriage plans of Lysander and Hermia, who escape into the woods to sort out difficulties they didn't even know they had, finally to return home, reconciled to each other and to the society which had forced them to flee.

Hermia and Lysander are followed by Demetrius and Helena. Demetrius is in love with Hermia, and has fallen out of love with Helena, who is still in love with Demetrius. While in the forest, one of the fairies, Puck, puts a love potion in the eyes of Demetrius and Lysander, with the result that both fall in love with Helena, and spurn Hermia. Puck later sets matters straight between the bewildered couples, thus facilitating the marriages of Helena and Demetrius, and Hermia and Lysander.

Puck is an imp of disorder. He takes great delight in the bedevilment of human couples in love. Those things best please him that "befall preposterously": all the quarrels, jealousies, mutual accusations, infidelities, and paranoid fantasies. He represents that part of ourselves that trips us up, and creates havoc in our relationships. He is the trickster, our shadow self. He is, as Shakespeare says, a knavish lad, thus to make poor females mad!

But Puck is also a guardian and guide of those deeper mysteries of love into which our relationship takes us. He presides over the painful follies of our marital journeys.

Puck is in the service of the King and Queen of Faeries, Oberon and Titania, who are estranged from each other. Oberon wants a mortal child, a changeling boy, from Titania, who has taken the boy after the death of his mother. Titania refuses, and the contention between the King and Queen disrupts the seasons and wreaks havoc upon the natural world. Floods and pestilence plague the world.

Jealousy and feuding in the family have consequences that extend far beyond the husband and wife. All of our relationships—professional, domestic, recreational—are affected by what happens in our marriages. It's like dropping a stone in a pond: the ripples radiate to the farthest reaches of the shore, for better or for worse.

All the painful perplexities of the play have their root in this dissension between Titania and Oberon. Their separation is like the splitting of the atom—what happens to the 'nuclear' family under these circumstances? Could there be some mysterious connection between the escalating rate of divorce and single parent families after World War II, and the ignition of nuclear bombs?

In Shakespeare's play, the fairies represent the fundamental forces of nature—such as those that reside within the nucleus. When they divorce, all hell breaks loose. When they're reconciled, harmony returns to the waste land.

During the course of their journey from city to woods and back to city, the Athenian lovers encounter the great themes of transformation, the reconciliation of opposites, and the powerful duplicities of the imagination.

Numerous oppositions work their way into the action and language of the play, eventually to be reconciled ('married') at the climax of play, when the lovers return for marriage festivities in Athens.

Theseus begins the play by contrasting the "merriments" of the marriage rites, to be awakened by the "pert and nimble spirit of mirth," with its "pale companion," the spirit of "melancholy," associated with "funerals.". He then bids Hermia choose either the chastity of the nun, "For aye to be in shady cloister mewed, / To live a barren sister all your life, / Chanting faint hymns to the cold fruitless moon," or the "earthlier" happiness of "the rose distilled."

The oppositions between love and hate, animal and human, comedy and tragedy then create havoc during the forest journey, and are compounded by the social oppositions between the rude mechanicals and the Athenian aristocrats, and between the fairy kingdom and the world of humanity.

The play within the play, performed by Peter Quince and his crew to celebrate the marriages at the end of the play, uses the grammatical figure associated with the reconciliation of opposites, the oxymoron. Theseus wonders at Quince's description of his play as "'tragical mirth' / Merry and tragical? Tedious and brief?" and of his need to find the "concord of this discord."

The play itself (Pyramus and Thisbe) combines comedy and tragedy, and its language constantly lapses into such comic oxymorons as the "sunny beams" of the "Sweet moon." But the ultimate goal of the play is the reconciliation between opposites, which is as characteristic of the marital journey as it is of alchemy, in which the mysterious union of Sol and Luna signifies the achievement of the philosopher's stone.[36]

Hence, Theseus speaks of the baying of the hounds on the May Day morning as a "musical discord," and Helena refers to her relationship with Hermia as a "union in partition." A union in partition! What a marvelous way of posing one of the central dilemmas of marriage—how to maintain our identity in the midst of relationship.

Both phrases epitomize the conjunction of opposites which constitutes the climax of the marriage mysteries.

All of these oppositions, however, tend constantly to reverse themselves, a movement typical of marriage, which involves the rapid revolution between extremes, as one quality (love, humanity, comedy, life) turns into its opposite (hate, bestiality, tragedy, death) in the blink of an eye.

Shakespeare uses a variety of synonyms to elaborate upon the changes from one extreme to another, and their ultimate reconciliation in marriage: words such as "translated," "transpose," "changeling," "change," "changed," "transformed," and "transfigured" are repeated to emphasize the rapid metamorphoses of marriage and relationship.

One of the principle metamorphoses—in the play as in marriage—is of man or woman into beast. Bottom becomes a beloved ass, in Titania's domain. Helena becomes a fawning "spaniel" in the forest, and urges Demetrius to use her as he would his "dog." Hermia calls Demetrius a "dog," a "cur," and a "crawling serpent." Lysander, in turn, calls Hermia a "cat" and a clinging "serpent." Hermia compares Demetrius to an "adder." And, finally, in a forest wildly populated by a variety of species, Helena sees Hermia as a conniving "vixen," a female fox.

While these transformations suggest the violent oscillations between love and hate, which reduce the lovers to animals in the forest, the transformations can also proceed in more subtle directions.

A principle theme of the marriage mysteries is the transfiguration of matter into spirit: Demeter puts the baby boy Demoophon into the fire to make him immortal in the Homeric Hymn, just as Isis puts the baby she is hired to nurse in Byblos into the fire each night, while she flits around the erica tree in which Osiris lies entombed.

These are the essential images of the mystery rites of the Ancient Mediterranean, which typically evoke that profound transformation of consciousness which marks the passage from the mortal to the spiritual realm.

Hence it is curious to find those traditional powers of the Great Goddesses of the mystery rites ascribed to the Fairy Queen of the play, Titania, who promises Bottom that she will "purge thy mortal grossness so / That thou shalt like an airy spirit go." With Bottom, she has her work cut out for her!

All of the lovers in the woods experience a parallel transformation, one which takes them out of the rational, materialistic realm of Athens, into the bewildering labyrinth of the imaginal forest. Theirs is a journey from reason into the dominion of dreams—and the play ends with a marriage of the two.

Shakespeare uses a diverse vocabulary to evoke those powers of the imagination activated by relationship and marriage: words like "fantasy," "fantasies," "fancies," "fancy," "fancy's images," "dream," "vision," and, finally, "imagination" itself.

The recurrence and variety of these words suggests that the play is about the imagination. For the marriage mysteries create an intensely activated imagination—producing, yes, delusions and trivial or paranoid fantasies, but also the more profound visions of a spiritual realm which permeates and transcends the mortal realm of daily rationality.

For that reason, Bottom reverts to the language of the New Testament when reflecting upon his dream vision of Titania and her domain: when he says "The eye of man hath not heard, the ear of man hath not seen, man's hand is not able to taste, his tongue to conceive, nor his heart to report what my dream was," he paraphrases St. Paul, who, in 1 Corinthians 2:9 uses such language to evoke a spiritual reality.

It is a reality which transcends the senses, like the imagination.

When Queen Hippolyta comes to recognize the "constancy" within the changes wrought upon the lovers by their dream visions in the forest, she says their minds have been "transfigured," a word with immediate biblical overtones for the Elizabethan audience, evoking, as it does, the Transfiguration of Jesus on the mountain, when, as he prays, "the fashion of his countenance was altered, and his raiment was white and glistening" (Luke 9:29).

Such evocative language to describe the activation of the imagination by marriage and relationship suggests conventional images of revelation and transformation.

It is a revelation not just of the bestiality of men and women in love, but also of the spiritual dimension which sustains their relationships, and which permeates the natural world.

For there is both a Minotaur and a Goddess at the center of the maze through which Bottom and the lovers travel in the forest. The maze, of course, is an archetypal image of the marriage mysteries, and it is frequently alluded to in *A Midsummer Night's Dream*: Titania mentions the "quaint mazes in the wanton green," and notes that the rapidly changing seasons have produced a "mazèd world." Hermia twice declares herself "amazèd" by the fickle affections of friends and lovers in the forest.

It is appropriate, therefore, that Hermia calls Helena a "painted maypole," for, like the "nine men's morris" to which Titania alludes, there is an ancient connection between May Day marriage dances and the maze. The winding and unwinding of the ribbons by which the dancers are connected to the Maypole creates labyrinthine spiral dance. And in the Morris dances, the dancers are usually accompanied by a hobbyhorse, half human, half animal, representing the Minotaur.

Coming to the center of the maze, therefore, constitutes the climax of the hero journey of marriage. We may find there either the Minotaur of sexual aggression (half animal, half human), or the Maypole of rejuvenation, which connects the earth to the heavens, "mortal grossness" to "airy" spirits. Thus reconciling the opposites our relationships evoke within us—for we are at our best and our worse during the hero journey of marriage, which takes us into, then back out of, the labyrinthine depths of the forest.

The Redcrosse Knight and Una

Edmund Spenser's great poem, *The Faerie Queene,* takes us deeply into the labyrinth of marital mysteries. The poem begins with the meeting of the lovers, proceeds to their separation, and ends with their final reunion.

At the beginning of poem, in the first of its seven books, the Redcrosse Knight and Una seek shelter from a tempest in the "covert" of "A shadie grove," just off the "plaine" upon which they are riding. The "loftie trees" spread so broad a foliage as to completely block out "heavens light," casting an ominous darkness over their descent into the forest, which is reinforced by ending the catalogue of trees which follows with "the Cypress funerall."

The forest is a labyrinth of "pathes and alleies wide, / With footing worne, and leading inward farre." The couple is quickly lost, unable to "finde that path, which first was showne, / But wander too and fro in wayes unknown, / Furthest from end then, when they neerest weene," which is a characteristic feature of treading a maze. The path leads at first happily right in to the center, but then veers around to the outermost periphery, until the couple is completely lost—"So many pathes, so many turnings seeme, / That which of them to take, in diverse doubt they been."

The maze represents the confusions of marriage, the bewildering passage through its painful forthrights and meanders. The Redcrosse Knight resolves to take the path "that beaten seemd most bare, / And like to lead the labyrinth about," but it quickly leads them to the "hollow cave / Amidst the thickest woods" in which Spenser's version of the Minotaur dwells.

Una—who allegorically represents the true Church—plays the role of Ariadne, guiding her Theseus (the Redcrosse Knight) into and out of the maze of heresies which the forest represents. The dragon dwelling in "the wandering wood, this *Errours den*," is both the monster that threatens marital relationship with lust, rage, and violence; and the Minotaur of theological controversy, derived from the beast of the Apocalypse (Rev. 9: 7-10).

After slaying the dragon, the couple again looks for refuge, this time coming upon "A little lowly Hermitage [...] Downe in a dale, hard by a forests side." We begin to suspect the Hermit who dwells within this "holy Chappell edifyde" when he tells of "Saintes and Popes, and evermore / He strowd an *Ave-Mary* after and before," terrible words indeed for an Anglican Protestant!

And when, after "drouping Night" comes, along with the "Sweet slombring dew" of Morpheus, the Hermit retires into his study to consult "His Magick bookes and artes of sundry kindes" in order to seek "out mighty charmes, to trouble sleepy mindes," we know for certain that we are dealing with a popish version of the Renaissance Magus, much feared by Spenser as a master of the black arts of necromancy, though celebrated by Shakespeare, in *The Tempest*, as a benign master of providential magic (1.1.36).[37]

His name is Archimago, and he uses "wordes most horrible," "verses," and terrible "spelles" to summon Hecate, Goddess of the underworld and of witchcraft. She is also the witch within, waiting to emerge during the duress of relationship to disrupt—but also enrich—the marriage.

The descent to the underworld which follows is very important for the study of the marital journey in literature, since it develops a psychology of myth (and of dreams) far in advance of, and yet in many ways similar to, the work of Freud and Jung.

Archimago uses his incantatory verses to "call by name / Great *Gorgon*, Prince of darknesse and dead night, / At which *Cocytus* quakes, and *Styx* is put to flight," allusions which firmly relate the dream to the underworld. Archimago proceeds to summon two spirits "out of deepe darknesse dred," one of which he will use to shape a pleasing female incubus. The other he sends down to the house of Morpheus, in order to "forge true-seeming lyes" in the form of a dream.

Spenser draws heavily upon the kind of water and threshold imagery which we have frequently seen in our history of the marital descent into Hades: the spirit speeds downwards "through the world of waters wide and deepe" to the very "bowels of the earth full steepe," where Morpheus has pitched his palace. Tethys, wife of Oceanus, "Doth ever wash" the "wet bed" in which Morpheus lies, steeped in the "silver dew" of Cynthia, goddess of the Moon. "A trickling streame" and "ever drizzling raine" drowns out all "other noyse," leaving Morpheus to sleep in peace.

On the way down, Archimago's spiritual slave comes upon the house of Morpheus, "Whose double gates, he findeth locked fast, / The one faire fram'd of burnisht Yvory, / The other all with silver overcast; / And wakeful dogges before them farre do lye." Archimago's spirit passes into the underworld, like so many spirits before, through a pair of doorways, "returning by the Yvorie dore" with a "diverse dreame out of his prison darke," which Spenser refers to as a "fit false dreame, that can delude the sleepers."

While the one spirit has been retrieving the false dream from the house of Morpheus, Archimago uses his "charmes and hidden artes" to fashion a very erotic woman indeed. Her "tender partes" are "fram'd of liquid ayre," and she is so lively as to quite ravage any sleeping male!

She is surely a creature of delight, fashioned by the repressed desires of the Redcrosse Knight, who now dreams "of loves and lustfull play, / That nigh his manly heart did melt away, / Bathèd in wanton blis and wicked joy." It seems to him as if "Faire Venus" had stepped into his bed, a "loose Leman to vile service bound," whose "uncouth sight" and "shameless guise" inspire the Knight with a "great passion of unwonted lust." She disturbs his sleep with a "troublous dreame" of "bowres, and beds, and Ladies deare delight."

Where does she come from? Who is she?

She looks like his fair beloved, Una—but she doesn't act like Una. She's too sexy.

When the Knight wakes up, he admonishes Una for trying to seduce him, and is unable to distinguish the seductive "woman of his dreams" from the real woman of his daily life.

In other words, the woman of his dreams comes from within himself, produced by his own unacknowledged fantasies and desires. He then confuses this imaginary woman with Una, with the final result that he is separated from her, and goes off with the false illusion of his dreams.

This is a marvelous, acutely psychological episode in the poem. How many marriages and relationships have been disrupted by delusions generated by the mind? How often do we find ourselves relating more to a projection of ourselves, than to the real person lying opposite us in bed? How long does it take to sort it all out?

Spenser's descent to the underworld evokes the psychological and spiritual problems of the human unconscious—problems aroused by relationship and marriage—during its quest for meaning. And it takes the Redcrosse Knight a very long time indeed to sort it all out. He does so only with the help of King Arthur, who represents the higher authority of the inner Self, which, in the end, dispels the delusions of the world, making possible a marriage between the Spirit and the Flesh.

Mercury and Venus

The union of earthly and divine beauty vastly enriches the philosophical symbolism of marriage in the paintings of the early

Renaissance, such as Botticelli's wonderful masterpiece "Primavera," which hangs in the Uffizi Gallery in Florence.

The painting is set in an orchard of fruit trees. The Goddess Venus occupies the direct center of the composition, framed by Zephyr on the right border and Mercury on the left. Zephyr represents the force by which the spirit is propelled into the material world, forced out of the heaven of the intellect, which hovers above the labyrinth of fruit trees in the orchard.

Mercury, on the left border, represents the process by which the spirit returns from the material to the intellectual world. He stands with his left hand on his hip and his right hand holding his wand, pointed upward into the fruit-laden boughs, where the hidden light of intellectual beauty shines.

The painting, therefore, is framed on either side by the separation and return phases of the hero journey of the spirit, while the center of the composition is devoted to its marriage with the forms of the material world.

This marriage is a mixed blessing. The material world is a kind of prison where the pure forms or ideas are "drowned," "submerged," "perturbed" and "disfigured beyond recognition." However, by being infused with the spirit, the material world is redeemed. The figures of earthly beauty serve to recall to the mind the pure forms of the supercelestial realm. This is exactly the function of Venus, standing in the center of Botticelli's "Primavera," with Zephyr, Chloris, and Flora on one side of her, and the three graces on the other.

She represents the earthly and the divine forms of love in one figure, and thus constitutes the central revelation of the marriage between spirit and matter. Like Mercury, she stands gracefully with her right hand pointing upwards into a little clearing in the maze of the orchard, and her left hand resting gently on her thigh.

It is a gesture frequently to be found in the images of the Goddesses of art history—the right upward-pointed hand signifies transfiguration, the return of the soul to its spiritual home, initiated by the loving contemplation of earthly beauty; her left hand, resting on the thigh, represents incarnation, the descent of the soul into the womb of Anima Mundi. The goal is to marry the two, in full recognition of the radiance of the spiritual in the forms of earthly life.

At the beginning of the 17th century, there was a revival of these philosophies of the Renaissance, during the Rosicrucian Enlightenment, when the Neoplatonic, Gnostic, and Alchemical symbolism of marriage became a skeleton key to unlock the mysteries of world mythology and religion.[38]

The beautifully illustrated manuscripts produced at this time often used the metaphor of the marriage of the King and the Queen, or the Sun and Moon, to represent the fulfillment of the alchemical work. The plates from the *Rosarium Philosophorum*, produced in Frankfort in 1550, provide a splendid example.[39]

The first plate shows the alchemical version of the archetype of the fountain, always symbolic of the mysterious source of life. In place of what would be the four rivers of Paradise radiating out from the Garden of Eden in the Genesis, we have four six-pointed stars at each corner to symbolize the four elements (earth, air, fire, and water), with a fifth star, in the center above the fountain (between the sun and the moon), to represent the quintessence.

In the second plate, the King stands on the sun, the Queen on the moon. A crested dove descends from the star of the quintessence, as Sol and Luna join left hands, while holding interlacing branches of the tree of life in their right hands.

The marital mysteries begin in Figure 3, which shows Sol and Luna stripped down, still standing on sun and moon: the stripping down begins the descent into marriage. In alchemical terms, the divestiture symbolizes the first breakdown of the molecular compound—formed by the marriage of two elements—as it undergoes the various operations in the alchemical vessel.

In the *Rosarium*, the hermetic vessel takes the form first of a seven-sided bath, in which the couple sits, and then later as a bath on top of a coffin (both representing the alchemical crucible). The conjunction of Sol and Luna follows these episodes in the bath. They are shown joined in coitus on the surface of a flowing river in a mountainous landscape.

In the numerous marital mysteries we have examined, the crossing of the river, or the passageway into the mountains, represents the descent into the underworld. Hence, after the lovers sprout wings on what is now the small surface of a pond, the next plate shows them as a hermaphrodite floating dead on the waters of putrefaction in

Hades. The caption to the plate reads "Here lie King and Queen dead / The soul in great distress is fled." The waters float now on top of a quadrangular sarcophagus, in which the couple is broken down into the four elements, while the soul ascends into the clouds of heaven.

These two plates represent the lowest point of the marital journey, for the entire sequence represents not only the journey of individuation and the processes of psychoanalysis, but also the rigorous ordeals of marriage (both follow the rhythms of the descent into—and return from—hell).

Marriage breaks the ego down into the repressed complexes of the unconscious. Then the reconstruction of the relationship begins, along new lines, as the Self begins to emerge, purified by the trials of the journey.

These purifications proceed through the various alchemical operations, from putrefaction, to ablutions of heavenly dew, to the sublimation effected by the return of the soul (which itself undergoes a complete cycle of separation, ascent, and return in the sequence). The last plate shows the rebirth and reunion of the hermaphroditic couple, who emerge from the coffin to stand together upon a crescent moon, having completed the descent into marriage.

Several archetypal symbols of relationship are included in this plate: the couple holds a crested serpent in the left hand, and a cup with three crested serpents emerging in their right. The serpent represents renewal, by the power to shed its skins. The cup represents the Grail, or Chalice, symbol of the highest spiritual fulfillment of marriage. Beneath the base of the cup we see the alchemical tree of life, with seven branches and thirteen happy faces—a baker's dozen of children. Beneath the serpent in the left hand sits a little bird, symbol of the soul coming to rest in fulfilled relationship.

The same scene is magnificently illustrated in a famous picture from the *Aurora Consurgens* in Zürich, which shows the hermaphroditic couple standing in a pile of putrid eagles with a marvelous Phoenix spreading its wings protectively behind them. The dead eagles represent the morbid passage through Hades; while the Phoenix represents the new life emerging from the grave of the marital crises. The couple is joined together by a wound at the waist—as if to suggest that the deepest bonds of marriage are created by the painful injuries all true relationships inflict upon us.

The Chemical Wedding of Christian Rosencreutz

One morning, after prayers, Christian Rosencreutz has a vision of a woman standing on a globe, her right hand chained to the heavens, and her left to a monkey sitting at her feet. She has stars like apple blossom in her hair, and a crescent moon covers her womb. She holds a golden trumpet in one hand, and a wedding invitation in the other.

Christian puts on a white coat with a red ribbon drawn crossways over his shoulder, and then sticks four red roses in his hat, before setting out for the castle in the mountains, where the wedding is to be held.

He gives his invitation to a porter at the royal entrance, who leads him into another gate guarded by a lion. The porter drives the lion back, and Christian passes through it. A Virgin holding a lamp leads him through a courtyard to another gate, which claps shut just as he walks through it into a splendid castle. There are staircases and rooms everywhere, many of them filled with marvels and odd, eccentric guests. One guest says he's seen Plato's Perfect Forms. Another that he can hear the music of the spheres. And a third sits counting the atoms of Democritus.

The Virgin who led Christian into the castle comes in to weigh all the guests in a balance. When she gets to Christian, who still wears the roses in his hat, she declares him to be the one, and prepares him for marriage. He then sits down to a banquet table covered with golden and silver cups.

Looking around, he sees that everyone at the huge table is regally dressed—but that none of them have any heads!

Then servants come through the swinging doors of the kitchen, carrying silver platters, each of which bears the head of the person to whom it is served at table. After all the guests put their heads on, two pages present everyone with a golden fleece, a gift from the bridegroom. Then the banquet proceeds.

After the meal, Christian walks outside to see some musical statues, and to listen to the water organ beside the Lion Fountain in the middle of a hedge maze. The Virgin with the lamp appears and washes Christian's face with some water from the fountain, and then gives him a golden cup to drink with.

When he returns to the castle, Christian puts on new clothes, and is given an even more splendid fleece to drape over his shoulder. It is studded with precious stones, twinkling like stars set in a golden sky. He sees a sun and a moon inscribed on a pendant hanging from the Golden Fleece.

Then Christian follows the Virgin into a great hall, where he finds six coffins, and watches spellbound as six people are beheaded and put into the coffins.

Pallbearers arrive to carry the coffins into the vast underground chambers below the palace. Each coffin is placed upright, in its own niche, beneath a flaming torch, in a large vault illuminated by bright red carbuncle stones. There is an alcove in the grotto with a musical waterfall, and a large sepulchre in the middle of the room. It is made of sheer crystal, carved with elaborately ornate inscriptions, and inside it lie a dead King and Queen.

A candlelit procession marches slowly into the room, and a mysterious service is performed over the glass coffin, at the climax of which a golden bird descends from the ceiling bearing a lily in its beak. When the lily touches the glass coffin, the King and Queen come back to life, and are greeted by a chorus sung by the six persons who step out of the coffins, their heads restored.

Christian then follows the procession back up the steps and out the castle doors. It is sunrise, and a ship flying twelve flags with the signs of the zodiac on them waits by the riverside below. On board, the Princess waits for Christian beside a bed made of white, red, and green cross posts.

They are married in a chapel on board, and set forth on the river. A man stands on rock downstream, fishing for coral with a long shepherd's crook. As the boat passes, he pulls a crimson specimen from the depths of the clear water. The boat reaches the mouth of the river at twilight, and, as it passes into the sea, a full moon rising in the east balances the round disk of the setting sun in the west.

In the middle of the sea, the evening star shines over the island of their destination. When they arrive, one half of the island is dark, and the other light. A Hermaphrodite stands in the middle of the island on top of two lions joined at the single head they share. The Hermaphrodite is wearing an ornate star-studded robe, dark blue on the left side, and bright yellow on the right. The left side of its face is female, the right male, and it holds one side of a double-bladed axe in each hand.

The Hermaphrodite stands in a grove of seven trees, each of which bears the alchemical sign of one of the planets. Three trees to the left bear silver apples, and the three trees to the right golden apples.

Directly behind the Hermaphrodite, the Golden Fleece hangs from a tree with a dragon coiled around its roots.

Above the fleece, an enormous wheel of fire revolves in the sky, circling the four letters of the Hebrew name for God. The wheel contains signs of the zodiac, and symbols of the angels, the Trinity, and of Jesus—a pelican feeding its young by drawing blood from its breast.

The landscape to the Hermaphrodite's left is dark. Westminster Abbey can be seen in the distance, rising above the waters of the Thames. A naked woman holding a bunch of grapes in her right hand receives a moon in her left, handed to her by a creature with a man's body and the head of a buck, with 12 stars at the tips of its antlers. Her right hand is chained to the wheel of the heavens. She stands at the mouth of a river, with an eagle at her feet, and the wings of the eagle are draped over symbols of two of the four elements—water and earth.

To the right side of the Hermaphrodite stands a naked man. His left arm is chained to the wheel of the heavens, and with his right he receives a sun from a lion standing on its hind legs. The landscape behind him is bright. Heidelberg Castle can be seen in the distance, and a phoenix at his feet covers the signs of the two other elements— air and fire.

Both the naked man and the naked woman have suns covering their left breast, and moons covering their right. The woman has a crescent moon covering her genitals, and the man a six-pointed star, Solomon's seal.

This little fable is adapted from an alchemical allegory of the early 17th century, and from one of the most beautiful illustrations of the sacred marriage of the same period, by a man named Merian. Both the fable and the engraving use the mythological images of the union of the sun and the moon as symbols of the mystical marriage of the soul.

These mysteries revolved around the court of the Prince at Heidelberg in Germany, where the Rosicrucian movement began. The fulfillment of the alchemical quest was symbolized by the Golden Fleece, and by the sacred marriage of Jason and Medea.

Jason and Medea

It's not an auspicious analogy, since the marriage begins and ends with adultery, betrayal, and murder.

The Golden Fleece comes from a winged ram sent by the gods to rescue the children of King Athamas, who has followed his second wife's step-motherly instructions to sacrifice the two children of his first wife.

The golden ram carries the children away. One falls off, but the other, Phrixos, reaches the town of Colchis on the Black Sea. There he sacrifices the ram and hangs its golden fleece on an oak in a sacred grove.

After Phrixos dies, he haunts a king called Pelias, who has stolen the throne from his brother, Jason's father, and killed off all his rivals. When Jason miraculously appears to demand his father's throne, Pelias sends him off to Colchis to fetch the Golden Fleece and lay the ghost of Phrixos to rest.

Jason agrees, and, with the help of the goddess Athena, assembles the famous group of Argonauts—including Orpheus and Hercules—to sail for Colchis. There's a piece of an oak from the sacred grove of Zeus carved into the prow that can talk, prophesy, and provide guidance.

On the sea voyage to Colchis, the Argonauts stop off at an island where the women have murdered all their husbands, in revenge for having been reviled and abandoned. Jason takes Hypsipyle to wife, and begets a son, before abandoning the island.

At the next island, the Argonauts rescue old King Phineus, who is plagued by a group of harpies—winged, monkey-faced creatures that steal his food and foul his table. In gratitude for driving the harpies away, Phineus tells Jason how to navigate the crashing rocks that lead into the Black Sea: send a dove through first, and just as the rocks crash together, race through. The bird loses its tail feathers, and the ship its stern, but the entrance through the Bosphorus remains open to sailors forever after.

Arriving at last in Colchis, Jason is assisted in his quest for the Golden Fleece by Medea, daughter of King Aeëtes. Two goddesses, Hera and Athena, compel the royal sorceress to fall in love with Jason—with the fatal proviso that Jason swears eternal fidelity in marriage.

With Medea's help—she is mistress of a formidable pharmacology—Jason yokes a team of fire-breathing bulls and sows serpent's teeth in the furrows he plows. The teeth sprout a skeleton army which Jason defeats by luring it to the edge of a cliff.

Jason and Medea then proceed to the sacred oak where the Golden Fleece hangs, drug the dragon guarding it, and escape from the island. To distract their pursuers, Medea murders her half-brother and cuts his body up into a thousand pieces, which she tosses off the stern into the sea.

The pursuing ship then has to zigzag crazily around to retrieve the dismembered body parts for proper burial ceremonies.

Jason returns with the Golden Fleece to King Pelias, who has killed Jason's parents in his absence. Medea contrives his revenge, promising to use her magic to rejuvenate the aging Pelias. She appears to him in the form of a withered hag who mysteriously transforms herself into a lovely maiden.

"How'd you do that?" Pelias asks.

"Easy," answers Medea. She cuts an old ram into thirteen pieces and boils them up in her magic cauldron, out of which steps a freshly fleeced lamb.

"Now you get in the pot," Medea says, and his daughters carry the old man over to the cauldron, and drop him in! And that's the end of him, since (as William Gass put it) out of some ashes no bird rises.

Jason, however, subsequently breaks his vows, and marries another woman. Medea's revenge is to murder her children by Jason, and to murder his wife by sending her a flammable robe as a wedding present.

It burns her up—perhaps a symbol of the consequences of lingering premarital attachments.

The Rosicrucians of Heidelberg assumed that the images of dismemberment and rebirth in the magical cauldron were alchemical symbols, and that Medea represented the mysteries of medicinal magic. Her cauldron is a sacred vessel of the great goddess, like the Holy Grail—a feminine symbol of the womb of rebirth.

Medea is both, womb and tomb, a loving and a terrible goddess.

For the Rosicrucians, her cauldron was an alchemical vessel, like a beaker or crucible, in which molecules were broken down into the elements which, when recombined, could form new and miraculous substances—like the philosopher's stone.

The symbol of the philosopher's stone was the sacred marriage of the King and the Queen, of gold and silver, of the Sun and the Moon. Their union created a mythical being, the hermaphrodite—part male and part female.

But to return to our Rosicrucian fable.

In the engraving, the creature with the man's body and stag's head is Actaeon, the Greek hunter who was turned into a buck one day by the goddess of the hunt, Artemis. Actaeon spied upon her while she was bathing in a forest pool. Her robes lay on the bank, but she still wore the silver crescent moon in her hair. When she saw Actaeon peeping out at her from the reeds, she splashed water in his face, and turned him into a buck. He was then chased down and torn apart by his own hounds!

The goddess turns him into a "horny" guy—we still use the word stag for a young male in heat! Actaeon is torn apart by his own lust, those instinctively compulsive energies of sexuality which women naturally arouse in their men.

But, alas, as we know, those energies can be violent, destructive, and brutal. These marvelous myths of marriage remind us that relationship can bring out the brute in us—whether it be Circe's pig, Diana's stag, or Beauty's Beast.

They also remind us of the sacred dimension of our bestiality.

The deer, for example, has long been an animal sacred to the goddess, and a symbol of death and rebirth. The Greek goddess Artemis, who turns Actaeon into a stag, was called "She of the Red

Deer," or "She Who Strikes the Red Deer." Prehistoric deer cults have been excavated in Spain and in the British Isles, where the deer has long been affiliated with the great goddess and her ritual dances—some of them possibly connected to a spiral maze dance—celebrating death and rebirth.

There are also Greek and Scottish tales about goddesses who turn themselves into deer, and in Old Europe, the fact that the stag molts its antlers annually made it a symbol of regeneration. By the time of the Christian era, the stag symbolized the resurrection—the cross appearing between the stag's antlers to Sts. Hubert and Eustace.

Gawain and Morgan le Fay

In one the most beautiful of all the Arthurian romances of the Middle Ages—a poem called "Sir Gawain and the Green Knight"—the stag is the quarry of a noble hunt that occurs outside the enchanted castle where Morgan Le Fay lives. Morgan's man is the Green Knight, a gigantic creature who bursts into Camelot at Christmas time to ask if anyone wants to play a holiday game.

The game goes like this: if any of Arthur's knights may be so bold as to strike the Green Knight's head off, with an enormous battle-axe, the Green Knight will kindly return the favor a year hence, at the Green Chapel. Sir Gawain takes the challenge and chops the Green Knight's head off.

It rolls and bounces over the flagstones on the floor, kicked around by the assembly of pages and knights like a soccer ball, until the Green Knight retrieves it, gets on his horse, and turns the head towards Gawain:

"Next year, at the Green Chapel!" the head says, as the horseman rides out of the hall, striking sparks on the flagstones.

Gawain leaves to keep his promise the following Halloween, and rides southwards over hill and over dale, nearly slain by the sleet as he sleeps in his irons. He arrives at a marvelous castle, sitting in a grove of shimmering oaks, on Christmas Eve, and is welcomed inside.

At dinner, his host makes a deal: "You sleep in for the next three days, before your date at the Green Chapel on New Year's, and I'll go hunting. I'll give you what I catch, and if you should catch anything here in the castle, you'll give it to me."

And so a hunt goes on during the next three days—both inside and outside the castle. The Lord of the castle brings home a stag, a boar, and a fox, which he gives to Gawain. In exchange, Gawain gives him two kisses on the cheek for the first two days. He's gotten these kisses from the lovely Lady of the Castle, who appears each morning at his bedside, dressed for the hunt—she's wearing a transparent nightgown, with jeweled brocade!

Gawain tries to pretend he's asleep, but she tickles him under the cheek to wake him up.

On the third day, a bit frustrated, she offers him more than a kiss: "Take all my body," she says; but, courtly lad that he is, Gawain refuses. Instead, he takes a green girdle she gives him, and wraps it around his thigh the morning he leaves for the Green Chapel.

The girdle is magic. It protects its wearer from any harm—like having your head cut off by the Green Knight on New Year's Day. So Gawain doesn't tell the Lord of the Castle about it on the third day of the hunt.

As it turns out, the Lord of the Castle is the Green Knight Gawain meets at the Chapel, where he must bend down on his knees to receive the blow from the axe which decapitated the Green Knight in Arthur's court the year before.

The Green Knight warms up and strikes twice at Gawain, missing both times because Gawain flinches. On the third swing, the axe knicks Gawain's jugular, and a stream of bright red blood squirts out onto the white snow.

Gawain leaps up, happier than he had ever been since the day he was born of his mother. But then he confesses his sins—cowardice and covetess—to the vast amusement of the Green Knight—who, after all, is pagan, a supernatural consort of the Morgan the Goddess.

Gawain then returns to Camelot, wearing the Green Girdle as a sign of his shame. Caught between the codes of courtly love and Christianity, in a kind of limbo between a Celtic and an Ecclesiastical society, Gawain's had difficult territory to negotiate.

It's the territory of the marriage mysteries, which binds us often to conflicting codes and obligations.

That Gawain decapitates the Green Knight, whose head is restored by the power of the Goddess, brings us back to our little alchemical fable—to the headless banqueteers and the six knights decapitated in the palace of the chemical wedding.

Their re-capitation represents the resurrection, the power of life to survive death. The plants do it every year: we cut the head off the corn in the fall, and it comes back next spring. Nature is ruled by the "Jolly Green Giant," whose color is a symbol of both life and death.

In folktales and myths all over the world, the decapitated god is the sun—its head cut off every night, with the blood streaming all over the horizon, and then restored the next morning. In one Russian tale, the hero, Ivan, steals that head, which returns to the body of the god after a Princess returns three of its hairs.

It would seem then that death and rebirth are essential elements of the sacred mysteries of marriage and relationship. In all the myths, the mortal who marries the goddess dies to be reborn. Love demands the descent to, and the return from the underworld. Marriage has its ups and downs, a sine wave of more or less extreme amplitude. A manic-depressive rhythm none of us escapes, and which we must learn not only to accept, but also to celebrate.

For after all, the valley of the red deer is a vale of soul making.

In our alchemical fable, on the island Christian Rosencreutz sails to with his bride, the marriage is between the Rhine and the Thames, Day and Night, Gold and Silver, the King and the Queen, the Sun and the Moon.

Both heavenly bodies have cycles symbolic of death and rebirth. Diurnal for the sun, monthly for the moon. The sun is often personified as male (except in German!), and the moon female. The one gold, the other silver. The sun is transcendent, beyond the terrestrial rhythms of the sub-lunar world. For the moon dies to be reborn every night, while the sun shines eternally—though it too has its dark passage, daily, and through the twelve signs of the zodiac, as it negotiates the journey between the solstices.

In a marvelous little poem by W.B. Yeats, a Celtic tale called "The Song of Wandering Aengus," the marriage of the sun and the moon symbolizes unattainable fulfillment of relationship.

A young man goes out to a hazel wood at twilight, a fire burning in his heart. He hooks a berry to a line, and catches a little silver trout in a stream purling along beneath the stars. He takes the trout home to cook, bending down on hands and knees to blow on the fire. A rustling at the door makes him turn around. He hears his name called out, as a girl with apple blossom in her hair flickers away out the door.

The young man runs out the cottage, but the girl fades away in the early morning dew, still calling after him. And still she cries, and still he pursues her, "through hollow lands and hilly lands," until he grows wrinkled and old.

Driven by relentless desire and implacable remorse, the old man vows to stay on the chase, until such time as he may catch the glimmering girl, and they may walk together on an island of bliss, plucking "till time and times are done / The silver apples of the moon, / The golden apples of the sun."

Adam and Eve

Like Shakespeare in *A Midsummer Night's Dream*, John Milton uses the maze as a myth of marriage, in his great poem, *Paradise Lost*. The poet divides Book IX of the poem into three parts, representing the stages of marriage and relationship: Adam and Eve before the Fall; the Fall itself; and Adam and Eve after the Fall, as they begin to move towards reconciliation.

Before the Fall, Satan arrives in Eden and sneaks into the "mazy folds" of the "sleeping serpent," which he discovers lying "In labyrinth of many a round self-rolled." After possessing the body of the snake, Satan crawls towards Eve, coiling erect upon a "Circular base of rising folds, that towered / Fold above fold a surging maze."

Satan had come to Eve the night before, in the form of a toad that whispered into her ear while she lay dreaming. The toad inspires her with the desire to work apart from Adam the next day. Not to stand by his side as they toil in the garden.

She wants her own life, her own career, and prevails over Adam's need to keep her in sight.

Eve stands "amazed" when the serpent leads her to the Tree of Knowledge. When she first hears the serpent's eloquence, she is "Yet more amazed," listening to the story of how eating the fruit elevated the Serpent's powers of reason, speech, and thought. Hence, when the serpent slithers towards the forbidden tree, Milton compares its motion to the "wandering fire" of the will-o'-the wisp, which "Misleads th'amazed night wanderer from his way."

The serpent dazzles Eve in the Garden with his philosophical eloquence, which he attributes to having eaten the fruit of the Tree of Knowledge. He speaks of the increased power of reason and language, of the "speculations high or deep" to which the eating of the fruit enabled him to turn his newly "capacious mind."

The powers of reason, speech, and thought are associated with the seductive maze of the mind, which the Serpent represents, and which tempts Eve. When Eve resists the temptation to eat the fruit, it is again to the elevated powers of natural philosophy that Satan turns in his efforts to seduce her. He calls the Tree a "sacred, wise, and wisdom-giving Plant," the "Mother of science!"

Writing at the end of the 17th century, and after having traveled in Italy, where he spoke with Galileo, Milton was apparently uneasy about the emergence of modern science in his time. But his version of the Fall also brings the problems that language and the intellect can create in our marriages, when either is abused—as perhaps, they often are.

Language can mislead, or hurt our relationships, as often as the mind may interfere with mistaken fantasies and misperceptions.

But Eve reasons that increasing her intellectual power might make her more Adam's equal—or indeed, perhaps make her his superior.

After eating the fruit, therefore, Eve celebrates its "operation / Blest to sapience." If the plant can give "elocution to the mute" serpent, which, having eaten, "knows, and speaks, and reasons, and discerns," then surely she too might partake of that "sciental sap" which would enable her, a woman, to tread the serpentine mazes of philosophy, rhetoric, and scientific speculation.

Adam is of course stunned when Eve returns with the news of having partaken of the fruit of the Tree of Knowledge—which, as God has told him, means death. In noble resolve to share his wife's sorrow, and out of fear at the thought of living without her, he follows suit, and eats the fruit.

Once again, Milton emphasizes the rapid intensification of the couple's powers of intellect and imagination that results from eating the fruit. Their minds are opened to the vast secrets of the universe, and they become conscious, for the first time, of the mystery of their place within it.

But soon afterwards, they notice their nakedness in a new way, and retire into the woods to make love—ashamed and guilty for the first time in their marriage. It would seem that sooner or later, we do and say things in our relationships that make it all too clear how less than perfect we actually are.

This recognition leads to a "scene" all too common in our marriages. Adam blames Eve for the Fall, and she in turn blames him for having been so weak as to submit to her desires! They go round and round in an endless quarrel of guilt and recrimination, spoiling the beauty of the day with acrimonious vituperation.

How do we get out of the mazes our relationships lead us into? How do we cope with the jealousy, the rage, the despair, the guilt about shameful behavior?

Milton suggests we do so by remembering Paul's letter on faith, hope, and love. Only the hope of an improved future makes marriage possible after our fall from innocence. At the end of the poem, an Angel consoles the grieving couple with a vision of their descendants, who will reenact the Fall in the Garden, "till one greater man restore us," and we "regain the blissful seat."

CHAPTER FOUR

Folk Tales, Ballads, and Fables

In his commentary on the fairy tales collected by the Grimms Brothers, Joseph Campbell broke the interpretation of the myths and tales down into the scientific, social-political, metaphysical, and psychological categories.[40] All of these levels of interpretation can be applied to the mysteries of marriage, as we have seen, and in fact many of the traditional symbols of archetypal wisdom come down to us in folktales and ballads about relationship.

Many of the most important symbols of the sacred marriage were established in the folktale traditions of the *Arabian Nights*, originally collected in Baghdad, around 800 C.E., and enormously popular in Europe during the 18th century, when translations brought them in to the mainstreams of French and English literature. These marvelous stories capture the most profound wisdom about marriage and relationships, in a thoroughly delightful way.

Zubaidah and the Beautiful Boy

The *Arabian Nights* begins with a famous frame of great importance for the sacred mysteries of marriage. One of the harem girls, Scheherazade, tells her stories to King Shahryar—to delay her decapitation. He has been cutting off the heads of his harem girls one by one, night after night, in a jealous rage after a visit with his brother—whose entire harem has cheated on him—only to find that his harem too has been unfaithful.

Scheherazade's tales have a therapeutic result. By the end of the 1001 Nights of stories (many of which are about marriage and relationship, and reflect the King's own affliction), King Shahryar's murderous rage has been transformed into love.

"The Tale of Zubaidah" is an excellent story about a woman's marital journey. It is uniquely concerned with the plight of women in the Islamic world, and with the relationships between three sisters.

The tale begins with conflict and crisis. Two of three sisters use the dowry left by the death of the father to marry, while the third and youngest increases her inheritance with prudent investments. When the two older sisters return destitute, having been abandoned in strange lands by bankrupt husbands, the youngest sister takes them in, and treats them generously.

When the older sisters build up a second dowry, they marry once again, with the same results: bankruptcy, theft, and abandonment. It is upon their second return to their youngest sister that Zubaidah resolves to sail to Basrah to do business. Zubaidah prudently leaves half her money at home, in case some misfortune ruins her at sea.

Zubaidah's departure is related to her sisters' misfortunes. But more than that, it is inaugurated from within, at midlife, by the urge to see more of the world. A storm at sea (an old symbol for the emotional turmoil of midlife) drives the ship ten days across unknown seas (an old symbol for the unconscious realm of the spirit) to a strange city on an enchanted island.

While her sisters wander off into the marketplace, where all the inhabitants have been turned into black stone, Zubaidah makes her way towards the King's palace (an archaic symbol of the Self). Zubaidah enters the palace through a great door of solid gold with a velvet curtain hanging in front of it. Inside, she finds a petrified King, surrounded by furniture of gold and silver, and sitting upon a throne encrusted with pearls that shine like stars.

Silver is associated with the moon, gold with the sun, and the pearls with stars.

Passing through an open door made of silver, Zubaidah climbs a porphyry staircase of seven steps to a golden trestle supporting a brilliant diamond, large as an ostrich's egg. The passage through a sequence of doorways, halls, corridors, and staircases reminds one of the labyrinth, an archaic symbol of the marriage mysteries. The diamond at the top of this seven-tiered staircase, surrounded by torches, represents the light illuminating the seven planets and the host of starry torches which surround it.

The source of light is compared to an ostrich egg. In an Orphic creation myth, the goddess of Night hatches an Egg, from which the radiant god of love emerges. Zubaidah has climbed the seven steps of the planets into the heavens.

When night falls, Zubaidah is lost in the labyrinth of the palace, unable to find her way out and circling endlessly around the hall with the diamond. This chamber yields first a magnificent book, the Koran, written in magnificent gold script, with red devices and illuminations in all colors. Zubaidah passes through another doorway at midnight, into a little room where a beautiful young man recites the Koran in a sweet and learned voice.

The astronomical symbolism of the sacred marriage emerges in the description of the beautiful boy. This description is the climax of the initiatory phase of the journey. Each of his features have celestial origins: Saturn gave him his black hair, Mars bestowed the roses in his cheeks, the constellation of the Archer gave the arrows to his eyes, sagacious Mercury imparted his sweet intelligence, and Venus forged his heart.

The catalogue modestly stops here, but one can infer that the young man is a kind of microcosm, each organ of the body corresponding to a celestial body.

The young man explains that the petrification of the city actually resulted from the irreverence of his father, who worshipped fire and light and all the turning stars instead of Allah, who turned the city to black stone.

Zubaidah's task is now to bring her newfound wisdom and her husband back home to Baghdad. She succeeds in the former, but fails in the latter, retaining the wisdom, but losing her husband. Her jealous sisters throw her and the young man overboard in the middle of the night, and the latter drowns.

Zubaidah clings to a spar of wood from the ruined bed, and is carried ashore. Here she kills a large snake before it catches a smaller snake. The little snake turns out to be a Genie which sinks the ship, transports the riches home, and turns the wicked sisters into two black bitches. Zubaidah has to beat them everyday with three hundred strokes, when she returns to Baghdad.

The allegory here revolves around sibling problems, suggesting the sad necessity of breaking ties with in-laws who exploit us, and disrupt our otherwise happy marriages—which happens as often in life as it does in the myths.

The Dervish and the Princess

The journey to the underworld plays a central role in many of the other stories about marriage and relationship in the *Arabian Nights*. One is called simply "The Tale of the Second Dervish."

While working for a woodcutter, during his exile in a foreign land, the dervish starts digging around the stump of a fallen tree in densely wooded glade. His axe strikes against a ring of brass on a wooden slab, which, when lifted, reveals a flight of stairs leading down to another door at the bottom.

This door leads into the spacious courtyard of a magnificent palace, where the dervish finds a young woman more beautiful than a priceless pearl and radiant as the sun. The princess says she was abducted by the son of Iblis himself, and imprisoned in his underground palace. Iblis is the Arabic name for Satan, which suggests a parallel between the princess and Persephone, who was abducted by Hades, Lord of the Underworld.

The dervish attempts to rescue the princess, but the Genie kills her, and carries the dervish up to a mountaintop, where he turns him into an ape.

The Egyptian god of writing, Thoth, was often depicted with an ape or baboon head. In the tale of the second dervish, the ape finds refuge with a king and his daughter, and amazes them by composing couplets, each in a different script, for which feat he is invested with a robe of honor. After the ape improvises half a dozen verses in praise of the King, the King's daughter recognizes the ape as the dervish, an illustrious prince in exile.

The King's daughter is a female magician, trained from childhood by an old nurse, a skilled enchantress deeply versed in sorcery.

The daughter has memorized the codes of magic, and boasts of the power to destroy the King's city and scatter its stones as far as the Mountain of Kaf. Instead of destroying the city, however, she puts her magical powers of poetry to good use, by turning the enchanted monkey back into a prince!

Is it not the civilizing power of the feminine to turn all of us from monkeys into men?

The princess does so by using a knife engraved with Hebrew words to sketch a circle and to inscribe it with talismanic names and magic inscriptions. Then she stands in the circle while reciting an incantation.

The Hebrew letters provide a fascinating glimpse into the syncretic world of myth drawn upon by the Arabian tales, for we know of an ancient form of Jewish mysticism which combined geometric forms and the mystical letters of the alphabet. This tradition produced marvelous documents and amulets, which had mystical power.

The princess uses the magical letters to conjure up a terrifying Genie, who appears in a hideous shape, and who pursues and eventually destroys her. This occurs through a series of transformations. The Genie turns himself into a lion, a scorpion, an eagle, a black cat, a large red pomegranate, and a whale to pursue the princess, who takes the forms of a serpent, a vulture, a wolf, a rooster, and a burning coal.

The battle ends with the death of the princess, whose sacrifice, however, leads to the transformation of the ape. The entire episode suggests the Pythagorean notion of transmigration—the soul passes through a series of incarnations, from animal to man, in its progress towards spiritual perfection.

Readers of Arthurian literature will also recall the story of Ceridwen, who sets her apprentice, Taliessin, to stirring her magical cauldron. When he dips his finger to taste the brew, he instantly achieves the omniscience the Goddess had intended for her son. As a result, Ceridwen pursues Taliessin through a sequence of transformations, very like those recorded in the tale of the dervish, right down to the hen and grain, which the hen swallows—only to give birth to the transformed Taliessin nine months later.

Aladdin and Badr al-budur

Perhaps the most famous of the tales in the *Arabian Nights* is the story of "Aladdin and the Wonderful Lamp," in which two complete journeys to the otherworld lead to the consummation of marriage.

The first journey begins in a Chinese city, where Aladdin, a poor tailor's son, is lured out of the streets and gardens of the town by a dwarfish Moor, who appears near the entrance to the market. The Moor is a powerful magician from Morocco, an astrologer deeply learned in physiognomy.

The death of Aladdin's father coincides with puberty, a rite of passage leading to marriage and renewed paternity. Aladdin's journey also involves the timeless task of finding a profession. The Moor lures Aladdin into his care with the promise of apprenticeship as a merchant.

The Moor takes Aladdin to a merchant and buys him a costly robe, made of striped and shining silk; a white turban decorated with gold; a Kashmir belt; and boots of bright leather. The robe renders Aladdin more beautiful than the moon, an allusion which evokes the lunar cycles of death and rebirth.

Thus invested, Aladdin is ready for his journey. The next morning, Aladdin goes to the door of his house to await the Moor, and then walks off through the gates of the city to the noble houses and handsome gardens in the suburbs. Beyond them lies a mountain, at the end of a deserted valley, filled only with the presence of God, which is the Moor's destination.

Here, in the deserted mountain valley, the Moor instructs Aladdin to collect some wood for a fire, over which he sprinkles incense and mutters spells in an unknown tongue. A chasm opens up, with a huge marble slab with a copper ring in the bottom. It is a doorway to the underworld, which can only be opened after Aladdin grabs the ring and recites his lineage, naming himself, his father, and his grandfather (for the underworld is typically the domain of the ancestors).

Aladdin lifts the slab and descends twelve marble steps to a second double door of red copper, studded with bolts. This door swings open of its own accord after Aladdin lifts his robe to his belt.

He then passes through a huge cave, divided into three communicating halls. In the first, there are twelve jars—of bronze, silver, and gold—filled with gold liquid, dust, and coins. Aladdin holds his robe close about his waist, in order to avoid touching any of the jars.

The number twelve represents the sun's journey through the signs of the zodiac. The precious metals suggest the metallurgical mysticism of the planets (Sun-gold, Moon-silver, Venus-copper).

A third door lies at the end of the third chamber of jars. It leads through a magnificent garden of trees heavily fruited with gemstones infinitely varied in color. A midnight sun scatters its rays through these jewels, and the trees burn as if with magic fire. The colors are white, red, green, blue, and yellow. They correspond to the planets. In the mystical traditions, the metals were subterrestrial embryos of the heavenly bodies.

A subterrestrial or paradisal garden of gemstones as the destination of the heroic descent is a frequently encountered motif in the mythology of the marriage mysteries. We have seen it before, in "Sir Orfeo" (Pluto's underworld palace of gemstones reached by a hole in a rocky hillside), and we will see it again, often.

In the Grimms' tale of "The Twelve Dancing Princesses," for example, the hero breaks off branches from a silver, a gold, and a diamond tree. Persian and Arabic tradition describe a land of emerald cities hidden within, or at the summit of, a mountain called Kaf. The cities are illuminated entirely by an emerald, glowing in the place of sun and moon.

Kaf is an imaginal terrain, between the realm of the senses and the pure forms of the intellect. It represents an intermediary world where the soul ascends to the infinite light of the heavens, or, alternatively, where the soul comes face to face with its earthly self. It is a world of archetypal images, a world of the imagination, the place where soul mates are found.

Entering these caves at the climax of Aladdin's journey therefore involves images of the marriage mysteries. The soul goes down into the underworld, along the twelve steps beneath the marble slab, traverses the three chambers of the cavern behind the large copper door, and then ascends the thirty steps to a terrace and niche containing the famous magic lamp.

The descent represents the death of the body, its passage through the twelve spheres of the zodiac. The ascent symbolizes the resurrection of the soul, and its return to its divine source, which resides beyond and above the spheres of the creation.

Ladders and staircases had been used as symbols of the journey of the soul all over the Ancient Near East, particularly in Egyptian tombs and funerary papyri, in which we find Osiris depicted as the Lord of the Staircase. The thirty steps leading up to the lamp may be lunar, for we know that the ladders of Set, Osiris, Buddha, and the Pharaoh had fourteen steps for the waxing moon, and fourteen for the waning.

Aladdin's return from this underworld involves a threshold battle. He encounters the old wizard, standing high above him at the top of the twelve steps behind the copper door. The wizard becomes enraged when Aladdin refuses to give him the lamp, and throws incense upon the smoldering fire in order to imprison the boy beneath the marble slab. The second door into the garden claps shut as well, trapping Aladdin on the staircase between the copper door and the marble slab, effectively burying him alive.

The wizard is a black magician, skilled in the arts of sorcery and spells, geomancy and alchemy, astrology, and enchantment. Through these arts, he learned of the existence of the magic lamp, buried in the mountains outside the city of Kolo-Ka-Tse in China. It is this lamp, as the world well knows, which now effects Aladdin's resurrection, and the completion of his first journey on the road towards maturity and marriage.

We have already encountered the lamp as a symbol of enlightenment in the story of Psyche. Lamps were also associated with funerary rituals as symbols of the eternal flame of the soul. A Roman legend records the discovery of a lamp miraculously burning for centuries in the tomb of Tullia, Cicero's daughter. In the alchemical mysteries, a perpetually burning lamp illuminates the sealed tomb of Christian Rosencreutz.

A lamp called the "effigy of the Supreme Deity" is carried by one of the priests in the sacred marriage of Isis and Osiris. Its handle and spout are covered by hieroglyphs. And in the Bible, the Virgins awaiting the Bridegroom (Jesus) are instructed to keep their lamps trimmed and burning!

The lamp is also a cornucopia, a "horn of plenty," like the platter we saw distributing favorite dishes to the knights gathered in the Grail castles. It serves a marvelous meal to Aladdin and his mother, after he returns home from his ordeal in the mountains.

The Genie serves the meal on a great tray of massive silver, which holds twelve gold dishes of spiced meats, six warm loaves of bread, and two large flasks of vintage wine. The combination of gold and silver we recognize as a symbol of the marriage of Sol and Luna, Eternity and Time. The ritual celebrating this moment is a kind of Eucharist, with its foods symbolic of resurrection—wine and bread. The occasion for the feast is Aladdin's homecoming, a traditional symbol of the completion of the soul's journey.

But Aladdin's homecoming leads inevitably to another journey, motivated by love and leading to marriage.

On a certain day, heralds run through the streets, warning all citizens to hide immediately behind the closed doors of their houses, in order to avoid seeing the marvelous "Badr al-budur, youngest of the moons of God, daughter of our Sultan's glory!" Those who dare to disregard this order and peep through doors or windows will be executed on the spot.

Aladdin, however, is overcome by an irresistible desire to see the Princess, and runs to the hammam where she is going to take her bath. There he hides behind a great door, in such a position that he might look through the crack and see the Sultan's daughter in her bath—rather like Actaeon spying on Artemis bathing in her forest pool.

It is an equally fateful moment. So astonished is Aladdin by the vision of Badr al-budur's beauty, and by the discovery that all women don't look like his old mother, that he is turned to stone. This drama at the doorway initiates his journey towards marriage. Aladdin begins lengthy and clever negotiations which lead eventually to his departure from his mother and union with the Princess.

These negotiations require the assistance of the Genie in the lamp, who must disrupt the Sultan's plans to marry his daughter to a Wazir by abducting her on the wedding night and taking her from the palace to Aladdin's humble abode. Then the Genie provides the processional dowry that the Sultan requires as proof of Aladdin's worthiness to marry his daughter, Badr al-budur.

The procession involves numerical symbolism associated with the mystical rites of the sacred marriage.

Aladdin sends forty dishes of solid gold, filled with jeweled fruit, like those which he plucked from the trees in the garden beneath the mountain. The dishes are carried by forty slave girls, each as fair as the moon. They are guarded by forty handsome young black men, strong, well built, and magnificently dressed.

The procession enters the Sultan's palace in pairs of black and white, and forms a crescent in front of his throne, after setting their burdens of gold down, prostrating themselves, and removing the gauze coverings from the forty dishes.

Then Aladdin's old mother advances to the centre of the crescent, and negotiates her son's marriage with Badr al-budur. The Sultan sits opposite on his throne, for he is the Grand Patriarch of the Universe. She is the Great Mother, the Goddess from whom those opposites of black and white, and male and female, proceed. The female slaves are summer moons, and their black attendants kings.

The astonished Sultan summons Aladdin to court, as a member of his royal family, and Aladdin dresses and prepares a second symbolic procession.

He puts on a magnificent robe of many colors, which, along with the symbolism of the Sultan and marriage, signifies the soul's re-investment with a spiritual body, and its return to God, after its long sojourn in the prison of this world—a distant, poverty-stricken suburb of heaven.

The bathing ritual Aladdin performs before putting on this magnificent robe is elaborately evoked, and recalls the metallurgical symbolism of the bath in the alchemical marriage. The bath is made of jade and transparent alabaster, with pools of rose carnelian and white coral. It is ornamented with large emeralds, and its inner hallway is paved with jewels.

Aladdin emerges from the flower-scented waters with flesh glowing like Gawain's in the Castle of the Green Knight, or Parzival's in the Castle of the Grail, for the bath signifies that purification of the flesh which allows the radiance of the spirit to shine through.

He then summons the Genie, and orders a grand processional: a pure bred Arabian stallion for him to ride, with forty-eight slaves, elegantly clad, to walk in two groups of twenty four—two files of twelve in front of him, and two files of twelve behind. All forty-eight slaves carry bags with five thousand dinars of gold hanging about their necks.

Aladdin rides in the center of the procession, with a diamond feather in his turban streaming with light. Four slaves at his sides hold the bridles of his horse.

One can't help but recall Black Elk's "Great Vision" of forty-eight horses of four different colors streaming in from the four cardinal points of the compass to the rainbow tent in the centre of the universe. The procession is a symbol of wholeness, based on the two numbers (4 and 12) associated with the earth and the heavens—the sacred marriage of which constitutes the essence of mystical teachings.

But it is after the marriage ceremonies that the tough journey begins.

The mysterious Moor reappears on the scene after using his magic to find out about Aladdin's marriage. His magic involves the manipulation of geometric figures symbolic of the marriage mysteries. He takes some sand from his cupboard, sits within a red circle inscribed on a square mat, and marks the male and female points.

That gives us two interlocking triangles inside a squared circle. It is like Solomon's Seal, or the Star of David. The downward pointed triangle is female, and symbolizes incarnation (the descent of the spirit into the material world). The upward pointed triangle is male, and symbolizes transfiguration (the ascent of the spirit to the heavens). The circle represents the eternity of the heavens; and the square symbolizes earthly time and space.

Bring them all together, and you have the essence of the sacred mysteries of marriage—the union of male and female, of heaven and earth, of eternity and time.

But the Moor uses his spells to destroy Aladdin's marriage. He disguises himself as a peddler, and persuades Badr al-budur to exchange her magic lamp for a useless new one. Having stolen the lamp, the Moor takes the Princess (and her palace!) to Morocco, so that when the Sultan wakes up the next morning and looks out across the way, his daughter's palace is nowhere to be seen.

Abduction is one of the most universal symbols of marriage. It initiates the descent into the underworld, to liberate the heroine from the lord of death. She represents Anima Mundi, the soul of the world imprisoned in material things. Her liberation is a symbol of resurrection and redemption.

Hence, after the Sultan's police arrest him, Aladdin is given forty days to find the Princess, and wanders off into open country. He comes to a great river, and contemplates suicide. The river marks the threshold crossing into the otherworld. It is a basic rite of passage in any marriage and relationship—depression and despair!

Aladdin, however, keeps at it.

He does not give up.

And neither should we.

Instead, he rubs his magic ring—a symbol of marital fidelity, and a reminder of those vows we took (in sickness and in health, in death as in life, in age as in youth).

The Genie in the ring takes Aladdin to Morocco, where the Moor has transported the Princess and her palace. There Aladdin manages to retrieve the lamp by drugging the magician, and he then takes the Princess and Palace back to China, completing the second journey of his marriage.

An interesting detail of this abduction and rescue links it to the story of Lancelot and Guenevere, and to the Harrowing of Hell. The Sultan's heralds announce that Aladdin has freed all who had been cast into prison, and declare a day of universal amnesty. Aladdin has performed the same symbolic feat as Lancelot, who, as you remember, rescued Guenevere (the soul of the world) from King Bademagus (Bad Magic). Along the way, he liberated all the captives from the kingdom "from which no traveler returns," i.e. the kingdom of death.

Aladdin's journey into marriage ends with one final test: the ordeal of fertility problems.

Concerned by the fact that she has not yet conceived, Badr al-budur sends for an old female saint named Fatmah. She instructs the Princess to hang an egg taken from a Roc's nest, on the highest peak of the Caucasus, in the middle of the crystal dome in the hall of windows. (A Roc is a huge, mythical bird, big enough to carry off an elephant). She must then meditate upon the egg for many days, after which her "interior nature will undergo modification and the dead shall live."

But Fatmah turns out to be the Moorish magician's vengeful brother in disguise, who is attempting to ruin Aladdin's happiness. When summoned to get the Roc's egg, the Ifrit refuses, and reveals his true identity as a servant of the most holy Roc, whom the Ifrit refers to as "the Father of Eggs." However, since Fatmah (the disguised sorcerer) requested the egg, and not Aladdin or Badr al-budur, the Ifrit is able to obtain it for the young couple.

The symbolism of the egg recalls the "Second Voyage" of Sinbad, who was shipwrecked on an island with a huge Roc egg in the center, and then on another island with serpents coiled around eggs inside a cave. Sinbad reached that second island by tying himself onto a Roc's talons. He escapes from the valley—which is full of rotting lambs with huge diamonds stuck to the flesh—by the crawling inside a carcass, and being carried up to the top of the cliff by the Roc.

Eggs in the tomb paintings of Ancient Rome represented the creative rhythms of life, of becoming and passing away. As far back as 1000 B.C., Phoenician mythologies attributed the Creation to a watery slime which was twisted into a shining egg by the swirling winds of night. The Orphics of Greece pictured these winds as a serpent coiled seven times around an egg, until it hatched and split open, to produced the world.

The cave, the snakes, the carcass, and the valley are all vivid symbols of death. But the diamonds stuck to the rotting flesh represent our souls—which are also stuck inside rotting flesh (our bodies, after age 40!). The lamb is of course a sacrificial symbol of death and resurrection—and not just for the Christian world, as this little fable demonstrates.

The ascent from the valley of the shadow of death speaks for itself.

The Roc is a mythical bird, a kind of phoenix, whose home beyond the seven mountain ranges symbolizes the soul's celestial dwelling place. Stories of the hero's abduction by a mystical bird, and subsequent flight into the heavenly mountains, were quite common in Persian and Arabic cultures.

In Hindu mythology, the bird form of Brahma is called the Hamsa, or wild gander. As a symbol of the creator, one could call it the "Father of the Eggs." Its flight over the Himalayas signifies the transcendence of the soul. The Hindu saint freed from the bondage of rebirth is compared to the Wild Gander.

In meditating upon the Roc egg hanging from the crystal dome in the middle of the hall of windows (there are ninety-nine windows, with the aperture at the apex of the dome representing the hundredth), Princess Badr al-budur is meditating upon the Creator, the ineffable source of all sublunary life.

She becomes fertile thereby, spiritually and physically.

The dome from which the egg hangs is itself one of the great architectural symbols of the Near and Far East. It encloses the world within and beneath. Passing through the oculus, the soul achieves liberation, like an arrow piercing the bull's eye, like the Roc returning to its nest, like a hero returning home from his or her journey.

Like the spirit, married at last, and forever, to God.

Badr al budur's meditation on the egg hanging from the dome must have worked, for at the end of the *Arabian Nights*, two marriages are celebrated, Scheherazade has given birth to three children, and King Shahryar has been cured of his gynocidal jealousy.

Thomas and the Faerie Queene

The tale of "Thomas the Rhymer" is based on the legend of a 13th century poet who spent seven years in Elfland, where the Faerie Queene granted him the powers of prophecy and 'true speaking.'

In the ballad, Thomas sees a gay lady riding towards him over the "fernie brae." She is dressed in "grass-green silk," and fifty-nine silver bells hang from her horse's mane. Thomas mistakes her for the "mighty Queen of Heaven," until she identifies herself as the "queen of fair Elfland."

The silver bells that dangle from the mane associate her with the moon in the alchemical tradition; her brilliant green mantel and skirt link her to the Celtic otherworld; and her "milk-white steed" suggests the sacred mares of Irish and British folklore—like the Irish Goddess Macha, the Romano-Celtic Epona, or the Welsh Rhiannon, who rides a white horse.

Rhiannon, like the Queen of Elfland in the ballad, is associated with the underworld, and with poetry: her three magic birds have the power to awaken the dead with their singing. The marvelous white horse etched into the hillside of Uffington may also link the Faerie Queene and her hollow hills to the mythology of the mare and the Goddess. The cult of the divine mare persisted all the way up until the 12th century, when the king of Ulster's sexual union with a white mare was ritually celebrated, after which the mare was sacrificed and sacramentally eaten.

In other versions of the story, and in other ballads, the animal which carries the hero to marriage with the otherworld is the deer. In a legend recorded later by Sir Walter Scott, True Thomas follows a hind and a doe off into the forest, at the end of his life, and he is never seen again.

The deer appears again, in association with the sacred mysteries of marriage, in the marvelous ballad known as "The Three Ravens" first published in 1611, and then again in Sir Walter Scott's *Minstrelsy* of 1803.

In the ballad, three ravens tell of a dead knight lying in a green field, attended by hounds, hawks, and "a fallow doe, / As great with yong as she might goe." The doe is later called the knight's "leman," or lover; she lifts up his head, kisses his bloody wounds, gets him up onto her back, and carries him off to an "earthen lake," where she buries him before dying herself.

The symbolism here links the deer with marriage, death and rebirth (since it is pregnant), with the sacred springs (so precious to the Celts), and with the journey to the otherworld. The deer was long sacred to the Celtic peoples of pagan England; since it sheds its antlers in the spring, it became a symbol of rebirth. The doe of the red deer family was called a "hind," an animal naturally associated with the Goddess, who frequently led men into mystic adventures, nurtured them in infancy, or carried them off to the underworld in the form of a White Hind.

In the ballad, Thomas the Rhymer undertakes his journey to serve the Elfland Queen for seven years, riding off on her milk-white steed for forty days and forty nights, through a land with neither sun nor moon.

The couple reaches a threshold typical of marriage: rivers of red blood, which lead, however, to a "garden green." There is forbidden fruit in this otherworld, fruit which the Queen tells Thomas not to eat, because all "the plagues that are in hell / Light on the fruit of this countrie." She serves him instead two items frequently found in the sacrificial meals of the marriage mysteries: bread and wine!

After the meal, Thomas lays his head upon the Queen's knee, and the revelations of relationship begin. She shows him the two roads of righteousness and wickedness, between which passes the road to Elfland. The imagery of the crossroads is as frequent in myth and folklore as it is in marriage and relationship, marking a turning point of some kind, and a decision to be made.

Hermes, for example, is the guide of souls to the underworld in Greek myth, and stone altars were erected to him at crossroads. Aeneas, Virgil's Roman epic, must choose between two roads in the underworld—one that leads to heaven, and another that leads to hell.

Our marriages and relationships would perhaps profit from remembering Virgil's remark, that the descent to the underworld is easy, but the return most difficult.

Thomas, like Aeneas, eventually returns from the otherworld. He spends seven years in Elfland, and is given "a coat of the even cloth, / And a pair of shoes of velvet green" for the return journey. He is also given the gift of 'true speaking' and prophecy, so that his journey becomes a parable of that precious wisdom bestowed upon us by marriage.

Tam Lin and Janet

Another ballad about the mysteries of marriage is known as "Tam Lin." It begins with the symbols of clothing and the white horse, as a young lady carefully lifts her "green kirtle / A little aboon her knee" to ride off to Caterhaugh. There she meets Tam Lin at the well, who appears after she plucks two of his roses.

Magical events typically occur at wells, pools, and springs in Celtic myth and romance (such as the magical spring in the story of Yvain and the Lady of the Fountain). Like the fountain, such locales were sacred symbols of the source of life in Celtic mysticism, as we know from relief sculptures of the Goddess Coventina, found by a well at Carrowburgh near Hadrian's Wall, and of three water goddesses from the Roman fort of High Rochester in Northumberland.

In the Bible, sacred meetings and marriages of this sort sometimes occur at the well, as in the story of Rebecca in the Old Testament, and of the Samaritan Woman in the New. In both, the feminine is associated with the water of life.

This may help explain the girl's curt reply to Tam Lin in the ballad. When he chastises her for plucking the rose and breaking the wand by the well in Carterhaugh, she replies that "it is my own, / My daddie gave it me; / I'll come and go by Carterhaugh, / And ask nae leave of thee."

The site was apparently hers originally.

The plucking of the rose in this scene recalls Persephone picking poppies when she was abducted by Hades, and it also looks forward to a marvelous scene in Cocteau's film, *Beauty and the Beast*, in which the plucking of the rose initiates Beauty's journey into the forest.

When the green-kirtled lass in "Tam Lin" returns home from Carterhaugh—we now learn her name is Janet—she is apparently pregnant, and she finds "Four and twenty ladies fair" playing ball and chess. Janet herself is said to be the "flower among them all."

One remembers Persephone picking poppies with twenty four nymphs, the Grail Maiden surrounded by twenty four virgins, and the twenty four dancing nymphs Gawain chances upon in "The Wife of Bath's Tale."

In all of these tales, the twenty four nymphs emanate from the Great Goddess standing amidst them: She is the source of the twelve hours of the day on the one hand, and of the twelve hours of the night on the other.

She is the womb and the tomb—and the whole show in between.

In the ballad, Janet puts on her green kirtle for a third and final time, and rides back to Carterhaugh to pluck the roses by the well again. When she does so, Tam Lin appears and tells his story. He had fallen off a horse while hunting, when the Queen of Faeries caught him, and carried him off "In yon green hill to dwell."

These images associate the horse, the mountain, the Goddess, and the underworld with the marriage mysteries. Tam Lin returns at the end of seven years, on Halloween night and the following Hallowday. These are now our All Soul's and All Saint's days, which the French called "Toussaint," a time when the borderline between this world and the other breaks down, and souls journey mysteriously back and forth.

On that night, Tam Lin tells Janet, the "fairy folk will ride" to Miles Cross, where she will see him riding on a "milk-white steed." If she pulls him off the horse, and holds him in his arms—while he turns into an "esk and adder," a lion and a bear, and finally into a "burning gleed"—she will break the spell binding him to the Faerie Queen in the otherworld, and win his love.

The last step in his redemption involves throwing the burning "gleed" (a coal) into a well, and then clothing the naked Tam Lin with a "green mantle." Divestiture and re-investment merge here with the symbolism of marriage, the crossroads, and the well. The alchemical mysteries of the smith at the forge are also implied (the ore is transformed into Tam Lin).

The bridles on the fairy horses ring with an unearthly music to celebrate the marriage and Janet's disenchantment of Tam Lin. The uncanny music of the procession is a characteristic element of the fairy's ride, as in this marvelous passage describing an old woman's encounter with the 'little people' at the beginning of the 19th century: "They rode on little white nags, with uncommonly long swooping tails, and manes hung with whistles that the wind played on. This, and their tongues when they sang, was like the sound of a far away Psalm."

Apparently, the mysteries of music and marriage are inspired by the journey to the otherworld—which all vital relationships compel us to undertake.

———————

The Miller's Son and the King's Daughter

One tale from the Grimms collection which preserves and transmits the millennial wisdom of the marriage mysteries is "The Devil and the Three Golden Hairs."

The hero of the tale is marked at birth as one who will marry the King's daughter, a prophecy which provokes the usual effort of the King to rid himself of the child.[41] He does so by purchasing the infant from its poverty-stricken parents, placing the child in a box, and pushing the box out onto the lake, hoping the box will sink and the baby will drown. Instead, it floats over to the Miller's cottage, who, being childless, brings the baby up with his wife.

Like Moses floating in his basket down the Nile, or Perseus floating in the coffin with his mother Danae, the motif of the infant exile evokes the trauma of birth and the sociological tensions between the classes: to wash up onto the shore is to be born into a life of conflict between the powerful and the powerless.

The King tries for a second time to get rid of the boy when he reaches puberty, the age when the initiatory rites of passage are typically performed. These rites involve the separation of the boy from his parents and a journey into the forest.

The King sends the boy to deliver a letter to the palace. Unbeknownst to the boy, the letter instructs the guards to murder him. But that night, on the way to the palace, as the boy sleeps beside an old woman in the robber's hideaway in the deep forest, the thieves take pity on him and rewrite the letter, so that instead of being killed when arriving at the palace the next day, he marries the King's daughter, as foretold.

When the King arrives at the palace to discover the marriage, he furiously tries for a third time to rid himself of the boy by sending him to get three golden hairs from the head of the devil.

The boy encounters three problems during his journey to the devil's cottage. The first town he comes to is afflicted by the withering of a tree which used to bear golden apples. The second town has a dried up fountain that used to flow with wine. Finally, a ferryman at the crossing to the yonder shore is cursed, eternally rowing back and forth across the river.

All ask the boy what they need to do to remove their afflictions, and he promises to return in a few days time with the answers.

We have encountered both the tree and the fountain before as archetypal symbols in the marriage mysteries, and here both suffer from the pervading conditions of the waste land, which emanates from the tyranny of the King. It is the young lad's universal challenge to reform the conditions inherited from the older generation, and thus to revive the waste land created by his new father-in-law.

The crossing of the river is particularly interesting with respect to the archetype of the descent to the underworld upon which the tale is based, for, as we will learn, the afflictions are well known to the devil, who lives on the other side of the river.

When the young boy arrives at last at the devil's cottage, only the old Grandmother is at home. She takes pity on the boy, turning him into an ant, hiding him in her skirts, and promising to get both the three golden hairs and the answers to his three questions.

Freudians take note: the boy has literally returned into the folds of the maternal skirts, from which he will be reborn the next morning after the mysteries have been revealed! These revelations take the form of three dreams which the Devil interprets, for the underworld is also realm of dream.

The Devil, lord of the underworld, knows the source of the afflictions in the waste land (from a Christian perspective, it certainly seems appropriate that the Devil know the source of these evils). The Old Woman coaxes his knowledge out of him indirectly.

While the boy remains hidden in her skirts, she plucks a series of three golden hairs from the Devil's head. Each time, when he wakes up, she says she has had a nightmare, and recounts in sequence the stories of the ferryman, the town with the dried-up fountain, and the town with the withered apple tree. And each time the Devil provides the remedy, which the boy takes with him the next morning, along with the three golden hairs he had originally come for.

The golden hair symbolizes light, and the imaginal wealth of the underworld, which expresses itself in the archetypal forms of dreams. This Devil is not purely Christian, since he knows the answer to all things (the underworld is a place of knowledge and destiny) and can be tricked into revealing that wisdom.

But still, the young boy must never see the Devil directly: he is in the Grandmother's skirts when the Devil arrives, and he wakes up after the Devil has gone, as if to suggest that there are some manifestations of spiritual power which we as humans had better not attempt to face in their unmitigated power.

This is perhaps nowhere more true than in our marriages: some issues are better off left alone, or, at the very least, approached indirectly.

The boy finally sets off on the return journey homeward, after the revelations in the Devil's cottage. First he tells the ferryman to give the oar to the next person who comes along, who will then be the one stuck rowing back and forth forever and ever.

The curse of endless repetition which can be passed on magically from one victim to another is a very old one in the lore of the folktale. These tales combine the search for a special treasure, like the three golden hairs, with a sequence of special questions, like the ones the afflicted ferryman and townspeople ask, the answering of which entails the transmission of the curse (this time ultimately to the King).

Equally archaic are the afflictions of the fountain and the tree: the frog under the stone in the middle of the fountain, and the mouse eating the roots of the golden apple tree. With the removal of the frog, the fountain flows once more with wine, and with the removal of the mouse, the tree immediately yields its golden apples.

There are Norse precedents for both images, which themselves hearken back to Classical sources and beyond. In Norse mythology, a dragon guards the well of the underworld, and a snake and deer gnaw the roots of Yggdrasil, the world tree. In Greek myth, the dragons on the island of the Hesperides guard the golden apples of immortality.

By removing the afflictions and answering the questions, the boy in "The Three Golden Hairs" is performing the typical Arthurian task (and indeed the task we typically ask of all our adolescent males) of redeeming the waste land. When the toad under the fountain is killed, the wine flows again. And when the mouse is removed, the apple tree blossoms again.

Do we have things eating at us in our relationships? Things beneath the surface of things that gnaw away at the innards? What happens when we bring the beasts to light? The story tells us that wine begins to flow again, and apple trees to bloom, after the long winter of our discontent.

When the boy returns to the palace and gives the King the three golden hairs, he has completed his cycle of journeys, which can be linked together in clusters of three: three efforts to get rid of him, three questions, and three golden hairs. He has successfully navigated the return phase of the cycle by retrieving some special boon (the golden hairs) symbolic of his newfound wisdom, and he is therefore now well prepared for the rigors of marriage and kingship.

His first action tests his new sense of justice: when his royal step-father greedily asks where the boy found the large bags of gold he has brought back on his donkey, the boy lays a trap for the old tyrant by sending him to the riverside. The gold, he says, is in the sand on the yonder shore. So, when the King asks the ferryman to take him across the river, the ferryman hands him oar, and walks away. In his great greed, the King takes the ferryman's place, and thereby inherits the curse of Charon.

He is rowing that boat right now, and will continue to do so as long as fathers-in-law set up obstacles to protect their daughters, and so long as people continue to die.

Vasilisa and the Czar

Several beautiful Russian tales collected during the 19th century by Alexandr Afanas'ev record feminine versions of the descent to the underworld and the encounter with the Great Goddess who rules there. Many of the motifs of the heroine's journey originating in the Ancient Near Eastern world were transmitted along lines of trade into Northern Russia via the Crimea.

That many of the tales in this splendid collection take their protagonists to the Black Sea is significant, for it indicates a long tradition of storytelling, during which the rich variety of mythological motifs of the Mesopotamian and Mediterranean worlds—not to mention India, Persia, and the Orient—survived the Christianization of the Ancient world during the reigns of Constantine and Theodosius.

After Theodosius proclaimed Christianity the official state religion of the Roman Empire in 438 A.D.—to the exclusion of all other forms of worship—the archaic motifs of the ancient world passed on into rich treasury of the folktale. The result is a magnificent collection of Russian tales enriched by a deep reservoir of mythological imagery which flowed into Russia from the Turkish world and beyond during the many waves of cultural interface in the Crimea.

One of the finest of these tales is the little piece called "Vasilisa the Beautiful," which preserves the archaic lore of the Great Goddess and the mysteries of the descent to the underworld which prepares her for marriage with the Czar.

The journey begins with the death of the mother, who leaves her daughter Vasilisa a little doll. After the father remarries, the wicked stepmother and stepsisters torment their more beautiful sibling and constantly pass the work on to her. This is the domestic crisis—death and remarriage—that leads to Vasilisa's departure from home. She is sent into the forest to get some light from the witch Baba Yaga, so the sisters can sew at night—with the thought that she will never return.

Vasilisa sets out at twilight into the dark Russian forest. Three horsemen pass her along the way—a black, a red, and a white—until at last she arrives at Baba Yaga's hut. It stands on chicken legs and is surrounded by skulls on sticks, and by a fence made of human bones. Vasilisa carefully unhooks the fence's latch (made of finger bones) and enters the hut.

The old witch, Baba Yaga, comes crashing through the forest shortly thereafter, riding a mortar and holding a pestle in one hand, and sweeping up her tracks with a broom in the other. Like Psyche, Vasilisa must perform a sequence of tasks (separating poppy seeds from the dirt)—or be eaten by Baba Yaga.

Vasilisa has clearly entered the realm of the dead, but it is a realm where the Goddess presides. At first Baba Yaga appears to be a devouring Goddess, with the skulls and bones of Russians whom she has eaten surrounding her hut. But the fact that she is riding a mortar and carrying a pestle is a significant representation of her nurturing side, for she is associated with the grain (an old symbol of death and rebirth, very much alive in the New Testament), which must be ground (die) in order to make bread (to rise again).

Her poppy seeds connect her with the Oriental visions of the underworld drifting up along trade routes from Turkey. Hence, what we have in this little tale is a Northern version of the mysteries of Demeter and Persephone.

After Vasilisa performs the tasks enjoined upon her by the old hag, she is allowed to ask just one question: who were the three horsemen she saw on her way to Baba Yaga's hut? "My three servants," Baba Yaga answers: the black horse of the Night, the red horse of Dawn, and the white horse of the Day. These horses represent the powers of birth, life, and death traditionally associated with the Triple Goddess, and they all emanate from Baba Yaga in her cosmic domain.

Baba Yaga's gift to the brave Vasilisa is equally symbolic: she gives her a skull on a stick with bright beams of light radiating from the eye sockets.

Among the most fascinating forms of the archaic divinities of the Ancient world are the little eye goddesses that take us as far back as the Sumerian goddess of death, who kills Inanna with the "eye of wrath."[42]

The light that shines through the sockets of the skulls is the soul that shines in the darkness of death. The skull thus serves as a symbolic token of the mysteries of death and rebirth embodied by the Goddess, Baba Yaga. It is therefore appropriate that Vasilisa uses the light shining from the eyes of this skull to guide her homeward through the dark woods of the Russian forest.

She is just about ready to throw the skull away at the threshold of the forest, which she reaches at dawn, when the skull speaks to her and tells her to take it home and place it in full view of the family. Here the skull fulfills another task crucial to the Great Goddess: she becomes a Goddess of Justice. When the sisters and wicked step-mother walk into the room, the light blazing through the sockets follows them relentlessly and eventually incinerates them as punishment for their treatment of Vasilisa.

Baba Yaga, therefore, is not only a Goddess of death and rebirth, not only a cosmic Goddess of the diurnal cycle, but also a Goddess of Justice. The wisdom which Vasilisa achieves on her journey is many layered, and represents an intimation of totality, from the feminine perspective. The skull with which she returns is a talisman of this wisdom, and can be seen as a representation of her initiation into the mysteries of her own femininity.

Only now is she ready for marriage.

After the death of her stepfamily, Vasilisa weaves some lovely fabric, and sends it off to the Czar, who is so delighted by its beauty that he comes to the lowly hut and marries the humble seamstress.

Ivan and the Lioness

The Russian tales are particularly enriched by images of the Goddess inherited from both native and Ancient Near Eastern sources. These images revolve around the creative and destructive sides of the Goddess, and constitute the central revelation of several hero journey cycles in the tales.

In "Two Ivans, Soldier's Sons," Ivan follows a fleet-footed stag into a meadow, and then crosses a little stream with two ducks floating on it (the stag is his guide and the stream his threshold into the underworld). He shoots one of the ducks, and takes it with him into the white stone palace which he finds after riding a long while on the yonder shore of the stream.

When Ivan sits down to eat the duck, after roasting it in the oven, a lovely maiden appears out of nowhere and demands Ivan's magic horse. His refusal to give it turns her into a wrathful lioness (sister of one of the dragons Ivan had slain earlier in the story), and she devours the champion whole.

Ivan's twin brother is alerted to the crisis when his handkerchief turns to blood, and he too goes in pursuit of the fleet-footed stag, crosses the stream, shoots a duck, cooks it, and refuses to give the lovely maiden his magic horse.

But when she turns into the wrathful lioness, he draws his sword and forces her to regurgitate his brother. Although the brother is dead and beginning to rot, Prince Ivan sprinkles him with the water of life, and then returns home to end the journey.

The imagery here is of the Goddess who both devours and bestows life. She swallows Ivan, then vomits him back into the world—a bit battered by his descent into the belly of the lioness!

The lion is among the oldest of the animals sacred to the Great Goddess of the Ancient World. She is the sun-lion pouncing on the moon-bull, which dies to be reborn from the fire of her womb every month.

The image takes us as far back as 6000 B.C. to Çatal Hüyük, where we find a Goddess giving birth on a throne with lions on either side of her. The image survived right down to Roman times, in a sculpture of the Anatolian goddess Cybele flanked by lions.

In Ancient Egypt, Tefnut, daughter of the son god Re, goes into Nubian desert, where she takes the form of a savage lioness, drinking blood and puffing fire from her eyes and nostrils.

Marriage with the lion goddess is a perilous affair, as Ivan finds out in the forest hut on the yonder shore.

Relationships can swallow us up, and we can feel ourselves devoured and digested by the other person. But if we stick with it, there's a light at the end of the tunnel, and we can come back, renewed, from the belly of the lioness.

Ivan and the Indian Princess

Another image of Baba Yaga as the devouring Goddess occurs in the wonderful tale, "Ivan, the Cow's Son."

It concerns the coming of age of three sons, all born when their mothers (the Queen, the Scullery Maid, and a Cow) eat some meat from a golden pike that swims in the waters of the castle moat.

At adolescence, they undertake a journey to the Black Sea, where they find a white, hazel wood bridge, and a little hut standing backwards on chicken legs by the road. Ivan the Cow's son tells the hut to turn around straight, and the three brothers find a feast inside and spend three nights there.

On each day, Ivan the Cow's son takes the place of his cowardly brothers to slay the six-headed, nine-headed, and twelve-headed dragons which come surging up from the sea, on three consecutive days. The dragons appear when he goes out to the hazel wood bridge, taps with his stick, and smashes the magical dancing pitcher that appears at his feet.

When he smashes the pitcher, a duck quacks, the earth quakes, and a dragon emerges from the sea—each more fearsome than the day before.

After the third battle with the twelve-headed dragon, his brothers take him for dead, because the bridge is soaked with blood. Ivan, however, lies asleep in the stables. These are marvelous Gnostic symbols of the soul, drowned in the sea, or devoured by the dragon—both of which represent the material world, in which it has descended, from its heavenly home.

After the two brothers leave, Ivan wakes up, and begins his journey homewards. He first turns himself into a fly, and listens on the stove of the hut, as Baba Yaga appears and tells her three daughters (the wives of the three dragons) how Ivan killed their husbands.

The revenge the three daughters plan revolves around key symbols of the archetypal powers of the feminine—mysteries into which the male must be initiated in order to be made eligible for marriage.

The first daughter turns herself into a poisoned well with a silver cup floating on the surface. The second daughter into a poisoned orchard. And the third into a hut with a perilous bed inside that will kill anyone who tries to sleep on it. In case these measures fail to kill the three brothers, Baba Yaga resolves to turn herself into a giant boar and swallow each one of them whole.

We have seen the well before as a symbol of the source of life in the Arthurian tale of "The Lady of the Fountain," only here the well is negative. We have also seen the connection between the Goddess and the fruit tree (another symbol of the source of life). And the bed into which the third sister turns herself, the place where life begins and where it ends, reminds us of the Perilous Bed Gawain sleeps in to redeem the Three Queens.

Ivan thwarts the revenge plans of the three sisters by smashing the cup in the well, destroying the fruit on the orchard trees, and splintering the bed in the hut. But the old witch Baba Yaga still manages to devour the two brothers who follow the left-handed path at the crossroads the next day.

She transforms herself into one of the most ancient avatars of the Goddess of the Underworld: the wild boar. The boar represents the mystery of death and rebirth. In Homer, Odysseus is wounded by a boar during a hunt; and, in some versions of the abduction of Persephone, a herd of wild pigs covers up the tracks of the chariot, so that no one can follow her down into Hades. And pig-headed Goddesses of Old Europe have labyrinths inscribed upon their bodies.

Ivan follows the right-handed path to a village of blacksmiths, whom he instructs as follows. When the huge wild boar (Baba Yaga in disguise) comes charging into town, the twelve blacksmiths get her to stick her long tongue into the burning forge, by promising to feed her Ivan the Cow's Son!

When she does so, the smiths pin the tongue down and prod her mercilessly with red-hot irons, until she vomits up the two brothers—and their horses! The devouring tomb of the boar's belly has become the womb of rebirth. It is a kind of alchemical forge as well, in which the operations of calcination and dismemberment proceed.

The two brothers are inside the boar when she is incinerated, and eventually emerge from her out of the flames. I think here of the famous alchemical picture by Michael Maier, which shows a wolf put in the fire of the forge after eating a King, and the King emerging reborn from the flames.

After their rebirth from the fires of the forge and the belly of the boar, the three brothers return to their kingdom, completing the hero journey cycle.

All of these ordeals prepare Ivan for marriage with an Indian Princess. Ivan tells her father the King that he has come to woo his daughter. She rejects him at first, sending her army out to attack him. After Ivan slays the army with a ladle, he is invited to the palace for dinner.

During the meal, the Princess asks to leave for an hour, and Ivan sneaks after her. She turns into a sea gull, and Ivan into a falcon, to follow her. She flies to a distant seashore and strikes the ground to summon her Grandfather. He emerges from the sea with a golden head and silver beard (like the sun and the moon).

The Princess tells her Grandfather that she doesn't want to marry Ivan, and asks for three hairs from his head to show him. After she flies off with the hairs, Ivan strikes the ground, calls the Grandfather forth, and then decapitates him as he emerges from the sea.

In order to marry her, Ivan must "guess from what root this grass comes," when the Princess shows him the three hairs. In response, Ivan lays the Grandfather's head on the table!

The Princess asks permission to leave once more, and again turns into a gull and flies off. But as she does, Ivan strikes the head against the porch and says, "Where you were before, be now too," with the result that the head flies back and grows together with its body.

Hence, when the Princess summons Grandfather again, he says he has been asleep, unaware of his decapitation. She is now forced to marry Ivan, who tames her on the marriage bed by beating her with three rods—made of iron, copper, and pewter.

A sad note to end a marvelous story on, but one which, alas, has become all-too-common in a world torn apart by domestic violence.

Ivan and the Frog Princess

Others among the Russian tales present a rather gentler portrait of marriage with the Goddess.

In "The Frog Princess," three sons shoot arrows to find wives. Prince Ivan's arrow is retrieved by a frog which he must marry. She sloughs her skin one night to take on human form, in order to attend a feast thrown by the King to see which of his three new daughters-in-law can dance the best.

Prince Ivan's frog princess sits at dinner stuffing the bones of her meal up one sleeve, and the wine from her cup up the other.

When she is called upon to dance, she whirls around and around, waving her hands in the air. From her right sleeve, lakes and woods appear, while from her left sleeve, various birds begin to fly about. When she stops dancing, "all that she had created vanished," as if she were Shiva Nataraja, dancing the world into and out of existence.

What a lovely way for a Goddess to enact her two archetypal roles, life giving and life destroying. The frog of course is an old symbol of the waters from which all life emerges, and is hence appropriately linked in this tale with the world creative powers of the divine feminine.

In an extraordinary sequence of images, Marija Gimbutas shows that the archetype of the "Frog Goddess of Death and Regeneration" may be as old as the Upper Paleolithic, when engravings of females with frog legs first appear as symbols of regeneration. Egyptian myth even preserves a creator Goddess (like our Frog Princess), called Haquit, who was portrayed with the head of a frog.

Another archaic symbol of the creative power of the Goddess in Old Europe which has thrived in Russia is the egg. That the egg can symbolize both the womb and the tomb is evident in the splendid little Russian tale called "Dawn, Evening, and Midnight."

Three brothers (triplets born to a poor widow on the same night at the times named in the title) set off to find three princesses whom a whirlwind has abducted, nobody knows whither.

They come first upon a little man the size of a thumb with a long beard and preternatural strength. The old man thrashes the first two brothers nearly to death when they slaughter one of his rams. But Dawn manages to fasten him by the beard to an oak pillar with a big iron stake. When the three brothers go to see, however, the little old man has torn himself free, leaving a trail of blood to a deep hole which leads down into "the other world."

Dwarfs, trolls, and gnomes are typically servants of the Great Goddess, like the ones who assist Rhea as she gives birth to Zeus in the mountain caves of Ida on Crete. Hence, when Dawn convinces his brothers to lower him down into the hole, the revelation of the sacred mysteries of marriage begin.

Underground, Dawn finds three kingdoms—of copper, silver, and gold—each presided over by the three abducted princesses. After drinking from a phial of the water of strength, Dawn defeats the three-headed, six-headed, and twelve-headed dragons which guard, respectively, the copper, silver, and golden kingdoms.

Before leaving their kingdoms with Dawn their deliverer, each princess waves a red handkerchief and rolls her kingdom up into an egg (Fabergé, no doubt), which she then puts in her pocket!

Evening and Midnight then pull their brother Dawn and the three princesses back up through the hole in the hollow hills, and they all return to home to celebrate their marriages. When they arrive, each princess takes her egg out of the pocket and rolls it into an open field, so that "straightway three kingdoms appeared, a copper, a silver, and a golden one."

The three goddesses have thus fulfilled their dual role, recreating those worlds which they destroyed in the underworld, by rolling the egg or waving the handkerchief. The egg has become both the womb and the tomb.

Sir Gawain and the Loathly Damsel

A goddess of a very different sort appears in one of our most amusing fables about love and marriage. We know the folktale from Chaucer's Wife of Bath, who uses the story as a parable about sexual politics: as long as men submit to the sovereignty of women, she implies, everything will be just fine!

The story begins with a crime against women. Sir Gawain rapes an innocent maiden in a meadow, and is brought to court. Queen Guenevere says he will be beheaded, unless he can find the answer to a question within a year's time: "What do women want?"

Gawain sets off on his penitential quest, finding many possible answers to the question along the way. Some say women want to be flattered, some say they want money. Some say they want to know everything, and can't keep a secret.

That last one comes close, says the Wife of Bath, who knows something about the misogynistic traditions this uncomplimentary list implies. One of her five husbands spent all his time reading religious tracts about the inferiority of woman. This got on the Wife of Bath's nerves: she smashes him in the head and throws the books in the fire!

But that business about secrets, she says, comes close.

"Let me tell you a little tale about the marriage of King Midas," she digresses.

"You know Midas had donkey ears. No one knew except his wife. He always wore a cap covering his ears in public, so that his wife was near to bursting with her secret knowledge of her husband's true nature. To relieve herself, she ran down to the lake one day, and immersed her head in the water, so that when she screamed out 'My husband is an ass!' no one heard her. But she felt much better nonetheless."

After this little therapeutic tip, the Wife of Bath returns to her story about Gawain (who also turns out to be an ass of sorts).

With just three days left, and no answer to the question about what women most desire, Gawain rides into a dense forest, in the middle of which he comes upon a bright clearing. Sunlight streams down into the emerald green meadow, where he sees twenty-four lovely women dancing in a ring.

As he approaches, they vanish into thin air.

In their midst now sits the ugliest hag imaginable. She has the nose of a bat, the tusks of a boar, the ears of an elephant, and skin like an alligator. A long red whisker bristles sharply above her lip.

"What is it you want? she asks Gawain, coyly inverting the question he has been sent to answer.

"I'll tell you the answer," she says, "if you promise to marry me."

Gawain is desperate. He faces decapitation in three days time if he returns without his answer. So he capitulates, and the Loathly Damsel tells him what he wants to know.

When he stands three days later before the Queen in Camelot, he announces that what women want most in the world is power over men.

"My god, you've got it" the Queen replies, and everyone sits down to celebrate Gawain's delivery. He is, after all, the most popular ladies' man at court.

But just when the banquet is about to begin, in rides the Loathly Damsel on a mangy old mule.

"What about me?" she asks.

Gawain reluctantly fulfills his promise, and marries her on the spot. The entire court grieves as he goes sadly off to bed, where the loathly bride awaits him.

"Why won't you kiss me?" she asks, twirling the whisker growing from the mole above her tusks. "Is it because of my poverty, my ugliness, or my low birth? Shame on you. We love the lord Jesus who was a poor and lowly carpenter. And as for my ugliness, at least other men won't be tempted. You'll have a faithful wife whom you'll never have cause to doubt."

Gawain seems unappeased by her wisdom, but the Damsel persists, finally persuading him to kiss her. When he does, the ugly old crone is transformed into a radiant young beauty.

There's a great lesson here about marriage. It involves sickness and health, youth and age, till death do us part. Those vows broken in the divorce epidemics of the 50s and 60s. When we marry, we must accept each other completely, for better and for worse, in life as in death—for there cannot be the one without the other.

Gawain gets a little reward for risking to love life's darkness.

"Well, what'll it be," the now lovely damsel asks the astonished Knight. "Do you want me to be hideous during the day, but lovely at night, when we're alone together? Or do you want me lovely during the day, when everyone can envy you your beautiful wife? But then you'll have to come home to a grotesque, abusive wife at night, and share her repulsive bed."

Gawain doesn't know what to say.

He pauses a few moments, and then the muses speak.

"Have it your way, darling. However you want it to be is the way it will be."

"Then I shall be lovely day and night," the beautiful maiden answers, "for you have granted me sovereignty."

As all men should, the Wife of Bath concludes: "God give us all good husbands," she says, "generous, submissive, and fresh in bed."

Modern Mysteries

Many of the mythological symbols in the folktales and ballads find their way into the short fiction of the 19th and 20th centuries, particularly in the stories about marriage by E.T.A Hoffman, Nathaniel Hawthorne, and D.H. Lawrence. In all of these stories, the archetypes of the maze, the goddess, and the descent to the underworld are metaphors for the sacred mysteries of marriage and relationship.

Ellis and Ulla

Hoffmann's "Mines of Falun" begins with a young man grieving the loss of his mother, a grief that will eventually lead him to his wife. His name is Elis, and he has just returned from a sea voyage. Unable to celebrate with the other sailors, Elis sits outside the pub, sadly reflecting upon his mother's death.

At this point a mysterious miner, named Torbern, appears to Elis, and persuades him leave his life as a sailor, and to follow him to Falun, where he can start a new career as a miner. Torbern entices Elis with magical descriptions of the beauty of the world beneath the earth, and that night, Ellis dreams about the mines.

In his dream, Elis finds himself sailing on a crystal sea, which turns solid beneath his feet, so that he is able to walk out on to the water, and put his face to the surface. Peering down into the depths, he sees a bevy of beautiful maidens, coiling around each other in an ecstatic dance. Flowers of glittering gemstones sprout from stems rooted in the ruby hearts of the girls.

As the maidens sing an enchanting melody, the old miner expands into a gigantic man, who crashes downwards into the abyss with a terrific peal of thunder. And then the majestic face of an enormous goddess emerges from the depths.

Elis is filled with terror and joy, when he hears the voice of his mother calling to him with ineffable sorrow. Turning to look upwards, he sees that it is a beautiful young woman calling to him, Ulla, his future fiancé! He has been unable to distinguish her from his mother!

When he awakens the next morning, Elis follows the old miner off towards the mines of Falun. Torbern appears and disappears at each crossroads, until finally they arrive at the gateway to the mines.

Torbern is a threshold guardian, a wise old man, and a guide of souls to the underworld. Elis follows Torbern to an enormous abyss, yawning like the jaws of hell. Stupefying vapors rise from the Inferno below, and the miners look like devils.

Elis is momentarily taken aback, and wishes he'd not left his life as a sailor. But that night, when he falls in love with the foreman's daughter, Ulla, he takes heart, and vigorously pursues his new career.

He hopes to win a high position in the company, and soon learns all the mysterious tricks of the trade.

When Elis goes down to work in the mines the next day, the uncanny Torbern appears like a shadow to strike his hammer with the force of thunder upon the richest veins of ore. Then he disappears into the winding, black labyrinths of the mines.

Although Elis still sees a horde of horrible monsters, the "dire brood of hell" at the entrance to the caves, he perseveres in his new calling—intent upon winning Ulla, and drawn ever more compulsively into the mysterious mazes of the mine.

For the labyrinthine underworld of the cave is also the archetypal domain of the Great Mother. From prehistoric times on, caves were labyrinths of the great goddess—both her womb and her tomb.

Other feminine symbols of creativity in the tale include the images of cooking and brewing, old Germanic symbols of the union of the loving and terrible aspects of the Goddess—to be found for example in the witch's oven in "Hansel and Gretel."

Mythologically speaking, the ores extracted from the mines were embryos in the womb of the goddess. The kiln or furnace where the ores were smelted was called the "Mutterschoss," a word meaning "womb" or "maternal breast."

Elis ultimately collapses into the arms of the mighty Queen of the caves, who draws him to her breast. He is lured to her by the crystalline beauty of the veins of ore; by the sparkling gemstones, hanging like fruit from the metallic trees; and by the maidens who sing a spellbinding melody.

Elis has returned to the mother he lost at the beginning of his story, who has taken up residence in his unconscious, and who now competes with Ulla for Elis's affection. It's a natural dynamic of the psychology of marriage, and not unhealthy—unless it completely disrupts the relationship, as it does in our tale.

On the night before his marriage, Elis resolves to go down into the caves in order to retrieve the queen's heart, which he imagines as a glorious ruby, a magnificent crimson stone which is the source of all hearts and souls on the earth above.

Like Eve, the Metal Queen is the Mother of all Living, the Great Goddess of the Earth—from whom all life comes, and to which it returns. For she is also a Medusa, turning all to stone, as Elis finds out when he tries to explain to his fiancé why he so drawn to the underworld of the mines.

Part of him remains attached to Ulla, while the other is irresistibly drawn to the Metal Queen below. Elis is a poor divided soul, torn apart by the tensions of courtship and marriage.

When at last he goes down to the mines on his wedding night, it his final descent. He is buried in a rock slide, and his body is not found until fifty years later, when some miners dig it up, perfectly preserved in vitriolated water.

The body turns to stone when the miners bring it to the surface, and then turns into dust. The grieving and now much older Ulla collapses and dies, clutching the remains of her beloved to her breast.

The psychology of the male who remains unable to cross the threshold of marriage, because of a lingering attachment to his mother, or to some other woman from his past, is acutely explored in this marvelous fable.

But the sacred mysteries of marriage involve more than the Oedipal complex. Marriage with the Metal Queen takes Elis into realms of creativity that go beyond the maternal and the erotic.

Amidst the richest veins of the bottomless caves ruled by the Metal Queen, Elis comes to assume that "none but he understood the secret signs, the significant writing, fraught with hidden meaning, which the queen's own hand had inscribed on the rocks, and that it was sufficient to understand those signs without bringing to light what they indicated."

This is truly a knowledge which surpasseth all understanding! It may be understood, but not brought to light. Intuited, but not interpreted. Experienced, but not explained.

Like the mysteries of marriage and relationship.

The Metal Queen "engraves" these sacred mysteries on the parchment of her preference—the stone clefts in the rock. The German word in this passage ("eingraben") preserves the same pun we have in English (to engrave). "Grab" of course means grave, as in tomb, and "graben" can mean to dig as well as to engrave.

The word is therefore resonant: it means engraving letters on stone or metal, and, oddly enough, digging a grave. The same pun emerges at the end of the story, where Elis links the Metal Queen with a "cherry-colored sparkling almandine, on which the tablet of our lives is graven."

The word for her writing on the tablet is again "graven" (*eingegraben*). To engrave suggests a process of memorializing, of telling a sacred story, or, better, of singing a spellbinding song about the mysteries of love and death—which, after all is said and done, are mysteries of relationship and marriage.

Faith and Goodman Brown

One sunset, in centuries long past, Young Goodman Brown lingered at the door of his house with his wife Faith, who thrusts her "pretty head into the street" and detains her husband with a kiss. She begs him to stay home with her on this night of all nights, but he leaves her anyway.

When Goodman Brown looks back home before turning the corner, he sees "the head of Faith still peeping after him" from their "threshold."

The threshold guardian is a mysterious stranger whom Goodman Brown encounters on a dreary path leading into the gloomy forest. The "fellow-traveler" looks like Goodman Brown's father, he has "the indescribable air of one who knew the world," he has traveled from Boston with supernatural speed, and he carries a staff "so curiously wrought, that it might almost be seen to twist and wriggle itself, like a living serpent."

This mysterious stranger is a devil, but also Hermes, the Greek god of travelers and guide of souls to the underworld. He travels at twilight with his supernatural speed, carrying a serpent-twined staff—the magic wand of Hermes, called a caduceus.

Goodman Brown resists going with the devil further into the forest until the stranger reminds him that both his father and grandfather were his "good friends," and that the deacons, selectmen, governors, and ministers of New England are among his "general acquaintance." After Goodman Brown sees Goody Cloyse, the "pious and exemplary dame" who taught him his catechism, walking with the minister and Deacon Gookin on their way to the Sabbath in the Forest, his resolve is weakened.

But when he sees his wife's pretty pink ribbons floating down from the clouds above, where she has been demonically transported, it is broken, and he runs howling down the wild and dreary road into "the heart of the dark wilderness."

The wilderness is not only a place of temptation and sin: it is also a place where the powers of imagination and dream are intensified. The sounds of the forest are evoked in the most poetic and rhythmically periodic of sentences. The wind whispers with the sounds of magnificent music: there are church bells, the solemn tones of a hymn sung by many voices, and the deep rich swells of a mighty organ. All are mixed with the natural music of the wind and water of the wilderness.

A potent, periodic prose approximates the power of the music. The voices converge into the "harmony," "verses," and "unison" of a church "hymn" or "dreadful anthem," which turn out to be part of a demonic ceremony conducted by the devil.

At an infernal altar deep in the woods, baptismal and marriage sacraments welcome Goodman Brown and Faith into the demonic congregation. The pulpit is a rock surrounded by four blazing pine trees. Two men lead Goodman Brown, and two women lead a "veiled female" up to a basin hollowed in the rock, over which the "dark figure" of the devil stands.

Seven figures stand around the basin of blood carved in the rock, with Goodman Brown and the veiled woman—his wife, Faith—at the center. One thinks of the alchemical basin into which the Solar King and Lunar Queen descend, to undergo the torments of the various operations which transmute base metals into gold.

One also thinks of the mandala most common to Christian iconography (of which Hawthorne's image is clearly an infernal parody): the image of Christ surrounded by the four evangelists. Some of these are even closer to Hawthorne's icon: illuminated pages from several Medieval English manuscripts show the crucified Christ in the center, with a male and female personage on either side, at the foot of the cross, surrounded by the symbols of the four evangelists at each of the four corners.

In "Young Goodman Brown," we have the devil in the center (instead of Christ) with Goodman Brown and Faith on either side of the basin, surrounded by the four blazing pines (instead of the four evangelists)!

These geometrical arrangements symbolize the totality of the Self, which embraces and transcends the opposites warring within the psyche: male and female, conscious and unconscious, persona and shadow. The sacred marriage represents the union of these opposites. What Goodman Brown is unable to assimilate, however, is the shadow, the dark side of human nature, revealed to him by the devil.

Goodman Brown is invited to "penetrate, in every bosom, the deep mystery of sin, the fountain of all wicked arts" and together with Faith to receive the mark of baptism, so that "they might be partakers of the mystery of sin, more conscious of the secret guilt of others, both in deed and thought, than they could now be of their own."

Awful and prophetic words! And, alas, an all-too-familiar aspect of marriage—the quickness with which we condemn the mistakes of others, but overlook our own.

By refusing the baptism of sin, and hence the awareness of his own guilt, Goodman Brown fulfills the very words of the devil, henceforth more conscious of the "secret guilt of others" than of his own.

He ends his days obsessed with this secret guilt, which he sees in everyone else, but not in himself. The obsession and revelation of the forest journey permanently transforms him: "A stern, a sad, a darkly meditative, a distrustful, if not desperate man, did he become from the night of that fearful dream."

The revelation of the marriage mysteries has thus led to transformation, only when Goodman Brown completes the cycle by returning to his village, he brings with him no redeeming boon, and in this respect he looks forward to the ambiguities of modern marriage.

Aylmer and Georgiana

Another story by Hawthorne, "The Birthmark," portrays the marriage mysteries as an alchemical journey through a sequence of doorways. As in "Young Goodman Brown," the crucial task of relationship is learning to cope with imperfections in ourselves, and in each other.

In the story, a brilliant young scientist (Aylmer) attempts to remove a birthmark from his wife's cheek by the power of alchemy. He becomes obsessed with the birthmark shortly after his marriage, seeing it as a symbol of his wife's imperfection, of her "liability to sin, sorrow, decay, and death." It is a visible mark of mortality which he hopes to remove.

Others see the birthmark on Georgiana's lovely face quite differently. The mark looks like the imprint of a tiny hand upon her cheek. It blazes bright red when she blushes. Hawthorne calls it a "faerie sign manual," to be variously interpreted, "according to the difference of temperament in the beholders."

Most see the blemish as enhancing Georgiana's already stunning beauty.

Unfortunately for Georgiana, however, her husband is a scientist, and a perfectionist, who cannot tolerate flaws in his otherwise perfect wife. Aylmer wants to dominate nature—and his wife. He wants to "make new worlds" more perfect than the one we have been given.

And he wants a new, more perfect wife than the one he has fallen in love with and married.

So Aylmer resolves to remove Georgiana's birthmark. His "treatment" of Georgiana involves locking her up in the inner rooms of the house surrounding his laboratory, where he gives her drugs—Prozac? Xanax? More like St. John's Wort, subtle infusions of floral distillates, extracted by various alchemical operations.

The movement through a sequence of doorways from the outer to the inner rooms of the house is symbolic of the journey of marriage, which activates the archetypal depths of the imagination.

The story begins in the outer rooms of the house, those closest to the normal concerns of domestic life. Aylmer then dreams of removing the birthmark, and secludes his wife in the extensive apartments near his laboratory. The movement inward has been compelled by the "spectres" of the dream world, "affrighting this actual life with secrets that perchance belong to a deeper one."

When Aylmer leads Georgiana "over the threshold of the laboratory," the birthmark glows so intensely that he shudders convulsively. Georgiana faints dead away. The crossing of the threshold is a crucial rite of passage in the marriage mysteries. The doorway represents a transition from the domestic to the daemonic, a kingdom of dreams and death.

Marriage is always a journey into the realm of the imagination.

The "smoky, dingy, somber rooms" of the laboratory have been converted into "a series of beautiful apartments not unfit to be the secluded abode of a lovely woman." It's real anima territory, permeated by a "penetrating fragrance," darkened by "gorgeous curtains," suffused by "a soft, impurpled radiance," and shut off from the world in the "infinite space" of "a pavilion among the clouds."

Aylmer feels that he has drawn a magic circle around his wife, sealing her off from the rest of the world—and certainly from other men! But the inner apartment is also a sacred space, within which the rituals of the imagination can be performed. In these rooms, Aylmer entertains Georgiana with some small vanities of his art.

Using his alchemical powers, Aylmer conjures up "Airy figures, absolutely bodiless ideas, and forms of unsubstantial beauty." He creates illusions of the scenery and the figures of actual life, "with that bewitching, yet indescribable difference which always makes a picture, an image, or a shadow so much more attractive than the original."

These "spirit displays" represent a basic element of the marriage mysteries—our relationships, like our lives, are composed of such stuff as dreams are made on. Imagination plays a central role in marriage—sometimes disrupting our relationships with jealous fantasies, but by the same token sometimes taking us into mythical realms of surpassing beauty and love.

After the spirit plays are over, however, Georgiana violates a basic code of marital civility: she sneaks off to read her husband's notebooks!

Her reading inspires Georgiana to cross the last threshold that separates her from the heart of her husband's mysteries. She secretly follows him into the innermost chambers of his laboratory. This unexpected intrusion leads to their first quarrel: "Would you throw the blight of that fatal birthmark over my labors?" Aylmer demands; "Go, prying woman, go!"

It is difficult not to see in this "prying woman" the Psyche of Apuleius' *Golden Ass,* who holds up the lamp to her demon lover, exposing him to the light of conscious scrutiny, and forcing him to abandon her in the magical pavilion where he has secluded her from mortal life.

It is also difficult not to see this scene as typically marital, and perhaps autobiographical: the wife here prying into the secrets of the artist's heart by reading his journals, and Aylmer (Hawthorne) responding with the wounded rhetorical question "Have you no trust in your husband?"

To defuse the quarrel, Aylmer tells Georgiana about " the long dynasty of the alchemists," who spent so many years in quest of an "elixir of immortality," which is also "the most precious poison that ever was concocted in this world."

The elixir has the power to beautify "things base and vile." By implication, these are Georgiana's faults and foibles, as symbolized by the birthmark. Surely no one before her husband saw her as "base and vile"! She is quite stunned to hear her husband speak of her in this way.

Administering the potent drug leads to her death.

As Georgiana herself recognizes, "the stain goes as deep as life itself." A denial of imperfection is a rejection of life. Aylmer's misguided attempt to remove his wife's imperfection is a psychological allegory about marriage and relationship.

C.G Jung wrote that every marriage involves at least four people: the husband and wife, and the anima and animus (their unconscious inner feminine and masculine sides). Every marriage involves the mutual projection of unconscious images onto the partner: the husband projects his anima onto his wife, and the wife projects her animus onto the husband. The resulting reactions to these projections considerably complicate the marriage, for the mistaken images projected upon us by our mates force us to act as if we are someone other than we really are.

The "alchemical marriage" involves sorting all this out, breaking down these mutual misconceptions by recognizing their source in the unconscious. The goal is the withdrawal of the projections, and an acceptance of the marriage partner as he or she really is. It is a painful and laborious process of many years, involving an alchemical breakdown of the personality into its fundamental elements, out of which a new relationship can be forged.

Aylmer has an apprentice to help him remove Georgiana's birthmark. The apprentice is called Aminadab, which spelled backwards yields 'bad anima'!

That says it all!

There's something wrong with Aylmer's inner feminine. *He* is the one with the problem. *Not* his wife.

The apprentice represents "man's physical nature," Aylmer the "spiritual element." Aminadab is Aylmer's shadow, the feeling side of his otherwise highly intellectual personality. Both are needed for a healthy marriage.

But Aylmer's relationship with his new wife Georgiana is strained by a 'bad anima,' a negative projection of his inner feminine, which in turn indicates an imbalance in his relationship with his own shadow.

Like many young, newly wed husbands, Aylmer is not the icon of perfection he (or his wife) thinks he is. Marriage will make sure they both learn that!

Aminadab immediately recognizes that it would be a mistake to remove Georgiana's birthmark. Aylmer's unwillingness to accept his wife as less than perfect, and his readiness to see her one flaw as a symbol of feminine evil suggests that he has projected a 'bad anima' onto his wife. His wife should be perfect, he reasons, yet she is fatally flawed by an innate capacity for sin and decay.

The archetypal figure behind Aylmer's negative anima is his mother!

He has devoted his "toilsome youth" to an exploration of Mother Nature, extracting medicines from "the dark bosom of the earth." Behind his mother complex is an archetype, and behind the archetype a goddess—the "great creative Mother." She is loving and terrible, producing poison and antidote, combining earth and spirit, marring perfection with blemishes of evil.

In as much as Hawthorne lost his father at the age of four, and spent the next 33 years of his life as the solitary, reclusive child of a widowed mother, I think it safe to assume the importance of his Mother complex in his psychological make up.

Georgiana, on her side, accepts her husband's projection. All to ready to submit to her husband's negative judgement against her— does she have low self-esteem?—she is willing to undergo the ordeal of 'cosmetic' surgery.

Nose job, face-lift, tummy tuck, breast implants—whatever it takes. She will have the little mark removed, even though she knows it penetrates as deep as life itself.

Georgiana buys into her husband's misogynistic condemnation of women.

She in turn projects her animus onto him, seeing Aylmer as the ideal, authoritative male. She venerates her husband with a love bordering on "worship." She sees him as honorable, pure, and lofty, and hence unable to accept anything less than perfection. She prays that, "for a single moment, she might satisfy his highest and deepest conception" of her.

Georgiana's exalted estimation of Aylmer's love for her suggests a view obscured by the animus, and in acting out his corresponding anima projection upon her, she sacrifices herself on the altar of his religiously inspired alchemy.

The ultimate goal of the alchemical marriage, a renewed fully individuated Self capable of recognizing and withdrawing its projections, is not achieved in the story. Georgiana dies in the end.

The attempt to remove her "imperfections" kills her.

Beatrice and Giovanni

Another story by Hawthorne, called "Rappaccini's Daughter," suggests a similar constellation of moral, psychological, and aesthetic aspects of the sacred mysteries.

A young student, Giovanni Guasconti, takes lodgings near the University in Padua. His window looks out over the botanical garden of the renowned and feared Dr. Rappaccini, whose daughter, Beatrice, Giovanni sees wandering amongst the extraordinary splendor of flowers.

During the entire first half of the story, Giovanni sits at his window, looking down at Beatrice in the garden below. She and her father emerge from or vanish beneath the "sculptured portal" at the end of the garden. When Giovanni is finally tempted to leave the window and go down to meet Beatrice, he follows Lisabetta, his concierge, who leads "him along several obscure passages" to a "private entrance into the garden."

This descent—through a labyrinthine sequence of doorways and corridors—leads Giovanni to his lethal anima figure, Beatrice, who wanders the maze of the "infernal regions" her father has imprisoned her in.

Could this garden, Giovanni wonders, be Eden? And was Beatrice its Eve, her Father its God? And he to be its Adam?

But the flowers in the garden are all malignant, so poisonous that butterflies and birds drop dead in their presence. Even the flowers Giovanni throws to Beatrice from his window wilt and die in her hands. For she has been raised as "the human sister" to the most poisonous flower in the garden, which she tends like "one sister performing the duties of affection to another."

Her father, Dr. Rappaccini, is plotting to marry Beatrice and Giovanni, but to do so he must establish Giovanni's immunity to his poisonous daughter by secretly administering strong doses of the malignant flowers before allowing him direct access to the garden, and physical contact with Beatrice.

These make Giovanni progressively lethal to outsiders. When he discovers that he has been poisoned and cut off from the world, he blames Beatrice. He calls her the "Accursed one!" and the "poisonous thing" who has made him "as hateful, as ugly, as loathsome and deadly a creature as thyself—a world's wonder of hideous monstrosity!"

Giovanni then administers an antidote to Beatrice, which kills her.

He fails to recognize that the plot was not hers, but her fathers, who says to the two lovers, as Beatrice lies dying, "My science, and the sympathy between thee and him, have so wrought within his system, that he now stands apart from common men, as thou dost, daughter of my pride and triumph, from ordinary women."

He had meant her to be "terrible" and "beautiful," to transcend "the condition of a weak woman, exposed to all evil, and capable of none." As she dies, she replies that she "would fain have been loved, not feared," and she asks Giovanni a rhetorical question: "Oh, was there not, from the first, more poison in thy nature than in mine?"

Beatrice, then, is the victim of her father, and her first love.

Her father had meant to sever her ties with an evil world by secluding her in the garden of his love. We never hear of her mother, and can assume an intense relationship between father and daughter.

A Freudian interpretation is tempting, and the film version in "The American Short Story" series bites the bait by having Giovanni dream of Beatrice being kissed by her father. This interpretation puts

Giovanni in the Oedipal role of the son who must steal Beatrice from her father's sexual love.

Rappaccini has imprisoned his daughter in an anima fantasy that has cut her off from all normal human intercourse.

By the same token, Giovanni's fascination with Beatrice displays all the symptoms of anima fixation. Giovanni sees in her "gaze the mystery which he deemed the riddle of his own existence." From the first he is captured by the "witchery" of her "girlish womanhood." Though "worthiest to be worshipped," however, Beatrice exhibits "a frightful peculiarity in her physical and moral system." By falling in love with her, Giovanni "felt conscious of having put himself, to a certain extent, within the influence of an unintelligible power" which he cannot resist.

This description of Giovanni's perceptions of and reaction to Beatrice parallels Jung's description of the mother archetype as "loving" and "terrible." On the one hand, the mother is associated with fertility and fruitfulness: "the cornucopia, a ploughed field, a garden." She is "all that is benign, all that cherishes and sustains, that fosters growth." But, Jung adds, "On the negative side the mother archetype may connote anything secret, hidden, dark; the abyss, the world of the dead, anything that devours, seduces, and poisons, that is terrifying and inescapable like fate."

Beatrice is all this to Giovanni—as perhaps all women are to all men. She instills a "fierce and subtle poison into his system" that he sees as the "wild offspring of both love and horror."

But Beatrice is also Giovanni's muse, for she kindles the fires of Giovanni's dream life, and gives "a kind of substance and reality to the wild vagaries which his imagination ran riot continually in producing." In her presence, "There came thoughts, too, from a deep source, and fantasies of a gem-like brilliancy."

Giovanni is attracted, repelled, and inspired all at once, bewildered by a "lurid intermixture" of "simple emotions" that produces "the illuminating blaze of the infernal regions." For Beatrice leads him, as her namesake did Dante, into the underworld of his love, dread, and creativity. Hers is "an Eden of poisonous flowers," created by a "cold and purely intellectual" father, who "would sacrifice human life" in the name of his godlike science.

It is tempting to see the mother complex behind this portrait of a young woman wounded by her father, who in turn poisons and inspires his son-in-law. Beatrice combines the imagery of beauty, sin, death, disease and creativity characteristic of Hawthorne, whose stories record the stages of psychological growth which only marriage and relationship can foster.

Jack and Mabel

In the wonderful little story by D.H. Lawrence called "The Horse Dealer's Daughter," a plain coal miner's daughter, named Mabel, assumes the role of the great Goddess in the life of a young doctor, Jack Ferguson. Jack rescues her from the pond in which she attempts to drown herself, after the death of her parents, and the financial collapse of her family. The story offers a complete hero journey about the entry into marriage, a major rite of passage, which always entails a descent to the underworld.

For, as Lawrence once said, every great conquest of life demands a harrowing of hell.

The journey begins when Ferguson visits Mabel's house just after the death of her father, when the horses and furniture are being taken away, and the three brothers ponder their future. They wonder what will become of their sister, who wanders around the house in sullen, ineffectual solitude. The breakfast table is desolate and desultory; the brothers are imprisoned in an "air of ineffectuality"; their sister is morose and sullen.

All are frightened by "the collapse of their lives" and look around "with a glazed look of helplessness." A "stupor of downfall," and a "helpless silence" sets in, "of futility and irritation."

This is the Waste Land, which only the mysteries of the sacred marriage can bring back to life.

Jack Ferguson, the town doctor, arrives, releasing a few sad sparks of a new energy, and sense of hope. His cap is pulled down low over his forehead, and a new mustache bristles above his sensitive mouth. The dog gets up to bark, and the horse bells ring in the barnyard.

After the doctor leaves the house, Mabel goes to the churchyard to scrub her mother's tombstone. She works "under the shadow of the great looming church, among the graves." It is as if she is in "another country." Mabel goes into a trance, "mindless and persistent," "intent and remote."

Jack watches her "as if spellbound" as he walks by the graveyard, and the "vision" of her "portentous" face seems to "mesmerize him." Mabel and Jack have both left the little world of their "fettered" lives behind, to enter the strange hypnosis of "another country."

They've taken the first steps toward the new life of marriage and relationship. The journey has begun with the traumatic circumstances of the deaths in the family, and to get to the new world, their old selves must die.

It's near dusk; the smoke from the nearby mines smudges the damp horizon.

Ferguson watches fascinated as Mabel leaves the cemetery, descends a hill outside of town, and walks straight into a pond at the bottom. In the twilight of the cold winter afternoon, Ferguson races down the hill. It's the "dusk of the dead afternoon," when everything is "deadened, and wintry," and the houses seem "extinct," under a sky of "smouldering ash." The town looks like a "hellish hole."

As he runs down into the "sodden hollow" in the "falling dusk," he sees Mabel's small "black figure" moving "straight down the field towards the pond" in the bottom. He watches amazed as her "small black figure walked slowly and deliberately towards the center of the pond." Alarmed, he goes after her, running straight down "into the depression" (a marvelous choice of words!) and on into the "dead water" of the pond.

To rescue Mabel, Jack slips into the rank mud, and falls under the hideous, acrid water of the "dead cold pond," which "clasped dead cold round his legs."

We've gone down into the land of the dead, where the waters of life originate.

When Ferguson and Mabel reach the bottom of the pond, it turns suddenly from tomb to womb, as images of rebirth begin to replace images of death.

Jack rises from under the water, grasping the hem of Mabel's black dress, and gasping like an infant struggling for its first breath. Once risen, and partly restored, he laboriously pulls Mabel out of the foul water, to carry her up the hill to her home.

The verbs Lawrence chooses ("rose" twice, "risen" and "restore" once) suggest the resurrection, while the struggle for breath and the total immersion in the water suggest baptism and birth, both Christian symbols of the new life into which Mabel now leads Jack. She is a kind of Goddess of death and rebirth, whose elements are fire and water.

Jack struggles to resuscitate Mabel on the floor of her empty home. After he strips her of her sodden clothes and puts blankets in front of the fire, she comes to. Although Jack remains repulsed by the smell and feel of the clay and water in her hair, he warms up quickly when, noticing her nakedness, Mabel assumes Jack loves her, and draws her down to him by clinging to his knees.

She looks up at him with "flaring, humble eyes of transfiguration," her face suffused by a "delicate flame," and her body so hot to the touch that "A flame seemed to burn the hand that grasped her soft shoulder."

Along with the heat of freshly kindled flame, however, a "strange water" rises in her eyes, as if from "some slow fountain." Hot tears flow, wetting Jack's throat, and stirring the embers of his heart, which seems "to burn and melt away in his breast." Before going up stairs to change, Mabel's "eyes again slowly filled with tears" as Jack kisses her, and, as he watches a tear fall, "his heart flared hot."

Their personalities have been broken down to their base elements—fire and water—in order to be formed into a new relationship. The alchemical marriage has begun.

The first thing the couple does is to perform a very British ritual. Jack puts fresh coal on the fire and lights the gas lamp. Mabel offers to heat up some water for tea. Then Mabel goes upstairs to change, and to get Jack a dry suit of clothes

Relationship strips the ego down, removing its defenses. The old self dies so that the new may be born.

Lawrence's word for this process is "transfiguration," the movement from the flesh to the spirit, in biblical terms. But for Lawrence, transfiguration actually refers to a union of the flesh and the spirit effected by marriage. The essential myth of marriage in all of Lawrence's work is the journey to the underworld. The ego dies, so that a new identity may be born, like the Phoenix rising from its ashes.

The tomb becomes the womb. The relationship we feared would kill us, forces us into a new life. As in so many myths and tales about the mysteries of relationship, homecoming represents the fulfillment of the cycle: the end becomes a new beginning.[43]

Beauty and the Beast

One of the most important rituals of marriage is the crossing of the threshold. Passing together through the doorway, we leave the old life behind to step into the new. Windows, doorways, hatches, and arches as images of the descent to and return from the underworld connect a long mythic tradition—going all the way back to Sumerian and Egyptian roots—to modern films about marriage, like Jean Cocteau's *Beauty and the Beast* and *Orpheus*.[44]

In the first, Beauty's father travels to town in search of his fortune, only to find that a shipwreck has destroyed his investments. Lost in the forest at midnight, between the village and his home, the father stumbles through an opening in a hedge onto the grounds of a mysterious chateau.

The doorway to the stable opens magically for his horse, and the front door of the chateau opens into a corridor of candles held by human arms. The hall leads to a table, in a fire-lit room, lavishly set for dinner, during which the father is waited on by invisible servants, and watched over by statuary faces puffing smoke on the capitals of the columns beside the fireplace.

After awaking the next morning, the father walks out to the stables, and plucks the rose his daughter Beauty has asked him to bring home for her. The Beast immediately appears from behind a bush to demand the father's or the daughter's life in return for the rose.

"You can take anything from me," he says, "except my roses!"

The father grimly returns home, and tells his story. This story is Beauty's call to adventure, since she clandestinely departs that night to offer herself to the Beast as payment for the rose.

In the sequence where Beauty secretly departs on her journey to the magical realm of the Beast, doorways and corridors play a crucial role. The conditions leading up to her departure are again characteristic of the marriage mysteries: a sudden collapse of fortune, intense sibling rivalry, and the need to redeem a debt.

Beauty emerges from a back door in the house, walks through a gate into the barnyard, stops at the door into the stable, and walks through the door to the Beast's white horse, called "Magnifique." Mounting Magnifique, Beauty rides through the stable door, through the barnyard gate, and into the forest path that takes her to the concealed opening in the hedge that leads into the chateau grounds.

She dismounts, and runs through the front door and down the corridor of candles. As soon as she passes through the door, the film slows down, so that Beauty seems to float into the Chateau of the Beast.

Beauty passes the dining room to a long dark stairway with a large doorway at the top, where she pauses to turn back towards us, apparently blown by an invisible wind against the door.

She then turns to walk through the dark doorway into the second floor corridor, down which Beauty floats in slow motion, with the long white curtains of the four windows gently blowing in the wind, and a large dark doorway in the background, at the top of the stairway she has just ascended.[45]

The effect is of Beauty passing through a sequence of four veils blown from the four windows, until she arrives at another doorway. Here she pauses as a mysterious voice tells her that this is the door of her room.[46]

Passing through this door, Beauty walks into a luxurious room, and goes to a wonderful large window, which is half way open and frames Beauty as she sits down at a beautiful boudoir.[47] She looks into a mirror which reveals her father lying sick in bed at home and calling out her name. Startled by this image, and by the rustling of the fur quilt on her lavish bed, Beauty jumps up and begins her descent into the basement of the chateau.

This descent takes her back through the door in her room, out through the large entrance of the chateau, and down a curvilinear stairway to a doorway beneath the Chateau. There she finally comes face to face with the Beast, who emerges from another doorway in the basement.

When he glares at her, Beauty faints, and the Beast picks her up and carries her back up the curvilinear stairway to the entrance of the Chateau. He then carries her down the front corridor of candelabra, to the darkened stairway leading up to the second floor.

Light streams through a window on the lower right, as the Beast carries Beauty up the darkened stairway on the left, into the dazzling light coming from the doorway at the top of the stairs.

The camera then zooms into a close-up of Beauty's body. As the Beast carries her through the door into her room, three quick shots taken from inside, then just outside, and then again from inside the door reveal the transformation of Beauty's clothing from the rags of her domestic servitude to the riches of her queenly state in the Beast's chateau.

This magnificently detailed sequence devoted to Beauty's departure from home and arrival at the chateau gives us approximately fifteen passages through doorways in only a few minutes (some doorways, like the entrance and gateway into the stable where Magnifique is and the door into Beauty's room in the chateau, are passed through twice in the same sequence).

There are in fact exactly seven doors leading from Beauty's home to her room in the Beast's chateau, the same number of gateways through which Inanna passes on her descent to Ereshkigal in the Sumerian underworld. A further connection is suggested by the change of clothing (an archetypal image in the marriage mysteries) which occurs during the two journeys. Inanna is stripped down at each of the seven gateways, but Beauty is stripped down as she passes through the final door of the sequence, only to be reclothed in a glorious gown. Beauty collapses in a dead faint when the Beast emerges from the basement, just as Inanna is killed when Ereshkigal (the Queen of Death) fastens the "eye of wrath" upon her.

A marvelous relationship develops between Beauty and the Beast in the underworld of the Chateau. He comes each night to ask her to marry him, and to escort her on promenades around the lovely estate. He is kind, loving, and gentle, but also ashamed of his beastliness.

When he hears a deer scurry through the underbrush, the Beast cannot subdue the demon of pursuit that slumbers in a brute!

He excuses himself, and darts off into the woods.

When he appears later to mope around outside Beauty's locked door, he is smoking with fresh blood, and his eyes are burning.

"Don't look me in the eye! Don't look me in the eye!" he screams, when Beauty approaches to chastise him for violating her privacy.

"Take this," she says, "and clean yourself up," throwing him a scarf.

The Beast retreats, as ashamed of his brutality as any man whose rage, jealousy, or lust has been roused by his relationships. Beauty exploits his shame, treating him with cold disdain to gain power over him.

Indeed, she is driven to her own kind of cruelty by his obsequious behavior.

"I am the beast," she will later confess, when the monster has been subdued (both the monster within, and the monster without).

Beauty repeatedly rejects the Beast's proposals, and begs him to allow her to return home to see her sick father. But once home, she misses the Beast. When she looks into the magic mirror, she sees him dying on the turf beside a pond at the Chateau.

She puts on her magic glove, which transports her from her bed at home to her bed at the chateau. When she arrives, she quickly rises from her bed and runs first through the door in her room, then through the corridor of candles to the front door, and then through this door down the steps, pausing just outside the front portal to call out for her Beast:

"Ma Bête! Ma Bête!"

From the stairs in front of the Chateau entrance, Beauty runs down the curving stairway of the earlier sequence (when the Beast emerged from the basement doorway), but this time turns to run along an outdoor colonnade. She passes four arches, through which we can see, in the distant background across a meadow, another colonnade of arches. Beauty runs into the middle of a meadow, towards the four of the arches of the distant colonnade.

She then comes to a natural arch of trees, in a little copse below the colonnade of arches from which she has just descended. Stepping through the arch, Beauty turns a corner into a grotto, and then runs quickly to fall down upon the Beast, whom she finds lying on the ground, gasping, and near death.

This descent through passageways and chambers, down stair-cases and through arches, and on into a sacred cave leads to marriage, redemption, and transfiguration. The Beast lies nearly dead, and now it is Beauty who must stoop down to try to raise him up again.

But this can only happen when her old boyfriend, Avenant, has been killed, shot with an arrow by the goddess Diana, while descending into her pavilion, to steal her treasure. As Avenant falls to the ground inside the pavilion, we see the Beast transformed into Avenant, who rises magically from the ground outside the pavilion where he had lain dying.

Diana, therefore, plays the role traditionally assigned the goddesses of the underworld in the sacred mysteries of marriage, all the way back to Ereshkigal and Persephone. She is the agent of death and resurrection; she is the tomb and the womb, and consequently the means of transformation.

Like Circe in the *Odyssey*, Diana's role is to turn animals into men, after having turned them into animals. And these, after all, are two of the tasks which every woman must perform in marriage. Most importantly, she must make men out of beasts.

Orpheus and Eurydice

Jean Cocteau's marvelous film, *Orphée* (of 1950), also uses the journey to the underworld as a complex allegory about marriage, creativity, and psychological growth. The journey requires the integration of the archetypal energies of the unconscious—the common task of marriage, poetry, and individuation. This process of integration involves a sequence of four descents in the film, each of which uses mirrors, doorways, ladders, corridors, and stairways to represent the rites of passage in marriage and relationship.

The first journey begins after Cégeste, a young and popular rival of the successful and middle-aged poet Orpheus, is killed during a brawl in the Café des Poètes, somewhere in the suburbs of Paris in the 1950s. Cégeste is run over by some mysterious motorcyclists, and then taken away in a Rolls Royce belonging to a mysterious dark-haired lady, who commands Orpheus to help her.

When Orpheus gets into the car, he realizes Cégeste is dead, and looks at the dark lady in bewildered horror as the car proceeds into a twilight countryside beyond the city limits, pausing at a railway crossing as a locomotive screams by. Beyond this railroad crossing, the road narrows to a tree-lined avenue leading to a ruined country estate. Cocteau uses negative exposures of the landscape rolling by to suggest a journey into an inverse reality, into a realm of dark reflections. Heurtebise, the chauffeur, glances nervously into the mirror.

Two black clad motorcyclists precede the Rolls Royce to the ruined mansion, where the body of Cégeste is removed from the car to be carried upstairs. The two motorcyclists carry Cégeste out of the car door, through the front door of the house, then up a stairway with one 180° turn at a landing. When the men reach the top of the stairs, they carry Cégeste through a door into an unpainted room, where they lay him down on the floor.

The lady in black walks back through the door across the hall towards the bewildered Orpheus, whom she leads through another door into her room. She sits down first on her bed, and then at her boudoir, on which a round mirror reflects her face and Orpheus standing behind her shoulder. The mirror shatters as the radio says *"Les miroirs feraient bien de réfléchir davantage"* ("Mirrors should reflect to one's advantage"). The dark lady gets irritated, stands up, and pushes Orpheus down onto her bed, which has a full length mirror closet at its foot.

The imperious lady then leaves through another door which she must open and close, telling Orpheus to let his wife wait for him alone at home—she will be gladder to see him because he's been gone! Two Oriental servants then push a cart carrying champagne through another door, while the dark lady stands in front of a tall mirror that reflects her, with the two motorcyclists in black standing on either side.

Then she commands the dead poet Cégeste to rise from the floor.

"Do you know who I am?" she asks.

"Ma Mort," he answers—"My death!"

The tall mirror reflects Cégeste and the dark lady, both flanked by the cyclists. She leads Cégeste through the mirror, a gateway to the underworld, with threshold guardians on either side. The camera moves back and forth through the mirror, shooting first from this and then from the other side.

Just as the two cyclists pass through the mirror, Orpheus comes through the door of the room, drops his champagne glass in astonishment, and goes over to pound on the mirror. We see him from both sides of the mirror as he slumps down onto the floor, his contorted face reflected in the glass, against which he presses in anguish.

In the shot immediately following, Orpheus mysteriously wakes up somewhere far away from the mirror in the ruined mansion. He is lying beside a reflecting pool of water in the sand dunes by the sea.

How did he get there? Where is the dark lady of Death? Where has she gone with Cégeste?

What will he tell his wife about the night's adventure?

He is in limbo, between waking and sleeping, youth and middle age.[48] Orpheus is tired of his success, which he says stinks of death, and he wants to do something new that will "astonish" his audience. But to do that, new doorways need to be opened, new spaces entered, and new lines of communication opened up.

Orpheus runs over the dunes in which he has awakened, and finds the Rolls Royce with the chauffeur (Heurtebise) waiting to take him home.

When Orpheus finally comes home, he acts like a cranky child, tells his pregnant wife to leave him alone, and goes upstairs—he says to sleep, but he then sneaks out the window to climb down into the garage, where he sits in the Rolls Royce, and begins moodily recording the cryptic verses broadcast over the radio. We later learn the poems were written by Cégeste, now dead in the underworld.

Has Orpheus become a murderer and a plagiarist, in addition to philanderer, during his midlife crisis?

To clear up these suspicions, Orpheus must visit the police inspector who is investigating the death of the young poet Cégeste.

Lady Death's chauffeur, Heurtebise, drives Orpheus into the city. Heurtebise is a ghost who has been sent from the dead to watch over Orpheus and his wife Eurydice. Eurydice is blond, a domestic housewife frustrated by her imminent maternity, and worried about her husband. Heurtebise—who has committed suicide—falls in love with and consoles Eurydice.

After the police Inspector summons Orpheus to town, Orpheus emerges from the garage door where he has gone to record the broadcasts from Cégeste in Hades. Heurtebise goes through the same door into the garage to get the car. He swings open the large doors, as Orpheus climbs the steps through the trap door on the floor of his bedroom, and then back down through the trap after arranging his tie in the mirror.

Orpheus emerges between the garage doors, and then Heurtebise deliberately shuts and locks them. The two men then open the doors of the car (now magically not a Rolls Royce but a little convertible sports car) and get in.

The whole sequence has taken us up and down, and in and out, through gates, doors, and traps in a few deft frames. We are navigating a visual labyrinth that symbolically represents the complexities of the relationships that develop between Orpheus, Eurydice, Heurtebise, and the dark lady of Death.

Those relationships will take them all into the underworld.

The ensuing trip to the city begins and ends in the car driven by Heurtebise, and uses of the same visual symbols of the descent to the underworld.

The convertible pulls up beneath a steep flight of twisting stairs. Orpheus leaves Heurtebise in the car, and climbs the steps towards an arcade of windows in a large apartment building at the top. He stops in a plaza where he suddenly sees the dark lady, who is walking in front of a closed shop door across the street. Orpheus watches and then pursues as she walks directly into a cavernous doorway that leads into the adjacent plaza. It's labyrinthine, with a long corridor of arches on the right.

Emerging from the cavernous doorway, Orpheus sees the dark lady disappear under the nearest of four arches, into an interior corridor of the arcade. Orpheus runs after her to the inside of the arcade. We see patches of light streaming through the arches on the left, and a yawning arch directly at the end of the arcade, towards which Orpheus runs.

Turning right at the end of the colonnade, Orpheus pursues the dark lady through the twisting alleys of a deserted marketplace. While trapped in a sequence of dead ends and empty stalls, Orpheus bumps into a man carrying a ladder, bothers a pair of lovers kissing in a corner, gets ridiculed by an old crone (who accuses him of chasing after the girls), and finds himself surrounded by a mob of admirers clamoring for an autograph, while he watches the dark lady escape in the same convertible Heurtebise had driven him to town in.

The gauntlet of stairways, avenues, arches, and alleys through which the dark lady has led Orpheus again suggests the labyrinth, an extremely ancient symbol of the sacred mysteries of marriage.[49]

After Orpheus returns home from the city, his wife Eurydice is killed when she tries to escape her house in the country, and is run down on her bicycle by the demonic cyclists from Hades. Heurtebise sees this accident through the window of the house, and carries Eurydice up through the trap door to her bed. The dark lady walks in through the doors of a full-length mirror, followed by Cégeste, whom she instructs to close the doors.

While the dark lady closes the curtains of the windows and Cégeste closes the trap door on the floor, Heurtebise vanishes to warn Orpheus of the imminent death of Eurydice, and then reappears through the trap door. But the dark lady raises her left arm and crashes through the mirror to take Eurydice down into Hades.

Orpheus walks through the side door of the garage and looks up to Heurtebise in the window, who tells Orpheus to climb the ladder and enter his room through the window. After closing the window, Orpheus turns to find Eurydice lying dead on her bed. Heurtebise then tells him that he can go in pursuit through the mirror—apparently the dark lady of Death has fallen in love with Orpheus, and is using the death of his wife to lure him down to her.

Heurtebise leads Orpheus through the watery mirror into the corridor of a bombed military school with numerous doorways, ruined walls, and dark window jambs. It is a difficult descent, impeded by a mysterious wind that blows through the "Hall of

Men's Memories," and by a glazier who crosses in front of Orpheus and Heurtebise as they move towards a very large, dark door at the end of the corridor.

They emerge from the cavernous darkness of this door to descend a flight of some fifteen stairs, that leads them into the interrogation chamber where the Judges of the underworld have assembled (there are three of them plus a scribe). During the ensuing trial, Cégeste and the dark lady are escorted by the motorcyclists back and forth through two doors, as the Judges cross-examine them.

Orpheus and Heurtebise arrive through a full-length mirror, which reflects the three Judges and the dark lady. She confesses her love for Orpheus, who recoils with fear and desire when he hears the confession. He watches in stunned disbelief as the lady is escorted by the cyclists through the same doorway that Eurydice subsequently enters. Eurydice hears Heurtebise confess that he loves her.

Orpheus follows the dark lady back to her bed, where the two lie down and express their love for each other. But they are summoned to return through the two doorways that lead from her room to the inquisition chamber. The verdict is passed, granting Orpheus the right to return with his wife Eurydice (accompanied by Heurtebise)—providing he doesn't look at her.

This takes some doing.

Once home again, the couple take farcical measures to avoid looking at each other. Heurtebise helps them, while the dark lady of Death (now called simply the Princess) appears each night to watch Orpheus sleeping.

But eventually, Orpheus glances in the mirror at his wife, while recording messages from the car radio in the front seat. Eurydice immediately vanishes.

Then a raving mob—fans of the dead poet Cégeste, whom they think Orpheus has murdered—break through the front gate into the driveway and shoot Orpheus.

The two motorcyclists drag the dead Orpheus through the a side door into the garage, from the front door of which we next see the Rolls Royce emerging, to speed down a highway beneath a large Roman arch. The Rolls Royce carrying the dead Orpheus follows the two motorcycles beneath this arch, and then proceeds down the country road leading to the original ruined mansion, where the dark lady had taken Orpheus and the dead Cégeste at the beginning of the film.

From there, Orpheus and Heurtebise begin the final descent into Hades.

Once again they struggle along the outer wall of the bombed out military academy, past a sequence of three barred windows, in the third of which a mysterious shade sits drumming. After turning a corner, both are swept down a corridor by the same mysterious wind that had impeded their progress earlier.

Orpheus lands on his feet in front of the fourth window, and walks through the arched doorway to descend the same fifteen steps as he had in his first journey (though running in slow motion this time). The Princess runs to embrace Orpheus in front of an empty doorway, through which we see, in the background, a large ruined wall punctured by many dark windows.

It is on the large stone sill of one of these windows that the dark lady then orders Cégeste and Heurtebise to strangle Orpheus, so that he can be reunited in the upper world with his wife Eurydice.

The Princess sacrifices herself so that Orpheus may live.

Orpheus dies in the underworld, in order to return to life. He struggles back through the same labyrinthine passageways to the mirror leading into his room, which reflects the multiple windows in the ruined walls of Hades. Once through to this side of the looking glass, he is reunited with Eurydice. The two awaken happily from their midsummer night's dream.[50]

As they kiss, Heurtebise fades back through the mirror, and follows the dark lady down an enormous hall, with great large arches at the top of a huge wall in the background. They turn right into a corridor which leads them down into some inscrutably deeper circle of Hell—where they will be punished for intervening in the lives of the living.

All four of these journeys comprise an elaborate allegory about the relationships between the poet and his muse, and between the husband and his wife.[51] These relationships require reconciliation between the various oppositions which generate tension in the Self, and in the marriage.

All of the characters in the upperworld of daily life represent the conscious aspect of the personality, while those in the underworld represent the unconscious side of the Self.

What is above reflects what is below. In the alchemical marriage, the tensions between the conscious and the unconscious (caused by the reciprocal projections of the anima, animus, and shadow), are gradually integrated to produce moments of equilibrium within the Self. The marriage of these opposites is the goal of the individuation process, and of relationship.

The domestic kindness which Heurtebise exhibits throughout the film towards Eurydice contrasts sharply with the callous cruelty and egotism of Orpheus. Heurtebise repeatedly comforts Eurydice when she recoils from her husband's imperious selfishness, so that, in this case, Heurtebise represents a positive shadow of Orpheus, that loving and tender side of the obsessive poet which is repressed until the very end of the film.

This duality between Orpheus and Heurtebise is inverted in their relationships with the dark lady: Orpheus the fawning and fascinated lover, and Heurtebise the resentful and rebellious subject, who relates to the dark lady much as Orpheus seems to relate to Eurydice.

The dark side of the domestic, blond-haired Eurydice, pregnant and confined to kitchen and bedroom (when she tries to leave she is killed), is the dark-haired fury of the underworld—the Princess, Lady Death—passionate, petulant, and bossy. She roams freely between the two worlds, until confined to the underworld by the Judges.

The opposition between Eurydice and the Princess expresses the idea of the shadow as the negative side of the personality that must be repressed. That the male shadow is positive, and the female negative, contributes to the opposition between male and female in the film. It is another one of those reciprocal inversions caused by the reversal of images reflected in the many mirrors of the film.

The four couples mirror each other, though with the kind of inversions that occur when one holds a letter up to the mirror. Orpheus and Eurydice in the upper world reflect the animosity of Heurtebise and the Princess in the lower. While the tenderness between Heurtebise and Eurydice reflects the tenderness between

Orpheus and the Princess. These reciprocal reflections are caused by the mutual projection of anima and animus figures.

The dark lady is clearly an anima figure for Orpheus, a part of his underworld—i.e., of his unconscious. She leads him deeply into the labyrinth of his innermost dreams and fantasies. Like the dark lady of many romance novels, she is poetic, dangerous, deadly—a *Belle Dame sans Merci* who functions as a muse.

Orpheus is obsessed with her, driven compulsively to pursue her through city streets and into the underworld. Yet, as he himself says, she is really the unknown to him, the mystery of the dark side of irrationality which nourishes his poetry and offers it the hope of renewal. She is loving and terrible—positive in her enrichment of his verse, negative in her disruption of his marriage.

Heurtebise, on the contrary, is an animus figure for Eurydice (having committed suicide for rejected love, he reflects her own innermost fantasies about men). He is almost wholly positive. He is everything she would probably wish Orpheus to be: obsequious, tender, completely honorable, and devoted. He puts a shawl around her shoulder, lays her down to bed—not to make love, but to get her to take a nap! He constantly tries to protect her, both from death, and from the destructive, 'artistic' temperament of her husband.

His only negative attributes, in fact, are completely unconscious, coming out in his irritable relations with Eurydice's shadow side— the dark lady.

These complicated interrelationships between the four major characters in the film represent aspects of the alchemical marriage, the purpose of which is to sort out the unconscious from the conscious experience of the other person.[52] The reconciliation of opposites (life and death, male and female, anima and animus, persona and shadow, conscious and unconscious) is gradually approximated during the marriage—which moves towards, but never fully achieves wholeness within the Self.

In the film, this process of reconciling conscious with unconscious contents is represented by the sequence of descents to the underworld, each of which, as the closing frames suggest, are aspects of a single archetypal dream. Whether the dreamer is the living husband and poet Orpheus, his wife Eurydice, or the hidden god with whose nightmares the dark lady identifies herself, is a question left unanswered. We are left to walk through the yawning arches into the abyss of mystery with which the film ends.

This mystery is essential to the film, to poetry, and to marriage.

Only those symbols, and those relationships rooted in the unknown retain the power to engage us.

Hence the film is an allegory of marriage, and of creativity in relationship.[53] The journey into the underworld is a journey into the archetypal depths of the imagination—where it becomes necessary not to comprehend, but to believe.[54]

Orpheus must stop questioning the Princess, Lady Death. He must accept his mortality, and relinquish his desire to know and control everything—both in his poetry and in his marriage. The broadcasts from Hades offer him lines he says he would give his life to have written.

The traditional task of the Orphic poet is to charm death, and to sing a particular kind of song that is haunted by passionate metaphors and mysteries—the kind of poetry that pierces the heart with the precious evanescence of life.[55]

To write such poetry, and to bring such passion into our marriages and relationships, we must go down—again, and again, and again—into the underworld of our innermost vulnerabilities. We must accept the psychopathology in our relationships, and attend to the messages from the unconscious which those symptoms communicate.

We must, our filmmaker suggests, surrender rationality and control. We must submit to the painful processes of reverie and reflection, which take us through the mirror of art into the underworld of the soul.[56] Only such openness to the archetypal depths of the psyche allows the poet to astonish us, and keeps our love alive.[57]

Redeeming the Waste Land

T.S. Eliot's poem *The Waste Land* has been regarded for many years now as a monument of modern literature. It has also been misrepresented as one of the most difficult and complex poems ever written.

Nothing of the sort.

It's one of the simplest.

Once one recognizes the importance of marriage and relationship in the poem, all the broken pieces of the puzzle fall into place.

There are more couples in this poem than in any other ever written. And their relationships all relate to the title, "The Waste Land," which comes from the Arthurian Romances of the Middle Ages.

According to the myth, the Fisher King was wounded one day while fighting in the service of love. It is a sexual wound. A pagan Knight drives a lance into his groin. The tip has to be surgically removed, and leaves a gangrenous poison nothing can heal.

But since the Maimed King (as he is also called) lives in the presence of the Holy Grail, he cannot die. Nor can he be healed, until Parzival finds the Castle and asks, "Uncle, what ails thee?"

This spontaneous act of sympathy heals the King, and rejuvenates the land around the Castle, which has been laid waste by his afflictions.

Sympathy is the great task of marriage and relationship.

All of the couples in Eliot's poem find it difficult, or impossible, and hence remain stuck in the waste land.

There is a nameless man who meets a "Hyacinth Girl" by a pool in the garden. He cannot speak to her, and her eyes remain empty, unresponsive, accusatory. Without communication, it's impossible to redeem the waste land.

Then, there's Tristan and Isolde, one of the great couples of the medieval romance. Tristan is sent from Cornwall to Ireland by his uncle, King Mark, to bring Princess Isolde back. Brangwen, Isolde's maid, wants to make sure the marriage works out OK, and so cooks up a love potion to give the middle-aged King Mark on the wedding night—a dose of Viagra, let's say, to put some spark in the old man.

On the boat ride back across the Irish Sea, however, Isolde mistakenly shares the love potion with Mark's ambassador, young Tristan. Isolde knows right away what's happened, but it takes the young man a while to catch on. "I feel funny," he says, "as if I've drunk l'Amor!"

He slurs his words: has he said "L'Amor?" Love? Has he said "La Mère?" Mother? In which case the psychologists will prick up their ears. Has he said "La Mer?" the Sea? Mother of us all? Or has he said "La Mort?" Death?

Whichever it may be, Tristan nobly swears, "if by this love I may meet my death, I shall not fear, even if it means my eternal damnation!"

And meet his death he will, for love and death are twins.

When the lovers return to the court of King Mark, their adulterous relationship is eventually discovered, and the two endure the unendurable agony of separation. Tristan later marries another woman—because she also is named Isolde, though of the white hands.

At the end of the tale, Tristan arranges a reunion with his truly beloved Isolde. But when he sails towards her castle on the shores of Brittany, he raises a black instead of a white sail, which Isolde takes to mean he is dead, and hence takes her own life. Tristan follows suit when he finds her gone.

This is the first of a handful of tragic lovers in Eliot's "Waste Land." Shakespeare's Antony and Cleopatra enter the poem next, the great lovers of antiquity. Antony was the Roman Emperor who would risk life, honor, and throne to pursue his obsession with the legendary beauty of Egypt, Cleopatra, who betrays him, when Octavius Caesar defeats Antony during the naval battle at Actium. She then commits suicide, out of grief, remorse, and unwillingness to be taken captive by Octavius. When Antony finds her dead, he too takes his own life.

Like Tristan and Isolde, Antony and Cleopatra are childless, and their love ends tragically in suicide.

Eliot introduces a modern, fictional couple into the poem next— well, not quite fictional, since the 'Nameless Narrator' and the 'Nervous Woman' might just as well be called Tom and Viv (Tom Eliot's first wife).

Nameless and Nervous can't get along.

She wants him to speak, but he can't. She wants to know what he is thinking, but doesn't. All he can do is mutter, under his breath, that they are "in rat's alley where the dead men lost their bones." That leaves her to threaten an hysterical scene: she will let her hair down loose and run raving in her nightgown out into the streets of London! Everyone will know what a mess their marriage is!

It would seem difficult to paint a more painful portrait of a love gone bad, but Eliot does, introducing next the mythical couple, Philomel and Tereus, the King of Thrace. Tereus cuts Philomel's tongue out to prevent her from talking about his adultery and domestic abuse, but the gods change Philomel into a nightingale, whose singing fills the desert at night.

Such is the "Waste Land," torn apart by domestic violence, adultery, suicide, sterility—and abortion.

A couple simply called Albert and Lil comes next into the poem. We overhear their story in a pub: Albert has been demobilized, and is coming home from the trenches of the First World War. He'll want to have a good time, and get his wife prettied up. To that end, he's sent her some money to get a new set of teeth! Otherwise, he couldn't bear to look at her, she looks so "antique"!

She looks that way because she's had five children, and has spent the money on an abortion, rather than on her teeth. The pills the chemist gave her have ruined her. She's never been the same since.

The pub episode concludes with another allusion to Shakespeare—to Ophelia, who drowned herself after the death of her father and Hamlet's rejection.

If there is to be any relationship at all in the Waste Land, it seems to be a matter of casual, mechanical sex, with neither love nor commitment. In the next section of the poem, therefore, a clerk visits a typist for afternoon tea, and seduces her on the sofa. She is unresponsive, but lets him go ahead with it anyway. He could care less, and welcomes her indifference. When it's all over, she straightens her hair, and says, "I'm glad that's done with."

Other couples in the poem don't fair much better.

Queen Elizabeth's love for the Earl of Leicester remains unconsummated. The two couldn't marry, for political reasons. Brunnhilde's love for Siegfried, in Wagner's opera, ended on the funeral pyre—after enduring betrayal, murder, and the cruel manipulations of power politics.

For society, power, and politics turn our love into a waste land. The problems in our relationships reflect the problems in the world around us, to which they may indeed contribute, in a vicious circle of pain.

How then do we redeem the Waste Land? How can we put it back together, and restore our relationships and marriages, and thereby contribute to the rejuvenation of a world torn apart by war, bigotry, and terrorism?

Eliot's answer is simple:

Give, Sympathize, and Control.

Remain unmoved by Fear and Desire.

And stay on the quest.

The poem ends with Parzival in the Chapel Perilous, on his way to the Grail Castle, where he will redeem the waste land by asking his sympathetic question of the Wounded King: "Uncle, what ails thee?"

Shortly afterwards, the thunder speaks, and we wait for the rain to fall.

The thunder says "DA," the Sanskrit word in the Upanishads for the Logos, the word of God. This single syllable is heard in three different ways—just as God takes three forms in Christianity. "DA" may be heard as "Datta," meaning to give; "Dayadhvam," meaning to sympathize; and "Damyata," meaning self-control.

It's the Hindu way of saying "Faith, Hope, and Love."

If we can manage those three things, our relationships and marriages will thrive, and the Waste Land the world is threatening to turn into will be redeemed.

Notes

1. See *Lilith: Die Erste Eva: Eine Studie über dunkle Aspekte des Weiblichen* by Siegmund Hurwitz, Zürich: Daimon Verlag, 1980.

2. As Erich Neumann wrote, the notion of a "patriarchal victory" over the "luciferian dragons" activated by the emergence of the earth archetypes of the Great Goddess is no longer "at the disposal of modern men and women" (33; my trans.). What is required is not the "conquest of the evils, rather their redemption, not patriarchal victory, rather a transformation of that which is below" ("Die Bedeutung des Erdarchetyps für Neuzeit" 33).

3. See Eric Erickson's *Youth: Identity and Crisis*.

4. For the mysticism of the date palm see Thorkild Jakobson, *The Treasures of Darkness*, and for the mysticism of ritual regicide, see the magnificent pages in Joseph Campbell's *The Way of the Animal Powers*.

5. See Joseph Campbell's discussion of this shift in the import of the imagery of serpent, woman, tree, and fruit in the first chapter of *The Masks of God: Occidental Mythology*. Since that ground breaking work, many other fine studies of the transition from matriarchal to patriarchal symbolism have appeared, such as *The Chalice and the Blade,* Gilda Lerner's *The Creation of Patriarchy,* and *The Once and Future Goddess.*

6. Homer's *Odyssey* has been the focus of many moving commentaries. James Hillman discusses the way wounding opens up the ego to the archetypal depths of the psyche, and he suggests that the scar of Ulysses (a thigh wound inflicted during a boar hunt in his youth) indicates the special relationship Ulysses has to the feminine, death, or the sea of the unconscious. This unique balance enables Ulysses to bypass the normal senex-puer conflict in favor of a unique harmony between the archetypal or human realms ("Puer Wounds" 100-128).

For Joseph Campbell, the *Odyssey* dramatizes the reemergence of the goddess during the 8th century B.C., after a long period of repression by the heroic patriarchs of Troy ("The Great Goddess" 84).

Murray Stein also focuses on the collapse of the patriarchal orientation of the persona after the Trojan War, taking the return of Odysseus to Penelope as a model for the mid-life crisis. His interpretation focuses on the roles Hermes plays in the *Odyssey* (guide, thief, protector, or companion) as aspects of the "liminality" of the mid-life transition (*In Mid-life* 129).

M.L. von Franz also provides a synopsis of Jung's notion that anima development occurs in four stages (CW 16: 174) in her chapter on individuation in *Man and His Symbols*: "The first stage is best symbolized by the figure of Eve, which represents purely instinctual and biological relations. The second can be seen in Faust's Helen: She personifies a romantic and aesthetic level that is, however, still characterized by sexual elements. The third is represented, for instance, by the Virgin Mary—a figure who raises love (eros) to the heights of spiritual devotion. The fourth type is symbolized by Sapienta, wisdom transcending even the most holy and the most pure" (185).

7. George Lord, for example, focuses on Odysseus' need for rehabilitation before returning to the domestic duties in Ithaca, a rehabilitation which is a crucial role of the feminine in the poem.

8. William Anderson, in fact, notes the connection between Ogygia and Elysium, and the close relationship between Calypso and death.

9. Howard Porter suggests that the olive tree symbolizes the rebirth motif, which he discusses as the central theme of the poem.

10. On the Argeiphontes epithet ("slayer of Argos," the thousand-eyed beast the jealous Juno sets to spying on Ino, after turning her into a heifer), see Gary Astrachan's fine article, in *Gorgo: Zeitschrift für archetypische und bildhaftes Denken*.

11. Several mythologists have seen in the story of Demeter and Persephone symbolic allegories of the cycles of the seasons: Jane Ellen Harrison pointed out that, in the tale Demeter tells the daughters of Keleos, she calls herself Deo, a name derived from the Cretan word for barley grains (272); Karl Kerényi suggests that the child in the fire and Persephone in Hades represent the grain in the oven, or the corpse in the winter earth, from which it emerges reborn in the spring ("Kore" 117); while Gordon Wasson sees in the symbolism of the mown ear held aloft during the Eleusinian mysteries an allusion to the hallucinogenic beverage Demeter consumes in the "Hymn," a compound of the fungus which grows on wheat. Psychological discussions of the myth (by Downing and Christ, among many others), see it as dramatizing the entirety of the female life cycle, with a unique focus on the mother-daughter relationship, as compensating for the patriarchal emphasis on fathers and sons in the Bible. These are rooted in Jung's analysis, in *Essays on a Science of Mythology,* and in the work of his female followers (like Esther Harding and Nor Hall). In his lectures, Joseph Campbell focused in great detail on the continuity

between the Eleusinian mysteries and the vocabulary of the rituals of the Goddess going back to Mesopotamian times: the pig motif, for example, points as far afield as to the Malekulan mysteries of the Goddess of the underworld (*Occidental* 171), and to the sacred vessels carried by the cherubim of Babylonian provenance (*Mythic Image* 285).

12. The story has attracted the attention of numerous critics and scholars, while writers from Marie-Catherine D'Aulnoy ("The Green Serpent" of 1697), to Walter Pater (*Marius the Epicurean* of 1885), and more recently C.S. Lewis (*Till We Have Faces*) have been tempted to create new versions of the story of "Cupid and Psyche." Early on in our century, in 1914, Richard Reitzenstein argued that Eros and Psyche were local deities in Greek cults (von Franz 64), while in 1962 Reinhold Merkelbach linked the story to the mysteries of the Isis cult in Egypt (von Franz 2). The tale has been studied both as an allegory of male psychological development, focusing on the mother complex and the integration of the anima (von Franz), and as an allegory of the psychological development of the feminine (Neumann and Johnson). James Hillman sees the story more generally as what he calls the myth of analysis, an allegory of the psychological creativity and growth characteristic of therapy as a whole. Christine Downing has very briefly discussed the relationship between sisters in the story.

13. In the Old Testament, the *Theogony*, and the Vedas, the serpent is associated with the Fall (*Occidental Myth* 9-41; *Mythic Image* 281-301). Campbell's work acknowledges the seminal work of Jane Ellen Harrison on the pre-Olympian deities of Greece, which has recently been amplified by Marija Gimbutas, whose *Language of the Goddess* devotes an entire chapter to the icon of the goddess and the serpent (121-37).

14. This is so in the *Odyssey*, in kundalini yoga, in Medieval representations of the Crucifixion, and in the alchemical traditions. See my "Alchemy and Modernism," along with Campbell, *Occidental Myth* 163 and *Inner Reaches* 70-92.

15. See the entire section devoted to "The Sundoor and Related Motifs" in Coomaraswamy's *Selected Papers*, Vol. 1, particularly Figure 18 of the Egyptian World Door and Sundoor" (480), and "Symbolism of the Dome."

16. Numerous recent commentaries have focused on the Grail quest in the romances of the Middle Ages. Edward Whitmont, Emma Jung, and Robert Johnson all agree that the Grail legends compensated for the excessive patriarchal orientation of the Church by exalting the feminine. Whitmont argues that the wounding of Anfortas, the Waste Land, and the sorcery of Clinschor, reflect a violation of the feminine principle, and that the legends point towards a healing reintegration of the feminine still necessary today. Emma Jung focuses on the split between the masculine and the feminine, between spirit and nature, and between good and evil as psychologically damaging aspects of dogmatic dualities which the reconciliations of the Grail legends tend to heal (Joseph Campbell goes so far as to equate Clinschor and Pope Leo III). Along similar lines, Robert Johnson suggests that Perceval's central task is the integration of the inner feminine which the Jungians call the anima. This involves the reconciliation between opposites which is also a common theme in alchemy, known as the sacred marriage (*hieros gamos*) or the *mysterium coniunctionis*.

For pictures and discussion on these various sacred vessels, see John Matthews, *The Grail: Quest for the Eternal* (46-52; 72-73), Joseph Campbell, *The Mythic Image*, and Hans Leisegang on "the Mystery of the Serpent." Adam McLean has charted the relationships between cauldrons, grails, and alchemical vessels in his article on transformation symbolism (64).

The perspective of comparative mythology on the Grail romances has also been illuminating, especially in the great work on the subject by Joseph Campbell, *Creative Mythology*. Campbell argues that Wolfram adapts religious imagery from a variety of traditions (Christian, Arabic, Oriental, Celtic, Classical, Alchemical) and applies it to the inner mysteries of human development over the course of a complete life cycle. In this view, the symbols in the romances become "archetypal, universal mythic images of spiritual transformation" which transcend theological sectarianism (453). Hence, the symbols serve as "paradigms of secular human experiences in depth dimension" (484) which are seen not as supernatural facts (in the way of dogmatic literalism, of whatever creed), but as "inherent in the episodes of men's normal lives" (484). In this sense, Wolfram's *Parzival* looks forward to the mythic method of Mann and Joyce, and is in fact the "first example in world literature of a consciously developed secular Christian myth" (476) which inaugurated a "new age of the human spirit" (480). The redemption of the Waste Land achieved by Gawain and Parzival then, brings about a new era of secular mythology, an age of the Spirit which sees through dogmatic creeds to the universal symbols of human transformation.

17. Grimaldi suggests that Orfeo is a Celtic folk hero, Christian Pilgrim, and Courtly King: as folk hero he undergoes initiatory experiences in the realm of faeric, the forest madness of the lover, and the visions of the faerie dance, hunt, and palace beneath the hills; as pilgrim, his sins of pride and lust are purged during ten years of penitential wandering as an anchorite, and the journey itself suggests the human pilgrimage from Eden, into Exile, and on to the restored Earthly Paradise; finally, as King, Orfeo enacts the fall of princes motif so popular during the Middle Ages, and he learns the value of the law and of obedient servants. In addition, the poem explores the courtly relationships between kingdoms, between subject and ruler, between patron and poet, and, most significantly, between husband and wife. All three of these levels of allegory enrich the underlying narrative of the journey to the otherworld.

18. James Hillman applies the phrase specifically to the story of Cupid and Psyche in his book *The Myth of Analysis*, but we use it more generally here since the hero journey as an image of the psychotherapeutic process (which Jung called individuation) takes a large variety of specific forms which are in themselves variations on the basic structure of the monomyth.

19. See Jung's *Psychology of the Transference* for a thorough discussion of alchemy as a myth both of marriage and of the individuation process.

20. The magic flute in Mozart's opera of that title is also made from a tree.

21. From the relief sculpture of the Cathedral at Otranto, to the ivory jewelry boxes of courtly ladies, to the illuminated manuscripts of the *Prose Lancelot*, all of which can be seen in Richard Barber's *The Arthurian Legends*.

22. For a comprehensive introduction to the problem of the three Marys in the Gospel and apocryphal traditions, and numerous examples of Medieval images of Mary Magdalen and her ointment jar, see Susan Haskins, *Mary Magdalen: Myth and Metaphor*.

23. See "Joseph Campbell on the Great Goddess" (78-79), and Marija Gimbutas, *The Language of the Goddess* (108-09).

24. There are of course innumerable examples of these two scenes in the history of Western art: my personal favorites are the Madonna and Pièta figures sculpted by Michelangelo, which taken together give us an extraordinarily beautiful portrait of the "loving and terrible" Goddess, mother our life *and* of our death, as envisioned by the Renaissance.

25. See Joseph Campbell's *Creative Mythology*, Chapter 4, where the contribution of the Minnesänger poets to the mysticism of the Arthurian corpus is celebrated.

26. The meeting of the sun and the moon is a frequent motif in Joseph Campbell's work: in *Creative Mythology* he discusses its role in Homer's Odyssey (163-64), and in *The Inner Reaches of Outer Space*, his discussion ranges from Dürer, to Kundalini yoga, to the sand paintings of the Navajo (Chapter 4).

27. I remember Lord Kenneth Clark's haughty proclamation, during his otherwise wonderful *Civilization* series on PBS, that the romances of Chrétien were "unreadable," a judgement which I (and many others) have found absolutely absurd: frankly, Francophobic!

28. Robert Graves notes in *The White Goddess* that "in all Celtic languages *trees* means *letters*; that the Druidic colleges were founded in woods or groves; that a great part of the Druidic mysteries was concerned with twigs of various sorts" (38).

29. See Edinger who provides the Latin version and translation of *The Emerald Tablet of Hermes* (230-32), Marie Loiuse von-Franz on the *tabula smaragdina* (*Alchemy* 113-14), and Jung's interpretation in *Mysterium Coniunctionis* (218-222). It should also be noted that in the symbolism of the *Kabbalah*, which is closely interwined with alchemical symbolism, the inverted tree becomes a symbol of the emanation of the deity in ten stages of manifestation. Several alchemical pictures portray the stages of the opus as branches on a hermetic Tree of Knowledge.

30. Many such images of the King as the Sun, and the Queen as the Moon, can be found in the wonderful anthology of alchemical illustrations collected by Fabricius.

31. See also Ariosto's *Orlando Furioso* for another splendid treatment of the theme.

32. The story of Parzival, as begun by Chrétien and revised and completed by Wolfram has proven irresistible to the critics and artists of our time. Emma Jung was the first to focus on Parzival's story as an image of the individuation process. Robert Johnson's Jungian commentary, entitled *He*, was a popular best seller of sorts. Joseph Campbell's illustrious career began with graduate studies in Paris and in Munich, where he discovered Wolfram's work, which would be a mainstay of his lectures for many years following. His *Creative Mythology* takes us through the entire story of

Parzival, with extended analysis and commentary. More recently, the story has been the subject of such films as John Boorman's *Excalibur*, Eric Rohmer's *Perceval* and Hans Jurgens Syberberg's *Parzival*, a cinematic version of Wagner's opera. It our task here, therefore, to indicate the main lines of the marriage theme in the story.

33. In his *Return of the Goddess*, Edward Whitmont has argued that a revival of the feminine in Western Culture began with the Grail romances of the Middle Ages.

34. See Anthony Roche on the Celtic otherworld in *A Portrait of the Artist as a Young Man*, in which Roche cites "the world of Celtic legend where the children of Lir were magically transformed into swans, and the souls of those who died young took flight to the Otherworld in the shape of birds" (328). The *aisling* conventions associate bird women with the land of faery in Gaelic poetry (329). Mozart's *Magic Flute* also employs the imagery of the bird catcher of souls (Papageno) as a servant of the Queen of the Night. She is modelled on Isis as the Death Goddess in Egypt, who is often depicted in sarcophagi as a magnificently winged bird.

35. Some of the influential titles and historical events in this area include George Ripley's *Cantilena* (1490), Petrus Bonus's *Pretiosa margarita novella* (1546), Cornelius Agrippa's *De occulta philosophia* (1533), John Dee's *Monas hieroglyphica* (1564), Ben Jonson's *The Alchemist* and Shakespeare's *The Tempest* (1610-11)— perhaps written for the marriage of Elizabeth and Prince Frederick of Heidelberg in 1613)—the *Fama Fraternitatis* and *Chymische Hochzeit* (1614-16), Robert Fludd's *Utruisque cosmi historia* (1617), Michael Maier's *Atalanta Fugiens* (1617), Mylius's *Philosophia reformata* (1622), the *Sapienta veterum* from the 18th century in Paris, the *Janitor pansophus* in the *Museum Hermeticum* (1678), John Milton's *Il Penseroso* (1645), Henry Vaughan's *Silex Scintillans* (The Sparkling Flint) (1650), Thomas Vaughan's translation of the *Fama* (1652; Reprinted 1923), Henry More's *Conjectura Cabbalistica* (1662), Abbé de Villars, *Le Comte de Gablis* (1670), Ralph Cudworth's *The True Intellectual System of the Universe* (1678), and Alexander Pope's *The Rape of the Lock* (1712-14). Studies and bibliographies of the subject may be found in Bonnefoy (211-222), Nicholl, Roberts, Eliade, von-Franz, Faivre, Smith, and, particularly, Frances Yates. Recently, Umberto Eco has attempted (not altogether successfully) to heap this material together in his novel, *Foucault's Pendulum* (in which several hero journey cycles occur).

36. Jung, for example, devotes all of his volume, *Mysterium Coniunctionis*, to the symbolism of the union of opposites in alchemy, which he takes to represent the achievement of harmony within the Self. Edward Edinger discusses the coniunctio symbolism in his article on *Romeo and Juliet*, and in *Anatomy of the Psyche: Alchemical Symbolism in Psychotherapy*, he saves the coniunctio to last, as representing the fulfillment of the journey of individuation.

37. See Dame Frances Yates, *The Occult Philosophy in the Elizabethan Age*, for the distinction between the handling of the Magus in Spenser, Marlowe, and Shakespeare.

38. On the transition from Renaissance to Rosicrucian hermeticism, see Frances Yates, *Giordano Bruno* and *The Rosicrucian Enlightenment*.

39. The complete plates and commentary may be found in Jung, *The Psychology of the Transference*, to which the figure numbers in the parenthetical citations refer.

40. These categories and much of the rest of this introductory material (I add the aesthetic category) come from Joseph Campbell's "Folkloristic Commentary" to *Grimm's Fairytales*, reprinted in *The Flight of the Wild Gander*. For more recent translations and historical commentary on the tales, see the work of Jack Zipes.

41. On the "infant exile" motif and its relationship to the birth of the hero see the selections from Raglan, Rank, and Dundes brought together in *In Quest of the Hero*.

42. A convenient collection of eye goddess figurines and icons is to be found in Laurence di Stasi's *Mal Occhio*. See also Gimbutas, *The Language of the Goddess*, Chapter 6.

43. See M. H. Abrams, *Natural Supernaturalism*, on the apocalyptic symbolism of weddings and homecomings in the literature of Romanticism.

44. Robert Hammond's edition of the shooting script of *Beauty and the Beast* reproduces many shots that illustrate the importance of arches and doorways in the film, though he does not reproduce entire sequences.

45. See shot 142 in Hammond's edition of the shooting script.

46. Shot 144 in Hammond.

47. Hillman notes that "The double Janus nature of the gate was also expressed as a door, neither open nor closed, ajar, waiting, always an open possibility" (226). As Beauty walks into her chamber (Shot 144 in Hammond) the door is halfway open.

48. See Murray Stein's *In MidLife* for a discussion of the descent to Hades as a period of liminality during the midlife crisis. His use of the term "floating" to describe the movements of the psyche during this phase is literally visualized by Cocteau both in *Orpheus* and in the sequence where Beauty goes to her room in the Beast's chateau for the first time. See also Livingston Paisley's discussion of liminality and the ritual scapegoat who threatens both violence and redemption in Bergman's films (92-100).

49. See for example the spiral labyrinths carved on the entrance stones of the tumulus of Newgrange outside of Dublin, dating back to approximately 3,000 B.C.E. For a quick overview of images of the labyrinth see Janet Bord.

50. Louis Carroll's *Through the Looking Glass* also conflates the journey to the otherworld with the labyrinth.

51. Jean Decock also suggests a multilevel and psychological approach to the use of myth and folktale in Cocteau's films: "the fairy tale genre expresses myths; that is crystallizations of psychological virtualities. Thus, every fairy tale can be interpreted on three levels: anecdotal, the miraculous adventure with an historical or profane moral; sacred, with a lesson attributable to psychology, be it conscious or unconscious; and finally initiatory, with a meaning acceding to metaphysics" (vii.).

52. See *The Psychology of the Transference* throughout, and especially the diagram on page 59 which outlines the complex dynamics of the relations between the conscious and unconscious contents of the personality during marriage.

53. See my books and articles in "Further Reading" below for an analysis of the descent to the underworld in Modernist literature.

54. Note the echo of Theseus in Shakespeare's *A Midsummer Night's Dream*: "Lovers and madmen have such seething brains, / Such shaping fantasies, that apprehend / More than cool reason ever comprehends" (5.1.4-6)

55. On the Orphic poet in the European tradition see Walter Strauss, *Descent and Return,* in which he argues that the journey downward is into nothingness.

56. With respect to mirrors and reflection, Hillman notes "entering the underworld is like entering the mode of reflection, mirroring, which suggests that we may enter the underworld by means of reflection, by reflective means" (52).

57. Ingmar Bergman acknowledged that Cocteau's work, while technically unsophisticated, remained "perfectly astounding" (*Bergman on Bergman 45*).

Suggestions for
Further Reading

Anderson, William S. "Calypso and Elysium." *Essays on the Odyssey: Selected Modern Criticism*. Ed. Charles H. Taylor Jr. Bloomington and London: Indiana University Press. 1963.

Apollonius of Rhodes. *The Voyage of the Argo*. Trans. E.V. Rieu. Penguin Books. 1971.

Apuleius. *The Golden Ass*. Trans. Jack Lindsay. Bloomington: Indiana UP, 1962.

Astrachan, Gary. "Dionysos in Thomas Mann's Novella, *Death in Venice*." *Journal of Analytical Psychology*. 35 (1990): 59-78.

_____, "Hermes der Argustöter." *Gorgo: Zeitschrift für archetypische und bildhaftes Denken*. 20 (1991): 29-46.

Athanassakis, Apostolos. N., Trans. *The Homeric Hymns*. Baltimore: The Johns Hopkins UP, 1976.

Bachofen, J.J. *Myth, Religion, and Mother Right: Selected Writings of J.J. Bachofen*. Trans. Ralph Mannheim. Preface by George Boas and Introduction by Joseph Campbell. Bollingen Series LXXXIV. Princeton: Princeton UP, 1967.

Barber, Richard. *The Arthurian Legends: An Illustrated Anthology*. Totowa, NJ: Littlefield, Adams, and Company, 1979.

Bergman on Bergman: Interviews with Ingmar Bergman. by Stig Bjorkman, Torsten Manns, Jonas Sima. Trans. Paul Britten Austin. New York: Simon and Schuster, 1973.

Bettelheim, Bruno. *The Uses of Enchantment: The Meaning and Importance of Fairy Tales*. New York: Alfred A. Knopf, 1976.

Biedermann, Hans. *Dictionary of Symbolism*. Trans. James Hulbert. New York and Oxford: Facts on File, 1992.

Bilibin, Ivan, illustrator. *Four Russian Folktales*. Trans. Robert Chandler. Boulder: Shambhala, 1980.

Bonnefoy, Yves. *Roman and European Mythologies*. Translated Under the Direction of Wendy Doniger. Chicago and London: The University of Chicago Press, 1992,

Bord, Janet. *Mazes and Labyrinths of the World*. New York: E.P. Dutton, 1975.

Branston, Brian. *The Lost Gods of England*. New York: Oxford UP, 1974.

Briggs, Katherine. *An Encyclopedia of Fairies: Hobgoblins, Brownies, Bogies, and Other Supernatural Creatures*. New York: Pantheon Books, 1976.

Budge, E.A. Wallis. *Amulets and Talismans*. New York: University Books, 1968.

_____, *The Gods of the Egyptians*. Vol. 1. New York: Dover, 1969.

Burkert, Walter. *Ancient Mystery Cults*. Boston: Harvard UP, 1987.

_____, *Structure and History in Greek Mythology and Ritual*. Berkeley: The University of California Press, 1979.

Campbell, Joseph. *The Flight of the Wild Gander. Explorations in the Mythological Dimension*. New York: The Viking Press, 1969.

_____, "Folkloristic Commentary." *Grimm's Fairy Tales*. New York: Pantheon Books, 1944.

_____, *Historical Atlas of World Mythology*. 2 Volumes, 5 Parts. New York: Harper and Row, 1988.

_____, Introduction. *Bullfinch's Mythology*. Compiled by Bryan Holme. New York: The Viking Press, 1979.

_____, *The Hero With a Thousand Faces*. Bollingen Series XVII. Princeton: Princeton UP, 1968.

_____, *The Inner Reaches of Outer Spaces: Metaphor as Myth and as Religion*. New York: Alfred van der Marck Editions, 1985.

_____, *Joseph Campbell and The Power of Myth with Bill Moyers*. Ed. Sue Flowers. New York: Doubleday, 1988.

_____, "Joseph Campbell on the Great Goddess." *Parabola: Myth and the Quest for Meaning*. 5.4 (1980): 74-85.

_____, *The Masks of God: Occidental Mythology*. New York: The Viking Press., 1964.

_____, *The Mysteries: Papers From the Eranos Yearbooks*. Bollingen Series XXX. Ed. Joseph Campbell. Princeton: Princeton UP, 1955.

_____, *The Mythic Image*. Princeton: Princeton UP, 1974.

Clark, R.T. Rundle. *Myth and Symbol in Ancient Egypt*. London: Thames and Hudson, 1959.

Cocteau, Jean. *Beauty and the Beast: Scenario and Dialogs by Jean Cocteau*. Ed. Robert M. Hammond. New York: New York UP, 1970.

_____, *Beauty and the Beast*. Lopert Films 1946. Embassy Home Entertainment.

_____, *Orphée: Film*. Photographies de Roger Corbeau. Paris: La Parade, Éditions André Bonne, 1950.

_____, *Orpheus*. (1950). Video Images.

Coomaraswamy, Ananda K. *Coomaraswamy: Selected Papers 1: Traditional Art and Symbolism*. Ed. Roger Lipsey. Bollingen Series LXXXIX. Princeton: Princeton UP, 1977.

_____, *Coomaraswamy: Selected Papers 2: Metaphysics*. Ed. Roger Lipsey. Bollingen Series LXXXIX. Princeton: Princeton UP, 1977.

_____, *The Dance of Shiva: Fourteen Indian Essays*. Revised Edition. New York: The Noonday Press, 1957.

_____, "The One Thread." *Parabola: The Magazine of Myth and Tradition: Labyrinth*. Summer 1992. 17 (2): 26-34.

Corbin, Henry. *Avicenna and the Visionary Recital*. Trans. Williard R. Trask. Princeton: Princeton UP, 1960.

_____, "Pour une Morphologie de la Spiritualité Shîite." *Eranos-Jahrbuch 1960: Mensch und Gestaltung*. Vol. 29. Ed. Olga Fröbe-Kapteyn. Zürich: Rhein Verlag, 1961.

_____, "Terre Céleste et Corps de Résurrection d'après quelques Traditions Iraniennes." *Eranos-Jahrbuch 1953: Mensch und Erde*. Vol. 22. Ed. Olga Fröbe-Kapteyn. Zürich: Rhein-Verlag, 1954.

Crossley-Holland, Kevin. *The Norse Myths*. New York: Pantheon Books, 1980.

Cunliffe, Barry. *The Celtic World*. New York: McGraw Hill, 1979.

Curtis, J.E. and J.E. Reade, eds. *Art and Empire: Treasures From Assyria in the British Museum*. The Metropolitan Museum of Art. New York: Harry N. Abrams, 1995.

Davidson, H.R. Ellis. *Scandinavian Mythology*. London: Paul Hamlyn, 1975.

Decock, Jean. "Preface." *Beauty and the Beast: Scenario and Dialogs by Jean Cocteau*. Ed. Robert M. Hammond. New York: New York UP, 1970.

De Rola, Stanislas Klossowski. *Alchemy: The Secret Art*. New York: Avon Books, 1973.

Di Stasi, Lawrence. *Mal Occhio (Evil Eye): The Underside of Vision*. San Francisco: North Point Press, 1981.

Doob, Penelope Reed. *The Idea of the Labyrinth: From Classical Antiquity to the Middle Ages*. Ithaka: Cornell UP, 1990.

Downing, Christine. *The Goddess: Mythological Images of the Feminine*. New York: Crossroad, 1981.

Edinger, Edward F. *Anatomy of the Psyche: Alchemical Symbolism in Psychotherapy*. La Salle: Open Court, 1985.

_____, "*Romeo and Juliet*: A Coniunctio Drama." *The Shaman From Elko: Papers in Honor of Joseph L. Henderson on His Seventy-Fifth Birthday*. San Francisco: C.G. Jung Institute of San Francisco, 1978.

_____, *Melville's Moby Dick: A Jungian Commentary*. New York: New Directions, 1978.

Eliade, Mircea. *The Forge and the Crucible: The Origins and Structures of Alchemy*. Second Edition. Trans. Stephen Corrin. Chicago and London: The University of Chicago Press, 1978.

_____, *Myths, Dreams, and Mysteries*. New York: Harper and Row, 1960.

_____, "La Terre-Mère et les Hiérogamies Cosmiques." *Eranos Jahrbuch 1953: Band XXII: Mensch und Erde*. Herausgegeben von Olga Fröbe-Kapteyn. Zürich: Rhein-Verlag, 1954.

_____, *Shamanism: Archaic Techniques of Ecstasy*. Trans. Williard R. Trask. Bollingen Series LXXVI. Princeton: Princeton UP, 1964.

Eliot, Alexander, et. al. *Myths*. New York: McGraw-Hill Book Company, 1976.

Eliot, T.S. *Four Quartets*. New York: HBJ, 1971.

_____, "Ulysses, Order and Myth." (1923). *The Modern Tradition*. Ed. Richard Ellmann and Charles Feidelson. New York: Oxford UP, 1965.

_____, *The Waste Land and Other Poems*. New York: Harcourt, Brace, Jovanovich, 1962.

Epic of Gilgamesh. Trans. N.K. Sandars. New York: Penguin, 1960.

Eschenbach, Wolfram von. *Parzival*. Trans. A.T. Hatto. New York: Penguin Books, 1980.

Evans, Sir Arthur. *The Palace of Minos*. 4 Vols. London: Macmillan and Company, 1921 and 1934.

Fabricius, Johannes. *Alchemy: The Medieval Alchemists and Their Royal Art*. Copenhagen: Rosenkilde and Bagger, 1976.

Fontenrose, Joseph. *Python: A Study of Delphic Myth and Its Origin*. Berkeley: The University of California Press, 1959.

Foster, Michael. "The Christian Doctrine of Creation and the Rise of Modern Natural Science." *Creation: The Impact of an Idea*. Ed. Daniel O'Connor and Francis Oakley. New York: Charles Scribner's Sons, 1969.

Faivre, Antoine. *The Golden Fleece and Alchemy*. Albany: State University of New York Press, 1993.

Feldman, Burton and Robert D. Richardson. *The Rise of Modern Mythology: 1690-1860*. Bloomington: Indiana UP, 1972.

Franz, Marie-Louise von. *Alchemy: An Introduction to the Symbolism and the Psychology*. Toronto: Inner City Books, 1980.

_____, *Creation Myths*. Dallas: Spring Publications, 1972.

_____, *On Dreams and Death: A Jungian Interpretation*. Boulder and London: Shambhala, 1984.

_____, *A Psychological Interpretation of Apuleius' Golden Ass With the Tale of Eros and Psyche*. Dallas: Spring Publications, 1980.

Friedman, Albert B., ed. *The Penguin Book of Folk Ballads of the English Speaking World*. New York: Penguin Books, 1978.

Fromm, Erich. *The Forgotten Language: An Introduction to the Study of Dreams, Fairy Tales, and Myths*. New York: Grove Press, 1951.

Frye, Northrop. "The Argument of Comedy." *Shakespeare: Modern Essays in Criticism*. Ed. Leonard F. Dean. London: Oxford UP, 1967.

Gennep, Arnold van. *The Rites of Passage*. Trans. Monika B. Vizedom and Gabrielle L. Caffee. Chicago: The University of Chicago Press, 1960.

Gimbutas, Marija. *The Civilization of the Goddess: The World of Old Europe*. San Francisco: HarperSanFrancisco, 1991.

_____, *The Language of the Goddess*. San Francisco: Harper and Row, 1989.

Godwin, Joscelyn. *Athanasius Kircher: A Renaissance Man and the Quest for Lost Knowledge*. London: Thames and Hudson, 1979.

Graves, Robert. *The White Goddess*. Amended and Enlarged Edition. New York: Farar, Straus and Giroux, 1948.

Green, Miranda J. *Dictionary of Celtic Myth and Legend*. London: Thames and Hudson, 1992.

Grof, Stanislav. *Realms of the Human Unconscious: Observations from LSD Research*. New York: E.P. Dutton, 1976.

Guénon, René. "The Language of the Birds." *The Sword of Gnosis*. Ed. Jacob Needleman. Baltimore: Penguin Books, 1974.

Halifax, Joan. *Shamanic Voices: A Survey of Visionary Narratives*. New York: E.P. Dutton, 1979.

Harrison, Jane Ellen. *Prolegomena to the Study of Greek Religion*. London: Merlin Press, 1980.

Haskins, Susan. *Mary Magdalen: Myth and Metaphor*. New York: Harcourt, Brace, and Company, 1993.

Hawthorne, Nathaniel. *Tales and Sketches*. Ed. Roy Harvey Pearce. New York: The Library of America, 1982.

Hillman, James. *The Dream and the Underworld*. New York: Harper and Row, 1979.

_____, *Healing Fiction*. Preface by George Quasha. Barrytown: Station Hill, 1983.

_____, *The Myth of Analysis: Three Essays in Archetypal Psychology*. New York: Harper and Row, 1972.

_____, "Pothos." *Loose Ends: Primary Papers in Archetypal Psychology*. Dallas: Spring Publications, 1976.

_____, "Puer Wounds and Ulysses' Scar." *Puer Papers*. James Hillman et al. Dallas: Spring Publications, 1979.

Hoffman, E.T.A. "Die Bergwerke zu Falun." *Sämtliche poetischen Werke*. Zweiter Band. Berlin and Darmstadt: Der Tempel Verlag, 1963.

_____, "The Mines of Falun." *Western Literature in A World Context: Volume Two: The Enlightenment through the Present*. Ed. Paul Davis, et al. New York: St. Martin's Press, 1995.

Homer. *The Odyssey*. Trans. Robert Fitzgerald. New York: Anchor Books, Doubleday and Company, 1963.

Hornung, Erik. "Auf den Spuren der Sonne: Gang durch ein äegyptisches Königsgrab." *Eranos Jahrbuch (1981): Aufstieg und Abstieg*. Ed. Adolph Portmann and Rudolf Ritsema. Frankfort am Main: Insel Verlag, 1982.

Johnson, Robert. *He: Understanding Masculine Psychology*. New York: Harper and Row, 1977.

_____, *She: Understanding Feminine Psychology*. New York: Harper and Row, 1976.

_____, *We: Understanding the Psychology of Romantic Love*. San Francisco: Harper and Row, 1983.

Jonas, Hans. *The Gnostic Religion*. Second Edition. Boston: Beacon Press, 1963.

Jung, C.G. *Four Archetypes*. Princeton: Princeton UP, 1964.

_____, *Memories, Dreams, Reflections*. Ed. Aniela Jaffé. Trans. Richard and Clara Winston. New York: Pantheon Books, 1963.

_____, *Mysterium Coniunctionis: An Inquiry Into the Separation and Synthesis of Psychic Opposites in Alchemy*. Second Edition Trans. R.F.C. Hull. Bollingen Series XX. Princeton: Princeton UP, 1970.

_____, *The Practice of Psychotherapy*. (The Collected Works of C.G. Jung, Volume 16). Princeton: Princeton UP, 1966.

_____, "A Psychological Commentary on The Tibetan Book of the Dead." 1935. *Psychology and Religion: West and East*. New York: Pantheon Books, 1958.

_____, *Psychology and Alchemy*. Second Edition. Princeton: Princeton UP, 1980.

_____, *Psychology of the Transference*. Princeton: Princeton UP, 1966.

_____, *Symbols of Transformation*. (The Collected Works of C.G. Jung, Volume 5). Princeton: Princeton UP, 1967.

_____, "The Transcendent Function." *The Portable Jung*. Ed. Joseph Campbell. New York: The Viking Press, 1971.

Jung, C.G. and C. Kerényi. *Essays on a Science of Mythology: The Myth of the Divine Child and the Mysteries of Eleusis*. Bollingen Series XXII. Princeton: Princeton UP, 1973.

Jung, Emma and Marie-Louise von Franz. *The Grail Legend*. New York: G.P. Putnam's Sons, 1970.

Kerényi, Karl. *Eleusis: Archetypal Image of Mother and Daughter*. Trans. Ralph Manheim. Princeton, NJ: Princeton UP, 1967.

_____, *Goddesses of Sun and Moon*. Trans. Murray Stein. Dallas: Spring Publications, 1979.

_____, *The Gods of the Greeks*. London: Thames and Hudson, 1979.

_____, *Hermes: Guide of Souls*. Dallas and Zürich: Spring Publications, 1976.

_____, "Kore." *Essays on a Science of Mythology: The Myth of the Divine Child and the Mysteries of Eleusis*. Jung, C.G. and C. Kerényi. Bollingen Series XXII. Princeton: Princeton UP, 1973.

_____, Preface. *Mythology and Humanism: The Correspondence of Thomas Mann and Karl Kerenyi*. Trans. Alexander Gelley. Ithaca: Cornell UP, 1975.

Kibler, William. "Introduction." *Lancelot, or The Knight of the Cart*. Chrétien de Troyes. New York: Garland Publishing, Inc., 1984.

Lagorio, Valerie. "The Apocalyptic Mode in the Vulgate Cycle of Arthurian Romances." *Philological Quarterly* 57 (1978): 1-22.

The Larousse Encyclopedia of Mythology. Introduction by Robert Graves. New York: Barnes and Noble, 1994.

Lauf, Detlef-Ingo. *Verborgene Botschaft Tibetischer Thangkas: Secret Revelation of Tibetan Thangkas*. Freiburg im Breisgau: Aurum Verlag, 1976.

Lawrence, D.H. "The Horse-Dealer's Daughter." The *Complete Short Stories*. Vol. 2. New York: Viking Press, 1969.

Leisegang, Hans. "The Mystery of the Serpent." (1939). *The Mysteries: Papers From the Eranos Yearbooks*. Ed. Joseph Campbell. Bollingen Series XXV. Princeton: Princeton UP, 1955.

Lord, George de F. "The *Odyssey* and the Western World." *Essays on the Odyssey: Selected Modern Criticism*. Ed. Charles H. Taylor, Jr. Bloomington and London: Indiana UP, 1963.

Maclagan, David. *Creation Myths: Man's Introduction to the World*. London: Thames and Hudson, 1977.

Marks, Richard and Nigel Morgan. *The Golden Age of English Manuscript Painting: 1200-1500*. New York: George Braziller and Company, 1981.

Matthews, John. *The Grail: Quest for the Eternal*. New York: Crossroad, 1981.

Meyer, Marvin, ed. *The Ancient Mysteries, A Sourcebook: Sacred Texts of the Mystery Religions of the Ancient Mediterranean World*. New York: Harper and Row, 1987.

Milton, John. *Complete Poems and Major Prose*. Ed. Merritt Y. Hughes. Indianapolis: The Odyssey Press (Bobbs Merrill Educational Publishing), 1957.

Mookerjee, Ajit and Madhu Khanna. *The Tantric Way: Art, Science, Ritual*. Boston: New York Graphic Society, 1977.

_____, *Yoga Art*. Boston: New York Graphic Society, 1975.

Neumann, Erich. *Amor and Psyche: The Psychic Development of the Feminine*. Bollingen Series LIV. Princeton: Princeton UP, 1956.

Opie, Iona and Peter. *The Classic Fairy Tales*. New York: Oxford UP, 1974.

Pater, Walter. *The Marriage of Cupid and Psyche*. Illustrated by Edmund Dulac. New York: The Heritage Press, 1951.

Panofsky, Erwin. *Studies in Iconology: Humanistic Themes in the Art of the Renaissance*. Icon Edition. New York: Harper and Row, 1972.

Pépin, Jean. "The Platonic and Christian Ulysses." *Neoplatonism and Christian Thought*. Ed. Dominic J. O'Meara. International Society for Neoplatonic Studies. Albany: State University of New York Press, 1982.

Poncé, Charles. *Kabbalah: An Introduction and Illumination for the World Today*. London: Theosophical Publishing House, 1973.

Popol Vuh. Trans. Dennis Tedlock. *The HarperCollins World Reader: Antiquity to the Early Modern World*. Ed. Mary Ann Caws and Christopher Prendergast. New York: HarperCollins College Publishers, 1994.

Porter, Howard. Introduction. *The Odyssey*. Trans. George Palmer. New York: Bantam, 1963.

Quispel, Gilles. "Der Gnostische Anthropos und Die Jüdische Tradition." *Eranos-Jahrbuch (1953): Mensch und Erde*. Vol. XXII. Ed. Olga Fröbe-Kapteyn. Zürich: Rhein Verlag, 1954.

Roberts, Gareth. *The Mirror of Alchemy: Alchemical Ideas and Images in Manuscripts and Books From Antiquity to the Seventeenth Century*. Toronto: University of Toronto Press, 1994.

Schama, Simon. *Landscape and Memory*. New York: Alfred A. Knopf, 1995.

Shakespeare, William. *A Midsummer Night's Dream*. Ed. Madeleine Doran. *William Shakespeare: The Complete Works*. Ed. Alfred Harbage. Baltimore: Penguin Books, 1969.

Smith, Evans Lansing. "Alchemical Imagery in Modernism." *Cauda Pavonis*. Spring (1994) New Series 13 (1):11-18.

_____, "Amazing Underworlds: Yourcenar's *Fires* and Nabokov's *Pale Fire*. *The Yearbook of Comparative and General Literature*. 45/46 (1997/98): 105-31.

_____, "The Arthurian Underworld of Modernism: Thomas Mann, Thomas Pynchon, Robertson Davies." *Arthurian Interpretations*. Spring, 1990. 4 (2): 50-64.

_____, "The Descent to the Underworld: Jung and His Brothers" *C.G. Jung and the Humanities: Towards a Hermeneutics of Culture*. Ed. Karin Barnaby and Pellegrino D'Acierno. Princeton: Princeton UP, 1990.

_____, "The Descent to the Underworld in Borges and Cortázar." *The Yearbook of Comparative and General Literature*. 40 (1992): 105-115.

_____, *The Descent to the Underworld in Literature, Painting, and Film: 1895-1950: The Modernist Nekyia*. New York: The Edwin Mellen Press, 2001.

_____, "Doorways, Divestiture, and the Eye of Wrath: Tracking an Archetype." *Janus Head: Journal of Interdisciplinary Studies in Literature, Continental Philosophy, Phenomenological Psychology, and the Arts*. 2.1 (Summer 1999): 11-28.

_____, *Figuring Poesis: A Mythical Geometry of Postmodernism*. New York: Peter Lang, 1997.

_____, "Form and Function in T.H. White's *The Once and Future King Quondam et Futurus: A Journal of Arthurian Interpretations*. Winter, 1991. 1 (4): 39-52.

_____, "Framing the Underworld: Threshold Imagery in the Films of Murnau, Cocteau, and Bergman." *Literature/Film Quarterly*. 24.3 (Spring, 1996): 241-54.

_____, *The Hero Journey in Literature: Parables of Poesis*. Lanham, MD: University Press of America, 1996.

_____, "The Lyrical Nekyia: Metaphors of Poesis in Wallace Stevens." *The Journal of Modern Literature*. XXI, 2 (Winter 1997/98): 201-08.

_____, "Myths of Poesis, Hermeneusis, and Psychogenesis: Hoffmann, Tagore, and Gilman." *Studies in Short Fiction*. 34 (1997): 227-36.

_____, "Postmodernist Revisionings of the Grail: Leonora Carrington, Umberto Eco, Thomas Pynchon." *Mythosphere: A Journal for Image, Myth, and Symbol*. 1.4 (1999): 507-22.

_____, *Rape and Revelation: The Descent to the Underworld in Modernism*. Lanham: University Press of America, 1990.

_____, *Ricorso and Revelation: An Archetypal Poetics of Modernism*. Columbia, SC: Camden House, 1995.

Speirs, John. *Medieval English Poetry: The Non-Chaucerian Tradition*. London: Faber and Faber, 1971.

Spenser, Edmund. *The Faerie Queene. The Literature of Renaissance England*. Ed. John Hollander and Frank Kermode. New York: Oxford UP, 1973.

Stein, Murray. *In MidLife: A Jungian Perspective*. Dallas: Spring Publications, 1983.

Stone, Merlin. *Ancient Mirrors of Womanhood: Our Goddess and Heroine Tradition*. Volume 1. New York: New Sybylline Books, 1979.

Strassburg, Gottfried von. *Tristan and Isolde*. Trans. A.T. Hatto. New York: Penguin, 1960.

Strauss, Walter. *Descent and Return: An Orphic Pattern in Literature*. Cambridge: Harvard UP, 1971.

Taylor, Charles Jr., Ed. *Essays on the Odyssey: Selected Modern Criticism*. Bloomington and London: Indiana UP, 1963.

The Tibetan Book of the Dead: The Great Liberation Through Hearing in the Bardo. Trans. Francesca Fremantle and Chögyam Trungpa. Boulder and London: Shambhala, 1975.

Treasures From the Bronze Age of China. New York: The Metropolitan Museum of Art and Ballantine Books, 1980.

Ulanov, Ann and Barry. "Bewitchment." *Quadrant: Journal of the C.G. Jung Foundation for Analytical Psychology*. Winter (1978): 33-61.

Virgil. *The Aeneid of Virgil: A Verse Translation by Alan Mandelbaum*. Berkeley: The University of California Press, 1981.

Wagner, Richard. *Tristan and Isolde*. English National Opera Guide 6. New York: Riverrun Press, 1981.

Wakeman, Mary K. *God's Battle With the Monster*. Leiden: E.J. Brill, 1973

Walker, Barbara. *The Woman's Dictionary of Symbols and Sacred Objects*. San Francisco: HarperSanFrancisco, 1988.

_____, *The Women's Encyclopedia of Myths and Secrets*. HarperSanFrancisco, 1983.

Wasson, Gordon, et al. *The Road to Eleusis: Unveiling the Secret of the Mysteries*. New York: HBJ, 1978.

Weston, Jessie. *From Ritual to Romance*. Mythos Series. Princeton: Princeton UP, 1993.

Whitmont, Edward C. *Return of the Goddess*. New York: Crossroad, 1982.

Wilkinson, Richard H. *Reading Egyptian Art: A Hieroglyphic Guide to Ancient Egyptian Painting and Sculpture*. London: Thames and Hudson, 1992.

Wind, Edgar. *Pagan Mysteries in the Renaissance*. Revised and Enlarged Edition. New York: W. W. Norton & Company, 1968.

Wolkstein, Diane and Samuel Noah Kramer. *Inanna Queen of Heaven and Earth*. New York: Harper and Row, 1983.

Woodroffe, Sir John. *The Garland of Letters: Studies in the Mantra-S'astra*. 7th Ed. Pondicherry: Ganesh and Company, 1979.

Wooley, Sir Charles Leonard. *Publications of the Joint Expedition of the British Museum and of the Museum of the University of Pennsylvania to Mesopotamia*. 2 vols. London: Oxford University Press, 1934.

_____, *Ur of the Chaldees*. London: Ernest Benn, Ltd., 1929.

Yates, Frances A. *Giordano Bruno and the Hermetic Tradition*. (1964). Midway Reprint. Chicago: The University of Chicago Press, 1979.

_____, *Majesty and Magic in Shakespeare's Last Plays: A New Approach to Cymbeline, Henry VIII, and The Tempest*. Boulder: Shambhala, 1978.

_____, *The Occult Philosophy in the Elizabethan Age*. London and Boston: (Routledge and Kegan Paul) Ark Paperbacks, 1983.

_____, *The Rosicrucian Enlightenment*. (1972). Boulder: Shambhala, 1978.

Yeats, W.B. *The Complete Poems of W.B. Yeats*. Ed. Richard Finneran. New York: Macmillan Publishing Company, 1983.

Zimmer, Heinrich. *The King and the Corpse: Tales of the Soul's Conquest of Evil*. Ed. Joseph Campbell. Bollingen Series XI. (1948). Princeton: Princeton UP, 1973.

_____, *Myths and Symbols in Indian Art and Civilization*. Ed. Joseph Campbell. Bollingen Series VI. (1947). Princeton: Princeton UP, 1974.

_____, *Philosophies of India*. Ed. Joseph Campbell. Bollingen Series XXVI. (1951). Princeton: Princeton UP, 1969.

Zipes, Jack. *Spells of Enchantment: The Wondrous Fairy Tales of Western Culture*. New York: Viking Penguin, 1991.

Index

About
the Author

Evans Lansing Smith received a B.A. in English from Williams College, an M.A. in Creative Writing from Antioch International (London and Dublin), and a Ph.D. in Literature from The Claremont Graduate School. He traveled with the late Joseph Campbell, on study tours of northern France, Egypt, and Kenya, and he studied literature in England, at Oxford and Cambridge Universities. Since then, he has taught at colleges in California, Switzerland, Maryland, and Texas, where he is currently Professor of English at Midwestern State University, in Wichita Falls. He has published five previous books, and numerous articles, on comparative mythology and literature. Lans is married to Michelle Ruppert, Director of the Honors Program at the University, and they have three children, Anita, Charles, and Angela. Lans and Michelle regularly deliver slide-illustrated lectures on mythology to a wide variety of audiences.

2215666R00117

Made in the USA
San Bernardino, CA
24 March 2013